EATONIANS

EATONIANS

THE STORY OF THE FAMILY BEHIND THE FAMILY

PATRICIA PHENIX

M&S

National Library of Canada Cataloguing in Publication Data

Phenix, Patricia
  Eatonians : the story of the family behind the family / Patricia Phenix.

Includes bibliographical references.
ISBN 0-7710-6995-2

1. T. Eaton Co – History.   2. T. Eaton Co – Employees – Anecdotes.
3. Eaton family.   I. Title.

HF5465.C34E358 2002   381'.141'092271   C2002-902509-5

We acknowledge the financial support of the Government of Canada through the Book Publishing Industry Development Program for our publishing activities. We further acknowledge the support of the Canada Council for the Arts and the Ontario Arts Council for our publishing program.

The author also wishes to thank the Canada Council for the Arts for its support in the form of a grant.

Typeset in Sabon by M&S, Toronto
Printed and bound in Canada

McClelland & Stewart Ltd.
The Canadian Publishers
481 University Avenue
Toronto, Ontario
M5G 2E9
www.mcclelland.com

1 2 3 4 5   06 05 04 03 02

Contents

Acknowledgements

It would be impossible for me to individually thank the over two hundred Eatonians across Canada who provided background information, letters, photographs, and poems for this book. In place of doing so, I dedicate this book to them. They formed the backbone of the Eaton's empire and were responsible for the company succeeding for as many years as it did. It is time that they received the recognition they deserve. In the few instances where individuals chose not to be named, I have complied with their requests.

There are several individuals I need to single out for their help. Many parts of this book could not have been completed without the advice and help of Jim Matthews. He is the epitome of a true Eatonian. His loyalty towards his former co-workers eclipses any negative feelings he may have developed toward the company after its collapse. Jim's kindness and selfless generosity will not be forgotten. Thanks also to Verna Matthews, for suffering through countless Eaton's powwows with endless good humour.

Others who deserve special mention include Jim Chestnutt, Sigi and Michael Brough, Manfred Buehner, Alan Finnbogason, Pierre and Ethel Witmeur, Hank Hankinson, Dorothy Ferguson, Joan Caruso, Jim Thomson, Judith McErvel, Patrick Blednick and Cathy Teolis, Tom Pezzack, Reg Collins, Rose Askin, Barbara Redlich, the late Rose Collins, and Peter Glen, who died in October 2001. I have chosen to retain Peter's quotes in the present tense for the sake of narrative continuity.

I am very grateful for the assistance of Christine Bourolias at the Archives of Ontario, George de Zwaan at the National Archives of Canada, Scott Reid of the Provincial Archives of Manitoba, Shelley Sweeney of the Special Collections section of the University of Manitoba Archives, Stéphanie Poisson of the McCord Museum in Montreal, Richard

Gerrard of Collection Services, Museum and Heritage Services Culture Division, City of Toronto, and Sharon Landry of Sears Canada Inc.

In reproducing photographs, I give my thanks to Rick and Isabelle Zolkower.

My thanks also to my agent Bruce Westwood and his associate Hilary McMahon, of Westwood Creative Artists. My editor, Pat Kennedy, deserves a medical licence for the expert surgery she performed on the first draft of this manuscript. Kudos.

I'm very grateful to Fred and John Craig Eaton for making themselves available for interviews. Their contributions added immensely to the final product.

And finally, I thank my family, including Ivy and Ebby.

Patricia Phenix
Toronto
March 2002

Foreword

by Jim Matthews,
Eatonian of forty-seven years and
collector of Eaton's memorabilia

As I write these words, Canada's Thanksgiving Day is approaching, giving me cause to recount the many reasons to be grateful. At the head of the list is that I am a Canadian, and blessed to live in this great land! Then, as I consider the title of this book, I am thankful to be able to call myself an "Eatonian," like countless thousands of citizens from sea to sea to sea.

Canada and the T. Eaton & Co. were born only two years apart – Canada as a nation in 1867 and the T. Eaton & Co. in 1869. Future historians will look back and view the impact of the Eaton name in two ways: first, it was given to a family-owned and -operated company; and second, it was associated with a collection of extraordinary individuals named Eatonians, who contributed immeasurably to the life and growth of this country.

An understanding of the inner workings of the Eaton's empire came early for me. My father started working at what by then was known simply as the Eaton's store, in 1920. As I grew up, my father used to take me downtown to the store, and over the years, as a young lad, I was introduced to many Eatonians during these shopping trips. Eaton's was, in fact, part of our family.

All of a sudden, one day I found myself working at Eaton's, on the fifth floor of the Queen Street store in the Grocery Department, doing what I believed was a summer job. Then, just as suddenly, I was transferred to a permanent job that provided me with a close-up view of Eaton's. I became the office boy in the executive office on the seventh floor. Here I found myself in awe as a seventeen-year-old at the nerve centre of this great Canadian company.

Within minutes of arriving on the job, I had my first meeting with Lady Eaton, when she asked that I open a window in the boardroom. Then I was responsible for the daily delivery of fresh orange juice from the Health Counter on the fifth floor to Mr. R. Y. Eaton, who was the president at that time. Oh yes, and there was the incident of setting a mousetrap in Mr. John David Eaton's office, much to his amusement. I learned quickly that those who bore the Eaton name were indeed human. These events helped me appreciate the wide variety of experiences that I would encounter throughout my forty-seven years with the company, during which I worked in five stores. I was also part of the planning group of two new stores in Oshawa and London, Ontario. In all, I worked for six of the ten presidents of Eaton's.

There was a break from my job, when, like thousands of Eatonian men and women, I did my military service. On my return to Eaton's, my job was still there, as promised.

Working at Eaton's throughout the decades, I got interested in the company's history and its growth as a Canadian institution. My interest set me to collecting Eaton's memorabilia. My membership in the Toronto Postcard Club led me to see how many postcards there were depicting some aspect of Eaton's in Canada, as well as its influence on people in many other countries. In the May 21, 2001, edition of *Barr's Post Card News*, one of the world's largest deltiology newspapers, with national and international distribution, was an article entitled "Eaton's of Canada" by Ronald Olin. The article was illustrated with photographs of eight postcard views of the Eaton's store in Winnipeg, Manitoba. The author pointed out that, "Since Eaton's had locations in 170 cities & towns, its post card views are found in most Canadian collections."

My earliest postcard, dated 1893, comes from a customer in Beatrice, Muskoka, writing about her catalogue order. Another Canadian postcard, dated 1897, from the Eaton's Catalogue in Toronto, is addressed

to a customer in British Columbia and contains a handwritten message advising the customer that his recent order is delayed but will be forwarded as soon as possible.

A postcard dated April 25, 1907, from Paris, France, and addressed simply "Eaton's Store, Toronto, Canada," contains this request: "Will you send me your general Catalog. I am to start for Manitoba and I will know the price of everything."

There are also postcards showing stores across Canada, community events, and window displays, to name only a few subjects. One of the most spectacular is a 1906 black-and-white photo card of a hanging

Easter egg in the Queen Street store, the egg holding an eight-piece orchestra and piano. The size of the egg was twenty-one feet by fourteen feet.

In my postcard collection, there are two unique cards: One, known as a "Buster Brown" card, was written by an employee of the Mail Order department in Toronto to a relative in the United States. The message on the front of the card reads, "Mr T. Eaton is dead. Died very suddenly, store is closed until Monday." The date on the card is January 31, 1907, the day Mr. Timothy Eaton died.

The second postcard is dated May 30, 1907, and is in the Sacred Songs Souvenir series. Printed on the card are the words and music to a special hymn written by Rev. James Wilkinson entitled "Someday When Life Is Over" and carries this printed dedication. "To the memory of the late Timothy Eaton, Esq., Toronto, a man much beloved in Canadian Methodism."

Collecting Eaton's memorabilia brings me in closer touch with the vastness of the company's influence. My collection numbers almost 4,000 pieces housed in 36 loose-ring binders, 2 boxes, over 700 Kodachrome slides, an 8-millimetre film, 65 Eaton's-related books, 142 advertising buttons, as well as innumerable postcards and catalogues, plus 144 copies of in-store magazines such as *Contacts*, *Eaton's Gossiper*, *Eaton News*, *Eaton News Quarterly*, *Eaton's News Weekly*, *Entre Nous*, and *Flash*.

Looking over my collection, I find it easy to link the family who founded, built, and ran the business to the "family" of Eatonians who worked for the store in a multitude of jobs, and to the extended "family" of customers who, for 130 years, shopped in Eaton's stores and bought with confidence through the catalogue.

Amidst my collection of Eaton's advertising buttons, one stands out as particularly significant. It is a 2¼" × 3" button on a blue and red background containing the words "Eaton's Timothy Days" above a sketch of the founder, Timothy Eaton. Included on the button is a record of the year the store opened, 1869, and the dates of the "Eaton's Timothy Days" promotion, June 4–21, 1986.

In refreshing my memory about the "Eaton's Timothy Days" promotion, I was reminded of a photograph in my collection showing Mr. John Craig Eaton cutting a ribbon for the opening of a display of items from my Eaton's collection. I was always grateful to Mr. Eaton for his kindness in taking the time and interest to share in this event.

As a collector, I have noticed that many Canadians have saved the last issue of the Eaton's catalogue, dated Spring 1976. I have two in my collection, one signed by Mr. Fredrik Stefan Eaton and one by Mr. George Eaton.

Eaton's collectibles move the imagination of those who come across them. This summer I noted three incidents of items arousing interest. A friend came across a vintage doll from around 1905 and wondered whether it was an early Eaton's Beauty Doll. The Doll, which originally had a bisque head and kid-leather body, was sold through the company's mail-order catalogue beginning in 1901, for the low price of one dollar. In later years, a badge or banner clearly distinguished her as an Eaton's Beauty, ensuring her future as a collector's item. Preliminary research has suggested my friend's doll isn't an Eaton's Beauty Doll, but my investigation continues. Then there was another friend who gave me a letter he found in a book he bought at a neighbourhood garage sale. The letter is on Hardy Amies (Canada) stationery and was written by an Amies executive to an Eaton's buyer. The letter talks about a line of clothing designed by the British designer Hardy Amies that was being introduced in Canada. The writer expresses his appreciation for Eaton's help in launching the line with these words: "We are indebted to you the founding retailers, who helped us realize our dream." Finally, there were two toy-collectors/dealers I met at a summer antique show who talked proudly of the Dinky Toy version of an Eaton's truck of a very early vintage that each had in his collection.

As I put these thoughts together, I can well imagine those "Eatonians" – each a member of the "family behind the Family" – who, as they read this book, will quickly identify with events the author has drawn upon to weave together her extensive research, and conversations with hundreds of people. This book will serve to trigger memories – both of events covered in the book and of people and events known to them personally.

For me, in addition to these things I have already mentioned, I remember the Eaton's War Auxiliary Fun Night, put on by employees at Varsity Arena; a fundraising Eaton War Auxiliary midway night on the grounds of Lady Eaton's home, Eaton Hall; a fall afternoon in 1946, again at the beautiful Eaton Hall, when the company presented gold rings to Eaton's veterans from the Second World War. Then, too, I recall the Eaton's Christmas receptions at the Hall; the visit of the Lone

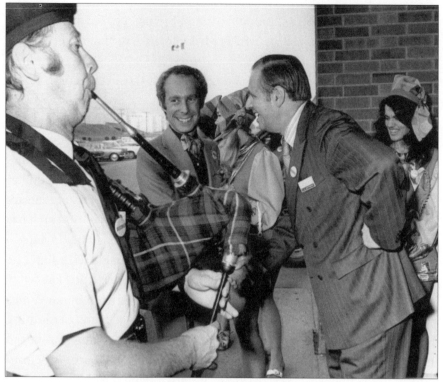

*Marketing guru Peter Glen being greeted at Eaton's
Warehouse store by Jim Matthews (Manager), mid-1970s*

Ranger to the employees; family picnics in Lakeshore Park in Oshawa; and the visit of Gordie Howe, Eaton's sports advisor, to the Oshawa store. Howe also took the time to visit the Eaton's store's family picnic in London, Ontario.

I remember the cold February morning in 1965 when, with proper ceremony, we raised the new Canadian flag on the flagpole of the Eaton's store in Wellington Square in London, Ontario. I recall too the night a tornado swept through Eaton's warehouse store, where I was the manager, wreaking havoc as it brought down store shelves and knocked over light fixtures.

I also remember attending the dedication of a plaque honouring Timothy Eaton in Kirkton, Ontario, where Timothy opened his first dry-goods store. The Ontario government hosted the event, and Lady Eaton was on hand to unveil the plaque.

As I seek to find suitable words to bring this foreword to a conclusion, I am reminded of the cover of the *Financial Post* magazine of

May 1978. Included on it was a photograph of the statue of Timothy Eaton. The title of the magazine article encapsulated Timothy's power over Canada: "In the Beginning There Was Timothy Eaton."

This sentiment is expanded on by Arthur Hailey in "The Radical Storekeeper," an essay contained in the book *Great Canadians: A Century of Achievement*: "When poets and politicians are long forgotten, the name of Timothy Eaton is likely to endure," he wrote.

Meanwhile, in his book *Who Killed Canadian History?* J. L. Granatstein wrote, "There are no heroes in our past to stir the soul, and no myths on which a national spirit can be built – or so we are told."

I say, Canada does indeed have heroes, and Timothy Eaton is one of them.

I conclude where I began. I am thankful to be a Canadian. I am thankful to have been a member of the "family behind the family," and especially thankful to those who encouraged me along the way.

October 2001

Introduction

AMONG MY MOTHER'S POSSESSIONS is a triptych of photographs showing my two brothers and me in separate years, sitting on Santa's knee. The "real" Santa, that is. Eaton's Santa. My brothers both look exhausted. Pale-faced and hollow-eyed from lack of sleep induced by over-excitement, they smile shyly at the camera, clutching the free gifts distributed by the store: in my eldest brother's case, a balloon, and my next-eldest brother's case, a box containing a "mystery" gift, probably a Dinky car.

As the youngest sibling, I had learned from my brothers' mistakes and had decided to face Santa without flinching. And my photo proves it. There I sit, hands clasped primly in my lap, my itchy wool hat knotted so tightly beneath my chin that it would leave a red mark in the flesh for the duration of the winter. As usual, my mouth is moving. "Santa," I might as well be saying, "let's get down to business." Disobeying instructions to look at the camera, I prefer to gaze inwardly at the imaginary loot I hope to receive on Christmas morning. Or does this picture really tell the tale? Am I just nervous? Am I talking, or merely chewing the corners of my mouth? Am I clasping my hands, or nervously kneading them?

Like photographs, anecdotal memories are not infallibly accurate. But they do convey the heart behind historical facts. By design, this book describes the funny, sad, or traumatic events that occurred over Eaton's history, as seen through the eyes of over two hundred Eatonians. The youngest employee I interviewed was twenty, the oldest, one hundred.

The Eaton's empire collapsed in 1999, yet the feelings of Eatonians for the store, both good and bad, remain strong. For single women, especially, the store was not merely a part of their lives, it *was* their lives, and when it closed for good, it took their pasts with it. Many continue to grieve its loss.

Where one Eatonian's recollections of an event have been controversial, I have attempted to corroborate them through the recollections of at least one other Eatonian – a challenge, considering the sheer number of events that occurred during the store's 130-year history.

Due to the constraints of both words and time, I have broken the book down into specific subject areas. These include the beginning and end of Eaton's sponsorship of the Santa Claus Parade, the rise and fall of the Eaton's catalogue, Eaton's fundraising activities during the war years, as well as the effect unions had on Eaton's famed entrepreneurial ethos.

In addition to interviewing former employees and customers, I performed extensive research throughout the massive Eaton's holdings that are stored in the Archives of Ontario. Sometimes from eight in the morning until ten at night I sifted through thousands of typed and handwritten letters, memos, official press releases, magazine and newspaper articles, and, of course, photographs. The material I found barely scratches the surface of what made the company tick. Some subject files, including those pertaining to the catalogue closure, as well as those dealing with union activities, remain sealed for seventy-five years, so to obtain information, I relied as much as possible on anecdotes provided to me by those directly involved in the events.

The affection among Eatonians is deep. It is evident in the number of employees who continue to meet on a casual basis. From Vancouver to Halifax, employees share barbecues, dinners, even group vacations. If former Eatonians need assistance, other Eatonians come to their aid, providing food, clothes, and emotional support. Their ties cannot be severed.

A few years ago, some former Eaton's executives threw a surprise birthday party for Marg Morison at her retirement home. Morison is the one-time matriarch of the Santa Claus parade. Now in her early nineties, Morison still keeps in touch regularly with her former colleagues. Even former company president Fred Eaton personally called Morison to announce the family's decision to close the company altogether.

Meanwhile, the former chairman of the Eaton's board, John Craig Eaton, continues to receive personal anecdotes from Eatonians concerning their experiences with the store. To this day, his interest in everything Eatonian remains strong.

To help comprehend why Eatonians felt a unique kinship not only with the store but with its owners, I interviewed both Fred Eaton and John Craig Eaton. Portrayed in the press as merchant princes whose crowns had slipped, both men were understandably wary of speaking with yet another writer. "I must be insane, but I'll talk to you," Fred said when I first contacted him about an interview. In both cases, however, each man was generous with his time and didn't flinch from answering questions put to him, no matter how blunt.

As a former customer, I have a lot of affection for Eaton's. Nevertheless, when the company closed, I was sad, but not devastated. Eaton's catalogues, Christmas windows, and Santa Claus parades had been features of my youth, but by the time I was an adult I dismissed Eaton's as just another retail outlet. When I called to inquire about the availability of an item, I was usually transferred from one department to another, before being cut off altogether. Stock always seemed to be low. In its final years, clothes were chained together, and sales staff were impossible to find. On my last foray to the Don Mills store with my mother, in 1998, the only time the sales clerk offered assistance was to deliver my mother's notice of complaint to the suggestion box at the other end of the store. In my complacency, however, it never occurred to me that the store could cease to exist.

My interest in Eaton's was reawakened in August 1999. I was driving in downtown Toronto, when, on a radio call-in show, I heard the announcement that the company was closing for good. Callers reacted with emotions ranging from rage to regret. An obviously elderly man described the day years before when he and his wife had received an unexpected phone call informing them that the next day they could pick up their new baby for adoption. "We were panicked," the man said. "We didn't know where to start in outfitting our nursery." In an emotional voice, he proceeded to credit an Eaton's employee with making sure that they had everything they would need to properly care for their new baby.

Not long after the radio show ended, I took a side trip past the Don Mills Eaton's store. All its doors were locked. The parking lot was empty – there was no life to be seen.

There is, however, plenty of life among Eatonians.

This is their story.

CHAPTER 1

Going, Going, Gone

Eaton staff loyalty • The decline begins • The final auction

I N THE 1970S, Rose Askin travelled from her home in London, Ontario, to the Toronto Eaton Centre, to attend a Product Knowledge meeting. Buoyed almost solely by the success of the Eaton Centre, the godlike image of Timothy Eaton was carried by juggernaut down Canada's corporate highway, its massive wheels crushing competitors and acolytes alike in its seemingly unobstructed path.

For more than twenty years, Askin had worked as a housewares sales clerk in the company's Wellington store, located in London, Ontario. An ardent CCF member, she would eventually participate in a failed union drive against Eaton's in the early 1980s, but for now she was simply in the mood for mischief.

During a break in the meeting, Askin turned to a co-worker with a proposition, "Let's take the executive elevator, just for the fun of it." Like errant schoolchildren, the two rode the elevator to the seventh-floor executive offices – the inner sanctum of the vast Eaton's empire.

With a thud and a ding the elevator's heavy steel doors rumbled open to reveal a floor sign bearing, in bold black lettering, the admonition: "Authorized Personnel Only." On a wall inside the executive offices hung an enormous wooden map of Canada, pierced with dozens of pushpins, each pin designating another Eaton's store. And by coincidence, beneath the map, with a suntan and a dazzling smile, stood Mr. John Craig Eaton, great-grandson of Timothy Eaton, Chairman of the Board of Eaton's, and onetime manager of Rose's Wellington store, in London, Ontario.

"You look familiar. What are you doing up here?" he asked Askin, his expression characteristically bemused. As a former store manager, he had long ago resigned himself to the fact that staff incursions such as these were part of the territory.

"We've come to see how the other half lives," Askin replied, laughing at her own audacity.

"At that point he sort of started to laugh too, and gave the two of us a short tour of the executive suites before putting us back on the elevator," she says.

Gregariousness and charm were trademarks of John Craig Eaton's management style. London store employees best remember him as the handsome, windswept figure who would dash into the store late on Monday mornings, accepting a freshly laundered and pressed shirt from an admiring female employee.

"He was the John F. Kennedy of the company, that's the kind of charisma he had," confirms Sigi Brough, Eaton's former vice-president of corporate public relations.

Lloyd Bull, then manager of the Don Mills store, and Fred Eaton would be caught watching a horse race on TV during business hours.

John Craig's chummy sociability sometimes elicited unexpected responses. Once, while handing out a certificate honouring a female employee's twenty-five years with the company, John Craig was startled when, instead of returning the kiss on the cheek he had given her, the employee pinched his buttocks, cooing admiringly, "Nice buns."

"I got a big kick out of that," he says today. "I thought, 'What the hell. If she's got that kind of gumption, why not?'"

John Craig's younger brother Fred was also capable of kicking back and enjoying a few jokes with staff members. One day, in the late 1960s, Fred Eaton arrived at the Don Mills store to take over management duties from outgoing manager, Lloyd Bull, who was moving on to another position within the company. Shortly after Fred had arrived, he convinced Bull to sneak a store television into Bull's office during business hours to watch a Fort Erie horse race that featured one of Fred's horses. The two men had just settled down with their feet propped up on Bull's desk, when company president Bob Butler burst in to break up the party.

"You should have seen Fred's face," says Bull. "For a second, he definitely looked like the kid with his hand caught in the cookie jar. We both did."

"It was mortifying," agrees Fred.

Despite being one of the company's owners, Fred Eaton gave his managers considerable autonomy. Even today, Fred still refers to the Toronto Eaton Centre store as manager "Jimmy Robertson's store" or the Winnipeg store as operating manager "Alan Finnbogason's store." Former CEO Greg Purchase, meanwhile, exuded the same confident take-charge qualities as Robertson and Finnbogason, as well as that other quality most prized by the Eaton family: loyalty. When the Eaton's empire collapsed in 1999, critics accused the Eaton family of relying too much on the judgements of others, yet for more than 129 years, this "all for one and one for all" philosophy ensured the firm's success. It took a combination of market fluctuations, changing tastes, and poor corporate decision-making to destroy what had been a brilliant success.

Over its 130-year history, Eaton's became part of the social fabric of many Canadians' lives. Hundreds of couples that eventually joined for life would rendezvous at "Timmy's toe."

Unsure of where a city's employment offices were, immigrants learned quickly how to find jobs at Eaton's. Store founder Timothy Eaton's credo, "Goods Satisfactory or Money Refunded," could easily have been translated into "Service Exemplary or Goodwill Forfeited." Employees worked hard to gain their customers' trust, and worked even harder to gain each other's. For employees without families, the store became both their home and church rolled into one, a situation augmented by the various after-hours clubs and camps established by the company.

So indebted did they feel that, even years after they had left, conscience-wracked employees sought absolution for petty thefts they had committed while in the company's employ. In 1971, a former employee sent Eaton's president Bob Butler a cheque for fifty-five dollars to cover income the employee had earned by falsifying his number of work hours. Eaton's wrote back, offering not only their best wishes, but also a receipt for the money.

Meanwhile, in 1985, a ninety-year-old woman wrote to Eaton's worrying that, in 1917 while employed as a female forewoman in the lady's glove department, she might have marked down the price of soiled gloves too low. To rectify the situation, she enclosed a cheque for sixty dollars to compensate for what she thought she owed the company.

Employees fought to protect Eaton's stores from both natural and man-made disasters. During the night of June 8, 1954, a fire broke out in buildings located across the street from the Eaton's store on Portage Avenue in Winnipeg. The fire was only prevented from destroying the Eaton's store when male employees dangled from its rooftop by ropes, and hosed down the sides of the building with water pumped from the company's private well. As the men battled the blaze outside, female

Eaton's founder Timothy Eaton

John Craig Eaton (later Sir John Craig),
President 1907–22

Robert Young (R. Y.) Eaton,
President 1922–42

John David Eaton (son of John Craig),
President 1942–69

employees inside prepared sandwiches that they passed down a con-
veyer belt for wrapping and finally transporting to the men outside.

When a disastrous flood submerged much of Winnipeg in 1950, those
rendered homeless received funds raised through Eaton's employees'
donations. Eaton's delivery trucks, meanwhile, transported food and
other supplies to relief workers trying to erect dams against the water. On
two occasions, Eaton's stores also acted as an overnight refuge for commuters trapped downtown in paralyzing snowstorms that blanketed, on
separate occasions, the city cores of Winnipeg and Toronto.

The Eaton family reciprocated its employees' loyalty, particularly
during the First and Second world wars. Family members threw themselves into war-bond drives. During both wars, Eaton's paid servicemen
a portion of their regular salaries. When they returned from service,
most veterans found their original jobs waiting for them. During the
Second World War, fundraising events were held at Eaton Hall, the
estate of Sir John Craig Eaton's widow, Lady Flora McCrea Eaton, in
King City, Ontario. She also converted the house into a makeshift hospital to care for wounded veterans.

After it had built up decades' worth of goodwill through the actions
of successive family presidents – including Timothy Eaton (1869–1907);
his son, Sir John Craig Eaton (1907–22); Timothy's cousin, Robert Young
(R. Y.) Eaton (1922–56); and finally, John David Eaton (1956–69) – it
was shocking to see how quickly the company's grip on the imagination
of its employees, as well as on the buying public, slipped after non-
family-members assumed its leadership.

Shortly after Robert Butler became Eaton's first non-family-member
president in 1969, plans were made to demolish Eaton's flagship Queen
Street store, and, with it, the Georgian Room restaurant, the imaginative
Christmas windows, and, for some customers, a lifetime of memories.
Seemingly overnight, every tie that bound the Eaton's stores to the communities around them was being cut. Protest letters filled newspapers
shortly after Earl Orser, Eaton's second non-Eaton-family president, cancelled the Eaton's catalogue in 1976. Even being a member of the Eaton
family did not prevent then-president Fred Eaton from being assailed in
1982 when he withdrew the company's sponsorship of the Santa Claus
parade, one of the greatest promotional events in the store's history.

However, even by his own admission, it was when George Eaton
cancelled the company's popular "Trans-Canada Sales," in favour of

a strategy called "Everyday Value Pricing," that the store finally lost its premier status among department stores. Among the first Eaton's employees to understand the true extent of the damage were the sales clerks themselves.

"We were invited to watch a video about the Everyday Value Pricing strategy, and while it was running a co-worker leaned over to me and said 'There she goes!' referring to the stores. The public liked their sales, oh God, especially the Trans-Canada Sales, and we all knew that," says Donna York, then a sales clerk in the Guildford, British Columbia, store.

When Eaton's failed to live up to its promise to provide consistently lower-priced merchandise than its competitors, customers retaliated by shopping at discount stores such as Woolco (later Wal-Mart) and Sears. Gradually, Eaton's lost its status as "the" store at which to shop and became just "a" store. Even more alarming, Eaton's staff members, always its best immune system, could not warm to George Eaton as readily as they had to his brothers, John Craig and Fred.

In the mid-1990s, Donna York was part of a lineup of employees who shook George's hand as he toured the Guildford store's first floor around Christmas. As George moved on, the line broke up and employees, including York, went about their business in other parts of the store; in York's case, this was the second floor, where by coincidence she again found herself as part of a receiving line. "I shook his hand again," she laughs, "and knew right away that he didn't have a clue that he'd already met me. So I decided to make a game of it." When George had almost completed his tour of the third floor, he again met York, as she positioned herself just outside the manager's office. "He shook my hand and there wasn't a flicker," says York. "I stopped the game when my manager finally told me to knock it off."

Eaton's paternalistic legacy had become a liability. At the same time, the family grew understandably confused about how to satisfy a fickle buying public that expected the store to fast-track itself into the twenty-first century, while remaining in a fixed place as a historical icon. Attempts to modernize the store, by introducing computerized billing, designer fashions, and boutique intimacy, were derided by teenagers, the very demographic group that, in its later years, Eaton's wanted to attract. At the same time, Eaton's older customers recoiled at the slogan, "This isn't your mother's store any more."

A constant parade of outside consultants advised the family on how to fix the unfixable. The chaos of conflicting directives that resulted from their suggestions hobbled the company even more as it stumbled towards bankruptcy in 1997. By the time the empire toppled completely, virtually all of the company's veteran warriors of upper management had retired, or ceded the battle.

Those left to emerge from the trenches were the company's ground troops, consisting of its sales clerks and store managers, as well as its still impressive number of loyal customers, who watched dumbfounded in 1999 as Sears scooped up nineteen Eaton's stores, placing twelve of them under the name of Sears and seven of them under the name of "eatons," written this time in lower case and minus the apostrophe.

Some embittered customers lashed out at the family in letters to newspapers. Former staff members also offered their two cents. "I can forgive them for losing the business, but I can never forgive them for selling their name," says dietician Joan Caruso, a veteran employee of forty years, who left her job in 1995. Shortly after hearing the store was closing for good, Caruso visited the Marine Room cafeteria, located on the sixth floor of the Eaton Centre, for a last meal. Today, she still keeps the receipt from that lunch as a memento.

By far the majority of emotionally bruised former employees and customers, however, wrote letters of condolence to the Eaton family: "Sorry for losing your store," read one card that was left alongside dozens of bouquets of fresh flowers at the foot of the Timothy Eaton statue in Winnipeg. More cards and flowers were left at the Timothy statue located in the Eaton Centre in Toronto.

Many of the cards were signed simply: "From a Loyal Eatonian."

———■———

By April 18, 2000, the last hammer literally fell on the Eaton's empire. Inside the Toronto Eaton Centre executive offices, the painful task of burying old memories had begun.

On the main floor, sales clerks, still wearing their original red, white, and blue Eaton's nametags, rattled keys as they opened the store's large glass doors. Though the store was now under the ownership of Sears, it was business as usual – Eaton's business, it appeared – with lingerie, chocolate bunnies, and bedroom slippers all for sale, still bearing Eaton's price tags.

After they took the elevator to the seventh floor, visitors confronted the same sign – "Authorized Personnel Only" – but inside the reception area the wooden map of Canada, pierced with pegs showing the location of Eaton's stores coast to coast, had been dismantled. In its place hung a bright orange poster reading "Auction."

Two young girls withdrew and distributed auction catalogues from cardboard boxes stored behind a wooden table. An arrow pointed to an open doorway to the right of the table, beyond which stretched a long corridor bordered by executive offices. Outside the picture window of one office, a billboard advertising Celica cars featured giant bespectacled eyes, under which appeared the words, "Are You Looking at Me?" By grim coincidence or design, Joni Mitchell's elegiac "Both Sides Now" filtered from the PA system in the ceiling. Blue binders embossed with the Eaton's name in gold lettering were jammed under heavy glass doors to prop them open.

More blue binders, dozens of them, labelled "Eaton's Operating Reports, 1985–91," "Corporate Summaries," "Indirect Expenses," "Store Performance Binders," and "Product/Expense Reports," lay jumbled on bookshelves.

"You're not selling these, are you?" an employee was asked. "No, they're for shredding, unless you want them," she responded, grim-faced.

Moments later, an even grimmer-faced employee arrived swinging a wheeled garbage bin towards the bookcase, into which she swept the binders like so much deadwood. Yellow police tape was stretched across the area, discouraging snoops, while unwittingly conveying the not entirely false impression that a crime had just occurred.

Boxes of jumbled keys sat on desks that had been stacked in the corridor. Fake, dead, or dying green plants in quaint wicker baskets lined windowsills.

Dozens of paintings, in acrylic, watercolour, and oil, as well as prints by esteemed artists such as A. J. Casson and Ken Danby, hung from the walls. Alongside them were numbers showing the order of their auction placement. Few would raise more than $200 apiece.

"There were some nice pieces, but overall I was surprised at how little fine art there really was," says Bruce Lyle, President of Danbury Sales, the auction and liquidation company conducting the event.

Lending *gravitas* to the day was an enormous portrait in oils of the store's founder himself, Timothy Eaton, gazing benignly across the corridor at a smaller portrait of his son, Sir John Craig. The portrait of Timothy, painted by J. W. L. Forster, had once hung in a place of honour above the inside entrance of the Queen Street store in Toronto. J. W. L. Forster is still recognized today as one of Canada's premier portrait painters. Among the other famous subjects Forster painted are Wilfrid Laurier and William Lyon Mackenzie.

Bidding for the Timothy portrait would start at $500, "an embarrassment," says collector George Flie, who raised the bid to $1,500 and eventually secured the painting on behalf of an unidentified collector for $2,000. Amid congratulations from onlookers, Flie was stunned to receive the following advice, "If you take the painting out of the frame, you'll have a great mirror." "They were savages," Flie says of many of the people attending the event.

Following its purchase, the painting was wrapped in spun-polyester bubble pack and transported by truck along Kingston Road to its new temporary home, Scarborough's Guild Inn, one of the few repositories large enough to store it. Sir John Craig's portrait sold for an equally anemic $1,200 – again to Flie.

The auctioneer who sold John Craig's portrait got more than he bargained for when he began the bidding by joking, "This guy must have been somebody special, he rated a painting," prompting Judith McErvel, Eaton's former archivist, to shout, "It's Sir John Craig Eaton, you idiot," a comment that elicited some of the few smiles of the day.

"All the portraits went for way under what I would have expected. Whoever bought them did very well indeed," says Richard Gerrard, Registrar, Collection Services, Museum and Heritage Services Culture Division, City of Toronto. Gerrard was surprised that Eaton family members did not keep the portraits for themselves.

"I have the original portrait of Timothy and his wife and John and Lady Eaton, I don't need the big painting," says Fred Eaton, by way of explanation. "These guys all got their portraits painted big-time, and they were meant to be in the stores. There's nothing you can do with these damn things."

Rubbing additional salt in the wound that was Eaton's, former Hudson's Bay Company president Bob Peters arrived at the auction site accompanied by three suntanned and expensively besuited men. Together, they examined store blueprints and assorted posters leaning against a wall. "Old Timmy must be spinning in his grave," a member of the trio whooped.

Scores of photographs of George Eaton in cheap wooden frames lay on metal scaffolding. A full-length Christian Dior mink coat hung beside some stained and crumpled dresses. "What's the story behind that, that's what I want to know," a woman remarked. Before long another woman bought the coat for $600.

Instinctively understanding that suspense builds up desire, Bruce Lyle kicked off the auction by first concentrating on moving the more pedestrian items: computers, printers, photocopiers, cellphones; cardboard boxes filled with spools of thread, tape, staples, glue guns, and paper.

An expert at understanding that sentimental shoppers see beyond the price of things to their ultimate value, Lyle swung through the crowds on a movable stepladder, spitting out bids like a Gatling gun through a portable loudspeaker, pushed through the room by a Danbury employee. One asset after the other swiftly fell, proving that to the creditors – and the auctioneers – go the spoils.

When Lyle arrived at the memorabilia section, a kaleidoscope of emotions overtook both former and current Eaton's employees. "It's so

Vice-President of Corporate/Public Relations Sigi Brough and husband, buyer Michael Brough. The final Eaton's auction devastated both of them.

sad, it's just like going through a graveyard," one remarked tearfully to her co-worker. A more stoical employee, her arms crossed defiantly across her chest, either to keep out emotion or to keep it in, shrugged, "I've gotten used to tragedy. I'm immune to it now."

Suddenly a small commotion arose in one corner of the room. "Oh, my God, that used to hang just outside my office," Sigi Brough exclaimed, spotting a sad and substantially wilted Santa's outfit dangling from a hanger, weighed down by a foam belly that had seen too many rainstorms. "It's a disgrace. Oh, my God, look at these. These used to be in my office too." she said, picking up commemorative plaques that had been bestowed on the store by grateful recipients of Eaton's charitable fundraising.

There were plaques from the Children's Aid, National Mental Health, Learning for Life, the Toronto Board of Education, the Hospital for Sick Children, and bringing the proceedings thudding down to earth, a triangular statue bearing a plaque from 1997 reading: "Eaton's Restructuring Hall of Fame, $500 million of unsecured debt restructured, $625 million restructuring financing, $250 million in permanent financing. The Undersigned acted as advisors to Eaton's. Ernst & Young; Osler, Harcourt; RBC Dominion Securities; Goldman Sachs."

Sigi, who describes herself as "in diapers and on a trikey" when she started working at Eaton's, would experience the déjà vu of the damned mere weeks after the auction while visiting a country flea market with her husband, former Eaton's fashion buyer Michael Brough. There she spotted yet another commemorative plaque that had once hung from her office wall. When Michael Brough explained who his wife was to the seller, the seller merely responded, "Well, maybe if she signs the plaque, it will be worth more."

"I think that's when I finally had to say to myself, 'It's really over, Sig, it's time to move on,'" Brough says. But for her, like many other loyal Eatonians, moving on would involve innumerable sleepless nights and repeated Monday-morning quarterbacking.

Brough had worked her way up from being a shoe saleswoman in Eaton's budget Annex store in Toronto to become one of the few women in the firm to attain vice-presidential status. Her accession had been capped by the gift of her own company car. The afternoon she received it, she drove past her late mother's house crying softly, "I've made it, Mom." As soon as the company announced it was closing, cars such as Brough's were towed from their parking spaces by liquidators, often with employees' belongings still inside.

The greatest clamour at the Eaton Centre auction erupted over the sale of the catalogues. "If you don't want them for the contents, you can use them for wallpaper," Lyle joked, infuriating several onlookers.

Despite a few muttered protests against Lyle's ad libs, the bidding escalated quickly. Seated on a stool in the middle of the melee was flaxen-haired former child model Marilyn Elhart, who, along with her twin sister, Jacqueline, had been photographed for the cover of the 1945 catalogue. As a courtly gesture, a male bidder purchased the catalogue for the glamorous and jewel-bedecked Elhart, who attracted a small media scrum when she prepared to depart with a friend.

Another former child model, with long black hair and bottle-bottom glasses, obsessively flipped through the pages of a 1968 catalogue before locating herself alongside a fellow model, actress Jennifer Dale.

There had been two auctions conducted by Danbury prior to the one on April 18 at the Toronto Eaton Centre. The first two-day event took place on October 19 and 20, 1999, at Eaton's main distribution and warehouse facility in Weston, Ontario, where heavy equipment such as computerized sorting lines and forklifts were sold.

The second daylong sale occurred on November 23, 1999, at the Toronto Eaton Centre, and featured the sale of office equipment, and some memorabilia, including poster-sized prints of Eaton's catalogue covers, one of which sold for $450 to a Chicago businessman named Dan Moorehouse, whose mother had worked as a sales clerk for the store.

Danbury President Bruce Lyle conducting Eaton's Warehouse auction, October 19, 1999

Other auction companies across Canada sold what store fixtures and scattered pieces of memorabilia remained from Eaton's stores and warehouses in their cities. By just having the name Eaton's appear on their flyers, auction companies were assured of a healthy turnout. An auction at the main store in Edmonton, conducted by Real Auctions Inc., at which only 20 per cent of the items were owned by Eaton's, drew sufficient numbers of sentimental shoppers to make it the third-largest auction in the company's history. Shortly after the Montreal store's merchandise was liquidated in 1999, the building's new owners, Ivanhoe Inc., invested $150 million to renovate the store into a combined department store and retail office space. Meanwhile, Crescent Commercial Corporation sold what was left from Vancouver's warehouse store.

The Winnipeg store's former operating manager, Alan Finnbogason, attended the store's auction in the summer of 2000. He recalls seeing the auctioneers literally "tear the oak arches right off the store's steel pillars and sell them for $800," before he left the premises, sick. "God knows what they did with the oak-lined furniture in the executive suites," he says today. "People just didn't understand the value of these things."

It was a terrible comedown for the greatest retail store in Canada. Throughout the sales, one tantalizing question remained unspoken:

"What would Timothy have said?"

CHAPTER 2

Learning from the Bottom Up

The beginnings • Social activities • Working at Eaton's
• Eaton's and Canada • Modern times

WHEN TIMOTHY EATON ARRIVED in Toronto in 1869, he lived in a modest house on Gloucester Street, where he kept three egg-laying chickens in his backyard. By the early 1940s, his company had evolved into the fourth-largest employer in Canada, after the federal government and the CN and CP railways.

At its height, Eaton's employed on a full- and part-time basis over sixty thousand people, fifteen thousand of them located in Toronto alone. When the store closed for good in 1999, only fifteen thousand remained throughout all of Canada.

Born in 1834 in Ballymena, Northern Ireland, Timothy started his own retail career at the age of thirteen, working ten- to twelve-hour days as a draper. When only twenty, he emigrated to Canada, where he opened his own shop in Kirkton, Ontario, then later operated a shop with his brother James in St. Mary's, located in the farm county of Perth, Ontario. Bored with the slow pace of country commerce, Timothy decided to try his luck in the big city. On December 8, 1869, he opened a dry-goods shop at 178 Yonge Street in Toronto. Confederation was only two years old, and customers were already flocking to Toronto, thanks to the opening of the Toronto, Grey, and Bruce Railway, which

Sketch of Eaton's first store in Toronto

allowed them to commute from small Southwestern Ontario towns. Transportation lines would continue to be one of the biggest keys to Timothy's early success.

Trolley-car drivers travelling up Yonge Street announced the name of the T. Eaton store as they came to a stop in front of it. Before long, Timothy's business became so popular that he had to extend the exterior of his first store forty feet. Later, he relocated his entire operation to 190 Yonge Street, where, after extensive renovations, the building took up a large portion of the northwest corner of Yonge and Queen streets. To discourage competition from moving into his old store, Timothy continued to pay its lease for a year.

As floors were added in later years, two hydraulic elevators were installed, as well as benches, where shoppers could relax as they sat beside one of the store's warm boilers. Beginning in 1887, Timothy announced in his catalogue the creation of a toilet room, where store "visitors," as Timothy preferred to refer to customers, could wash off the dust from their journeys.

In his new store, Timothy erected the foundations of an empire that would expand for several decades. Eaton descendants would open major stores in Winnipeg, in 1905; Montreal, in 1926; Hamilton, in

Eaton's Winnipeg store

1927; Saskatoon, in 1927; Halifax, in 1928; and Calgary, in 1929. Toronto's College Street store would open in October 1930, just eleven months after the great stock-market crash. With the building of the Vancouver store in 1949, and a store in Charlottetown in 1955, the empire could rightly be called a coast-to-coast operation.

As Timothy pursued his dream in Canada in the late nineteenth century, skilled workers, who had flocked to Europe's major urban centres to seek employment in the factories that had proliferated during the Industrial Revolution, were looking farther afield. Birth rates had soared, and death rates dropped, making for overcrowded living conditions that forced many of these workers to seek better job opportunities in Canada. By the late 1870s, new Canadians were ablaze with the notion that, if they merely applied sufficient elbow grease, they too could attain Timothy's success.

Timothy was as shrewd as he was shy. A deeply religious taskmaster, he possessed a gift for staging evangelical-style cheerleading sessions for his employees, both at his home and at his store. These not only provided psychological boosts, but ensured that the "Eatonians," as they came to refer to themselves, banded together like an extended family to fight off any assaults by outsiders, such as unions or other retail competitors. It was a psychology that miraculously endured up to the last

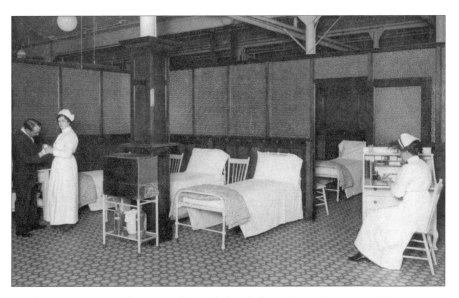

Tending to a patient at the in-store hospital, fourth floor, Queen Street store, Toronto, 1915

decade of the store's existence. Only then did marketing consultants, who were brought in to motivate staff members, succeed in pulling up Eaton's past by the roots.

One of Timothy's first and largest love-ins occurred on New Year's Eve of 1898, when 2,475 of his employees celebrated on the main floor of the store. In a speech he gave at the event, Timothy vowed to forever eliminate the term "employee" from Eaton's lexicon in favour of the term "associate." Raises were to be called "rate adjustments," while those employees who retired or were fired were referred to as "exiting" the store.[1]

If employees got sick, they were encouraged to visit the in-store infirmary, and infirmaries would eventually be set up in every store. Drugs were manufactured at the company's own factories and included, in the days before antibiotics, items such as smelling salts, Jamaican Ginger, and an infamous concoction known as beef iron and wine: a broth, alleged to be made of boiled rusty nails mixed with alcohol, that was used in the treatment of fainting spells.

The bonds between employees and management were further strengthened when Eaton's offered a 10-per-cent discount on merchandise, low-interest loans to employees who wanted to buy homes, a welfare department, and the firm's first pension and life-insurance plans.

Eaton's Deposit Accounts, established in 1904, also made employees and customers feel as though they were partners in symbiotically building the economic future of Canada. Itemized statements of purchases were mailed to Deposit Account holders at the end of each month. Years after the D.A. system was replaced – first by the Deferred Payment Plan, and then by credit-card capabilities – Eatonians could still rhyme off their D.A. account numbers as effortlessly as their birthdate.

In the store's early days, fourteen-and-a-half-hour workdays, from 7:30 a.m. to 10:00 p.m., were the industry norm. Prior to the days when "multi-tasking" became a catchphrase, employees hired as anything from bookkeepers to sales clerks were expected to heave boxes or sweep up the floors at the end of the day. The first three employees to work in the store – a man, a woman, and a boy – earned $8, $4, and $1.50 a week, respectively. Overtime pay was as foreign a notion as toothpaste.

The first challenge of a sales clerk's day was simply getting to work by the 7:30 start time. In the late nineteenth century, Toronto was referred to as "Mudtown." Instead of sidewalks, wooden planks were crudely laid across dirt. Cars were not yet on the scene, while horse-drawn carriages were owned only by taxi drivers or the rich.

William Fryer started working in the Toronto store in 1880 for $1.50 a week, which he used to pay for his daily cup of coffee, a sandwich lunch, and his transportation fare to and from work. Since Fryer lived in the Toronto suburb of Parkdale, a few miles from the store, he had to leave home by 6:30 a.m. to catch a ride in a horse-drawn cart, whose bottom was filled with straw to keep its occupants' feet warm. If he arrived a minute past 7:30 a.m., Fryer was locked out of the store for half an hour, and after the store closed, he was expected to sweep up before going home.[2]

While Fryer had straw to keep his legs warm on his ride to work, other employees weren't so lucky. A woman employed in the Winnipeg store in the 1930s remembers walking miles through sub-zero temperatures to get to the store. "I wore stockings just above the knee, and the portion just between my panties and the stockings was exposed. A lot of times I came to the store with white patches on my legs where they were frozen."[3]

Eaton's policy of punishing latecomers persisted throughout its history. Norma Rooke, an employee at the Winnipeg store in the 1940s, recalls that once, when she was a minute or two late for the 8:30 a.m.

store opening, the employees' doors were locked, and she was forced to walk around to the employment office to obtain a pass. To shame her out of arriving late again, Eaton's managers told Rooke that she must stay past the closing time of 5:30 to roll up draperies and straighten up tables before leaving – with no overtime pay. "We had to take it, because Eaton's wasn't unionized," she says.[4]

As gruelling as getting to work on time could be, getting from department to department on time was even harder. In 1914, when he was thirteen years old, Tom Pezzack was hired as a mail delivery boy in the Eaton's general office in Toronto. "Back then, you could leave school under fourteen if you had senior matric," he recalls. His salary was $3 a week. Pezzack noticed that athletic young mail-order workers used roller skates to travel down special ramps from the store's seventh floor to the sixth floor to distribute bundles of orders to the appropriate departments.

Eaton's oldest employee, Tom Pezzack, pictured here cutting the cake for his hundredth birthday. Pezzack worked for Eaton's between 1914 and 1917.

Shortly before the outbreak of the First World War, Pezzack was made responsible for filing numbered invoices in an office on Albert Street. As another part of his job, he was required to hurry down to the Customs Department at approximately ten minutes to three each day, to begin the painful task of coaxing a cheque out of executives, in order to pay that day's customs duties.

When the Eaton's treasurer, Mr. Bishop, wasn't available to sign the cheque, Pezzack was forced to approach Sir John Craig Eaton, who "always balked, he hated it," says Pezzack. John Craig's brother, William Fletcher Eaton, meanwhile, would scream, "Get somebody else to sign it," forcing Pezzack back onto the mercies of John Craig. Having finally secured a signature, Pezzack would run down to the Dominion Bank located at King and Yonge streets, just in time to get the cheque certified before the bank closed for the day. Clutching the certified cheque, Pezzack would then run down to the customs house, located a few blocks from the bank. Possibly for security reasons, after a few months an

Eaton's employee began picking Pezzack up in a company car, in this case a Buick, to drive him from the bank to the customs house.

Despite devoting the majority of his day to his job, Pezzack noted that he didn't even make enough money to afford a pair of ice skates. The majority of his money went to pay for essentials for his seven other family members, who all lived in the same small house as he did. "I was too young then to know any better, but it was no secret that most of my co-workers in the office felt terribly discontented and grossly under-paid," he says.

After being with the store for a year, Pezzack was called to the office manager's desk, "as though appearing before God," and told that, as a reward for performing good work, his salary was being raised to $3.25 a week, the bulk of which he used to pay off family expenses. "In those days, you took the pay envelope home without opening it. My mother let me keep the twenty-five cents," he says.

Home for Pezzack was a row house situated on Shuter Street, a slum area, where he recalls everything as "dark, dirty, and disagreeable," especially in the winter. His father worked for a steamship line, and when the water froze in the winter, the boats couldn't move. As a result, to earn money, his father shovelled snow at the Toronto City Hall for a dollar or two a day.

Each night after finishing dinner, the family left the father at the kitchen table to read his newspaper beneath the house's single oil lamp, which featured a state-of-the-art reflector. "When he was finished, my father would say, 'Well, Tommy, give us a song,'" says Pezzack, who during the evenings and on weekends sang with the St. James Cathedral choir.

To celebrate New Year's, Pezzack's father and brother pooled their money to buy a $1.25 bottle of whisky, their one treat in an otherwise dismal existence.

To provide some happy diversion for financially strapped employees like Pezzack, Eaton's established two camps in the early 1920s: for men, the Young Men's Country Club, and for girls, Shadow Lake Camp.

Reg Collins, who, as a teenager in the 1920s, worked as a drapery salesman, considered attending the Eaton Young Men's Country Club, but found even the modest fee of three dollars a week beyond his budget. Eaton's quickly offered a compromise: if Collins agreed to cut the grass and wash dishes for three weeks, he would be allowed to stay at the camp for free. When Collins displayed a preference for pranks over grass-cutting,

Sleeping camper becomes victim of a gag. He has been wrapped in mattresses by his fellow campers.

Horsing around at Eaton's Young Men's Country Club

Reg Collins (far left) in Eaton Men's Country Club dining room, 1920s

Eaton's allowed him to stay for free anyway. "They were good that way," says Collins. "They always gave a young guy an even break."

Located near the Scarborough Bluffs, the Eaton Young Men's Country Club featured hot- and cold-water showers, an open-air dining room, and a heated swimming pool, praised by campers as the last word in natatorial equipment. Weekend trips were organized to Wasaga Beach or Frenchman's Bay. Hijinks were the order of the day. Collins recalls that some of those who turned down field trips offset their boredom by setting fire to old cars and pushing them over the Bluffs.

Gathered in front of Shadow Lake Camp's tuck shop

Members of the Masquers theatre troupe

Meanwhile, those who slept outside to escape nighttime humidity could awaken to find they were bound up like human hot dogs between sets of old mattresses. New campers who slept out of doors experienced an even more embarrassing fate when they awoke to find they had urinated down the front of their pyjama pants after having one of their hands dipped in a bowl of tepid water.

Recreational activities such as horseback riding, tennis, and swimming at nearby Musselman's Lake were offered at the 225-acre Shadow Lake Camp for Girls, located just outside Stouffville, Ontario. A four-storey structure situated beside the camp's tennis court housed close to three thousand birds, whose eggs were served for breakfast or sold in the camp's Hostess Shop. In the evenings, female members of an in-store entertainment troupe called the Masquers, along with their male counterparts, who later travelled overseas to entertain Eaton's veterans during the Second World War, performed costumed skits and musical shows on a stage in the main cabin. Church services were conducted in the recreation hall on Sunday mornings. A nightly curfew of 10:00 p.m. was imposed, though it was relaxed in later years. Camping fees started at seven dollars a week. For an additional twenty-five cents, women could take a bus from the Eaton's store directly to the campgrounds.

Back in the city, those women who were as devoted to exercising their intellects as they were their figures could join the Margaret Eaton School of Literature and Expression. Begun by Timothy Eaton's wife in 1907, the club prepared women for careers by improving their diction, comportment, and manners.

Run out of the same YWCA building on Yonge Street in Toronto as the Margaret Eaton School, the Eaton Girls' Club, begun in 1923, offered a wide range of athletic and cultural activities. Toronto's central YMCA, meanwhile, played host to the Eaton's Young Men's Club. Its members' three favourite activities consisted of boxing, bowling, and basketball. Between playing sports, club members could listen to speeches delivered by various experts of the day on subjects such as civic-mindedness, and the value of developing good character traits. Annual Managers' and Parents' of employees nights were thrown each year, which attracted crowds of over five hundred. Meanwhile, St. Valentine's Day dances were offered to entice the opposite sex.

■

Because they needed to work at an early age to support their families, employees in the late nineteenth and early twentieth centuries were lucky even to complete Grade 8 or 9. Neither Timothy Eaton nor his son and successor, John Craig, who assumed the presidency after his father's death in 1907, viewed an employee's lack of formal education as a liability. Neither man, in fact, supported higher education among staff members. "I don't want anyone who has a college education, for any purpose," Timothy once informed employee Jean Story.[5]

Indeed, the Eaton's store's prejudice against college-educated employees lasted into the 1940s, possibly out of the fear that the more discontented a staff member, the more likely he might incite fellow workers into organized protests or strikes. A 1946 Eaton's memo warned:

> The other type of sales person to check carefully is the young man or woman of a poor background, who is attending school or college at night. This type is often aggressive and he cannot reconcile his scholastic and intellectual qualifications with the seemingly simple duties of a sales person. When too many young people of this type are brought together in one department, the keen competition may result in jealousies, disappointments and sometimes even in labour conflicts. Simple sales people, trained by the store, answer your requirements much better than sales people whose wasted education and abilities turn them into frustrated human beings.[6]

Harry McGee receiving his Rolls Royce for forty-five years of service, 1928.

Timothy did not offer formalized staff training, preferring to bestow bonuses above regular commissions on those employees who moved merchandise the fastest. This reward system provided both monetary and emotional incentives to succeed.

Harry McGee, Eaton's longest-term employee, remains the best embodiment of Eaton's philosophy that a man who receives encouragement from fellow staff members, as well as extra cash in the form of bonuses, will sacrifice almost every hour of the day to work his way up in the firm.

Eaton's hired McGee, then twenty-five, in 1883 to sweep floors, as well as to move furniture from 178 Yonge Street to 190 Yonge Street. Within days he was promoted to being a salesman, where he earned six dollars a week, which grew to seven dollars within two weeks. After seven months, he was promoted to the position of manager of the carpet section, where he received eight dollars a week, plus commissions.

Eventually, McGee became a director of the company, and in his position as vice-president of construction was instrumental in helping to build many of the company's major stores. Few employees could fail to be impressed when, to mark McGee's forty-fifth anniversary with the store in 1928, the Eaton family presented him with a new-model Rolls-Royce.

As Timothy's empire grew, job applications floated in like confetti. Many came from friends of friends, drawing upon their one-time proximity to Timothy in church. Some of the applications, scribbled in pencil, were delivered to Timothy's house itself. Inside were pleas from the parents, sisters, and brothers of young men and women desperate for employment.

One letter, dated 1897, came from a young woman who, in addition to raising three orphaned children, was supporting her ailing mother and father. The woman asked if Timothy might allow her to establish a lacemaking department in the store. Timothy politely denied her request, but invited her to send a few samples to the store for possible sale. Another letter arrived from a railway worker, and father of three, who had been laid off because of injuries he had suffered on his job. The worker now sought indoor work in Eaton's horse stables. There is no record of Timothy's response.

The colloquial tone of many application letters reveals that their authors viewed Timothy's store as more of a mom-and-pop boarding house than a commercial establishment, a testament no doubt to the carefully cultivated image of paternalism perpetrated by Timothy. The friend of an applicant wrote in 1897:

> Mr. T. Eaton: Dear Friend, I received your letter glad to hear from you before I would send Joseph Irvine down till you would see him. I think he will suit his apearence is good and you will find him all rite. [I] would like very much to have him with you as he has neither Father or Mother that are both dead and I am the only one he has to help him he don't like the farm he would like the store bisness and this city life and if you say I will send him direct, waiting your reply, Gerard Irvine.[7]

Despite the enormous time it must have taken, Timothy responded personally to every application letter he received, even if he had to refuse.

It didn't take applicants long to realize that, in the search for employment, one qualification became virtually foolproof: "You always had a better chance of getting a job if you knew anything about Ireland," says William "Taffy" Davies. In 1930, while still a teenager, Davies ran away from Wales, and soon after emigrated to Canada. His first job was wrapping parcels at Eaton's Hamilton store.

An Irishman named Mr. Leith was in charge of hiring at the Hamilton store when Davies arrived. "I understand you know something about Ireland," Leith said to Davies.

"My aunt and uncle had a cottage outside Belfast," Davies replied.

"If I got on the train from Belfast and took it to Larne, could you name the stations in between?" asked Leith.

"Yes I could," Davies replied, proceeding to do so.

"You've got the job," an impressed Leith said.

An Irishman named Fred Walls started at Eaton's as an office boy in 1910 and, when he left Eaton's fifty years later, had risen to become both the general manager of the Montreal store and vice-president of the company. At his retirement party in 1960, in the Montreal store's ninth-floor restaurant, Eaton's representatives presented Walls with a cheque for ten thousand dollars as a gesture symbolizing his value to the company. "I don't know if it was I, or because I was a simple Irish lad, but a lot of people took an interest in me and helped me,"[8] he told the hundreds of admirers who packed themselves into the restaurant. Walls

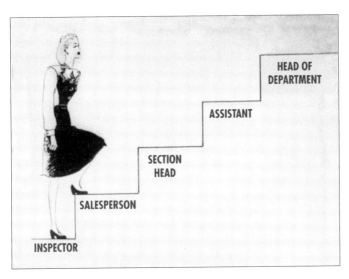

HEAD OF
DEPARTMENT

ASSISTANT

SECTION
HEAD

SALESPERSON

INSPECTOR

The hypothetical career path for female Eatonians: few would ascend higher than the second or third step.

confessed that he had never had a chance to gain much of a formal education, and reassured those present that diplomas were without much value unless their recipients had experience to accompany them.

Because of the company's fondness for Irishmen of any stripe, and its demonstrated propensity to elevate family members to executive positions, the media soon accused Eaton's of gross nepotism. The November 23, 1947, edition of the Toronto tabloid *Hush* called Eaton's "a hotbed of intrigue and double-cross," where favouritism decreed the hiring of members of a clique, over the hiring of qualified men and women. The paper went on to accuse the family of moving employees who had "fallen in the graces of the gods" from department to department, each less prestigious than the next, in an effort to break their spirits, while simultaneously hiring "rank novices" to take their place.

Eatonians countered that, since the Eaton family owned the store, it had the right to hire whomever it chose. "The Eaton family's name was over the door, on the walls, on books, napkins, and our pay packets. There wasn't any of us who was going to argue with what worked. If it wasn't broke, we weren't going to fix it," says George Carlyle, a menswear salesman in the 1940s.

Female Eatonians voiced equally vigorous defences, even though they were notoriously less well paid than men. In Timothy's day, a woman earned as little as $2.50 a week, compared to a man's salary of $7.00. While Eaton's certainly attracted a number of exceptional women, including Marg Morison, who supervised the yearly Santa

Claus parades as well as other Eaton's extravaganzas, Dora Matthews, who became a world-renowned fashion maven, and Hannah North, one of Eaton's most powerful and feared buyers, the bulk of female employees worked as sales clerks or as telephone order-takers.

Mildred Hamilton, who, in 1940, became the first woman hired to work in the merchandise-display department of the Winnipeg store, recalls receiving her first pay packet with her employee number on it. When she got home she was delighted to find $18 inside. The next morning, Hamilton was called to the wages office, where a supervisor informed her that, since there had never been a woman employed in the display department before, the department had mistakenly paid her a man's salary. "I was left with $11 once they took the difference out," says Hamilton, "which made a big dent when you consider that in those days shoes cost $8.50 a pair."

Over the years, the women who came closest to achieving wage parity with men were those who undertook commission selling. Latvian-born Barbara Redlich arrived in Canada in 1949 as a Displaced Person, or "Delayed Pioneer," as she rephrased the pejorative term. Her first job at Eaton's was as a sales clerk in the "Better Dresses" department of the College Street store, where she received a 1-per-cent commission on all sales, plus a salary of twenty-six dollars a week. To inaugurate the start of what turned out to be Redlich's brief career in commission selling, fellow staff members offered her the chance to sell evening dresses, among the most expensive items of apparel on the floor, and therefore potentially providing the largest commissions.

It didn't take long for Redlich to figure out she had been duped. Exploiting Timothy's famous credo promising "Goods Satisfactory or Money Refunded," within two or three days, up to half the customers would return the dresses, often soiled, and with the sales slips still attached. Each returned dress represented another lost commission. "You'd start out thanking your

Barbara Redlich

co-workers all over the place, and by the end you'd be cursing them," Redlich says.

Another facet of fashion sales offended Redlich. One of Timothy's Golden Rules stipulated that merchandise descriptions must be accurate: 100 per cent cotton must contain that – 100 per cent cotton, not 99.99 per cent – but Timothy didn't mention anything about clothes being guaranteed to fit. Redlich disapproved of sales clerks who pinched fabrics or clutched zippers tightly to make a garment cling to a woman's figure in a more flattering way while she was trying it on.

Disillusioned by commission selling after only three months, Redlich submitted her resignation. When her floor manager offered her a position as an invoice clerk, a job for which she would need to know bookkeeping, Redlich jumped at the chance, despite having no training. She learned bookkeeping by waiting for her colleagues to take coffee breaks, then going from desk to desk, analyzing the methods they used to complete their jobs. At stock-taking time, her arm would ache from repeatedly pulling on the adding machine's lever.

In the end, however, Redlich could only move so far up the corporate ladder. After three years of being refused a management position, she decided to explore job offers coming in from other firms, in the hopes that her chances of reaching management status might become easier to obtain. To her surprise, instead of wishing her well, some of her co-workers refused to speak to her or eat with her in the store's cafeteria. "I learned quickly that leaving Eaton's was just not done," she laughs. "They'd say, 'Eaton's has been good to you, how could you leave?'"

———■———

The length of Eaton's working hours became a highly contentious issue. To provide his staff with time to enjoy the fruits of their labours, in 1880 Timothy Eaton began closing his store at 6:00 every weeknight. By 1901, he proposed to the public the idea of shortening the store's hours by closing at 2:00 p.m. on Saturdays during the months of July and August. Special inserts were placed in the *Toronto Star*, beseeching loyal customers to show compassion by voting to allow Eaton's staff members half-days off on Saturdays. Completed ballots were to be deposited in a special box located just inside the Eaton's store. When the final votes

were tallied, it was found that the buying public sided not with the over-
worked staff, but with commerce. By a vote of 1,500 to 1,190, customers rejected Timothy's 2:00 p.m. Saturday-closing hour. Now in a
position to look more benevolent than ever, Timothy nullified the vote
by enforcing the 2:00 p.m. closing anyway, enshrining himself as a hero
in the eyes of his staff.

Grateful employees failed to notice, or perhaps failed to care,
however, that Timothy more than made up for the lost Saturday hours
by revoking his daily 6:00 p.m. closing time to keep the store open until
8:00 p.m. every weeknight throughout June, July, and August.

With success came public scrutiny, and soon a series of municipal
welfare agencies showed up at Timothy's establishment to ensure that
various rules were being followed concerning the health and welfare of
employees. Not long after Timothy inaugurated the special summer
Saturday-closing hour, representatives of Toronto's Humane Society
(formed in 1897, the society was originally committed to protecting the
rights of animals and young adults) arrived at his store to investigate the
welfare of female sales clerks. In a follow-up letter addressed to both
Timothy and Staff Inspector Archibald, the Inspector of Morals of the
City of Toronto, the society chastised Timothy for failing to protect the
welfare of young women by not placing stools throughout his store for
them to sit on when they got tired of standing.

Timothy's reaction was scathing. In addition to ordering the
company doctor to draft a letter supporting the theory that increased
blood flow could be derived from standing, as opposed to sitting,
Timothy penned his own four-page missive to Staff Inspector Archibald
that honed in like a torpedo on what he considered the self-righteous
hypocrisy of the society, some of whose members he recognized as
having opposed Eaton's shortened Saturday summer hours. He wrote:

> Through strong opposition from the outside, a great many of
> [sic] customers, and among them, many of the Humane Society,
> thought it very hard that we should close our store at two o'clock
> Saturday night. We find amongst the Humane Society persons who
> take their own afternoons on the boats, at the Island, or the various
> parks open for their accommodation during the cool of the
> evening, that they may buy their articles of attire for Sunday. We
> take no objection to any person or persons doing their shopping

during the cool of the evening, but what we have opposed and urged for years is the unthoughtfulness of the buying public to the long July day from 8 a.m. to 10 p.m. for girls working in the store. This rule we adopted at a great sacrifice to ourselves and to the displeasure of a number of our valued customers. Our store is run on the principle for the greatest amount of good to the greatest number of persons, and in this a visit to our place of business will prove to you that the sensible people of Toronto and the surrounding districts appreciate our efforts in striving to shorten by two hours per day and eight hours on Saturday during the hot months of July and August, the hours of labor, making them shorter by that amount, or eighteen hours per week, than the Humane Society demand.[9]

Timothy was correct. No matter how draconian Eaton's hours might have seemed, they were still shorter than the twelve-hour days, with one hour allotted for dinner, promulgated by the Humane Society and based on the Factories Act of 1890.

By offering ten-hour workdays, nine months of the year, Timothy was not only conforming to the law, but also bettering it. In 1904 Timothy again moved back his store's daily closing hour, this time to 5:00 p.m., an action that precipitated at Massey Hall one of the company's largest staff celebrations ever recorded.

—■—

Timothy was obsessed with keeping outsiders away from the inner workings of his store. This mindset also applied to his factories, which by the late 1800s manufactured everything from schoolbooks to military uniforms. The first factory was located on the top floor of 190 Yonge Street and contained fifty electric sewing machines that were initially used to produce children's clothing. With an increasing demand for adult apparel, a four-storey factory was soon built on the northwest side of the Queen Street store. Between 1909 and 1916, three more factories were built in Toronto; meanwhile, the Montreal factory opened for business in 1909, and the Hamilton factory in 1915.

Before long, virtually every type of suit and dress was manufactured in Timothy's factories, effectively cutting out the bane of Timothy's

Sewing-machine operators in Eaton's knitting factory. Hamilton, 1919

existence, the costly middleman known as the wholesale merchant. But if Timothy thought wholesale merchants were his biggest problem, he was about to confront a bigger one when he tried to perform end-runs around striking factory workers in 1899.

On the morning of July 14, 1899, American cloakmaker Alexander Reder filled the pockets of his jacket with stones and jumped into Lake Ontario. An employee working at the Gooderham Company's grain elevator nearby rushed to the scene and pulled Reder out of the water using a pike pole. Fifteen minutes after the rescue attempt, Reder was declared dead.

What began as a small news story grew when newspapers blamed Reder's death directly on Timothy Eaton. To subvert striking cloak-makers in his Toronto factory, Timothy imported scab machine oper-ators from the United States, Reder among them. The U.S.

Eaton's brand names

cloakmakers' contracts stipulated that they must remain employed at Eaton's for a minimum of six months, or else the cost of their transportation from New York to Toronto would be deducted from their wages. Documents presented at Reder's inquest revealed that neither Reder nor his fellow cloakmakers had been told in advance that a strike had already begun at the store. Pledging that he would rather starve than work as a "scab," Reder, lacking sufficient funds to pay his way home, killed himself.

Timothy was not violating any existing laws by hiring replacement workers from Canada, but, by importing American workers, he was in violation of the Alien Labour Act of 1896, which prohibited the importation of workers from countries other than Canada. In apportioning blame, the inquest's jury determined that being brought to Toronto under false pretences to work for the T. Eaton Company precipitated Reder's suicide. Critics ultimately cried foul, however, when the judge overseeing Reder's inquest imposed nothing harsher than a verbal reprimand on Timothy Eaton.

Ultimately, the most serious labour insurrection at Eaton's was the 1912 cloakmakers' strike, led by Jewish garment workers. They were protesting against what they considered poor working conditions within Eaton's downtown Toronto factory, as well as low wages (the average pay was $17.50 a week). But the breaking-point came when seamstresses watched their incomes diminish after Eaton acquired machines that could sew linings into suits in a fraction of the time that it took the seamstresses to do it by hand. Male machine operators, meanwhile, protested the lack of additional income they received for sewing in the linings using the new, faster machines. When workers walked out in protest, Timothy's son John Craig Eaton, now president, simply locked the factory doors behind the workers and refused them re-entry.

Vowing that he would rather shut down the entire company than rehire the locked-out factory workers, John Craig imported scab labour from England to complete work orders. Within five months, however, John Craig relented and rehired most of the striking employees, with the exception of most union leaders. Those union leaders, when finally allowed to return, suffered salary cuts.

In an attempt to downplay public criticism, during the height of the strike John Craig took out an ad in the *Evening Telegram* entitled "Let Your Easter Clothes Be Eaton-Made." The ad bragged about the "healthful modern features" that Eaton's twelve-storey factory offered its employees, including rooms John Craig praised as being "abundant in light and air." John Craig invited visitors to come and see for themselves its "wide, airy, lunchroom" and "fresh clean linen," and to savour the "full course roast meat dinner of guaranteed and excellent quality" that was offered to factory workers for only eleven cents.[10]

Generally speaking, employees of Eaton's factories considered working conditions better than those in factories run by some of Eaton's competitors. Agnes Pollock was hired in 1906 to make silk dresses. She recalls: "We were pieceworkers, but we were always very well treated. The managers were always very considerate in listening to our grievances. We worked hard and our efforts were appreciated."[11]

Eaton's factory workers were paid union wages in spite of the fact that Eaton's didn't recognize unions. Employees worked the same number of hours as sales clerks – 8 to 5 or 9 to 6, six days a week – and received one-hour lunches and two twenty-minute coffee breaks, one in the morning and another in the afternoon. While no paradise, even under the best of conditions, workrooms were nonetheless well-ventilated and clean.

In the Montreal factory, tea and milk were served from a cart that an

Women sewing in one of Eaton's factories (probably Montreal), 1930s

employee wheeled around twice a day. One factory employee marvelled at the sight of the first locker she had ever seen in a factory. In other factories, she had always hung her coat on a nail.

"I have no complaints about the working conditions in factories at Eaton's," said a Winnipeg factory worker who, at the age of sixteen, worked alongside thirty other employees making fatigues for servicemen during the late 1930s. Prior to coming to Eaton's, the employee had worked at a rival factory, which was kept so cold her hands were perpetually blue. "When I complained to the foreman, he said 'You're just a bunch of Bolsheviks.'"[12]

The Montreal factory was remarkable for operating under the auspices of several female foreladies. In her spare time, forelady Flore Allard collected remnants of fabric to sew bedspreads for the poor. After leaving Eaton's, Allard settled at the Sisters of Providence Monastery outside Montreal, where she became known as Sister Hippolite.

Meanwhile, the tone of the Montreal factory in the 1920s was set by its manager, Mr. Mann, who kept a framed cartoon on his wall depicting two carpenters and their dogs. The unhappy carpenter violently splintered wood with a scowl on his face, as his dog cowered beside him; the happy carpenter smiled as he tapped, his dog sitting contentedly by his side. A male factory worker interpreted the picture as an admonition that, to be successful, a man had to remain calm, even in the face of adversity.

Staying calm would become a full-time job during the Great Depression of the 1930s, when department stores such as Eaton's were forced to drastically reduce the amounts they paid to suppliers to have merchandise manufactured. In turn, suppliers slashed their factory workers' wages, creating sweatshop conditions across the country. In 1929 a worker in corsets and underwear averaged 33.9 cents an hour, but in 1934 they earned only 28.8 cents.

In 1934, a Wage and Price Spread Inquiry was instigated by Henry Stevens, the Minister of Trade and Commerce, to investigate the charge that Canadian department stores, including Eaton's, were unfairly using their bulk-purchasing power to buy merchandise at bargain-basement prices, selling it at exorbitant profits, and paying their employees a pittance in wages.

Defenders of Eaton's argued that it was a miracle the store remained in business at all, with so few people buying merchandise. Even

The lack of jobs at Eaton's, plus low salaries, were blamed for leading young women into prostitution during the Depression.

commissioned salesmen were kept on staff, though at the time it was impossible for them to sell big-ticket items such as furniture, or hard goods such as fridges or stoves. Eaton's Welfare Office also continued to distribute money to employees down on their luck, including coverage of their medical expenses if they fell ill. Critics argued that employees would have preferred to receive this money in the form of decent wages, rather than have it given to them as a form of paternalistic charity.

In the end, the commission concluded that, between 1929 and 1934, of Eaton's total takings across the counter, 76.3 cents out of each customer's dollar had gone to cover the actual cost of merchandise, while profit and interest on borrowings combined amounted to only 2 cents out of the same dollar. The balance, approximately 22 cents, was distributed in the form of wages or other merchandising costs.

Though Eaton's was officially cleared of taking advantage of extraordinary markups on merchandise, a *Winnipeg Tribune* reporter attending the inquiry recorded that a woman in the back of the room gasped upon hearing that the women's coats Eaton's bought for $6.30 eventually sold for $15, a markup of over 138 per cent.[13]

On top of that, a crisis was narrowly averted after reporters discovered that, while employees' discounts were reduced during the Depression from 10 per cent to 5 per cent, the 25-per-cent discounts enjoyed by direct descendants of the Eaton family were maintained. Such a public-relations gaff would have been hard to imagine in Timothy's day.[14]

Unable to convict Eaton's of unfair markups on their merchandise, the more sensational tabloid newspapers of the day turned their attention to the plight of Eaton's female employees. "EATON'S GIRLS SHAMED," blared the *National Tattler* headline of February 1, 1939. Inside, an article entitled "Store Girls Are Forced to Shame Selves!" chronicled – in lurid language, and sketches of employees in flimsy silk negligées – the "pitiful struggle" girls experienced remaining moral in the face of the poor wages they received on the job.[15] While the tabloid offered no precise figures concerning the number of women affected, social-service agencies reported that many "girls" were supplementing their meagre incomes by moonlighting as prostitutes.

Despite accusations of being anti-labour, Eaton's continued to receive thousands of applications a year for employment, both before and after the Great Depression.

As far back as the early decades of the twentieth century, the store had also been accused of discriminating against the hiring of cultural minorities, both for their factories and stores.

In her 1992 doctoral thesis, "The Most Prominent Rendezvous of the Feminine Toronto: Eaton's College Street and the Organization of Shopping in Toronto, 1920–1950," Cynthia Jane Wright speculates that, as a result of their participation in the 1912 garment-factory strike at Eaton's, Jews were rarely invited to work as sales clerks in the Eaton's stores. Instead, they were relegated to working almost exclusively in the store's factories. Wright points out that, in 1937, for instance, 128 of 148 Jewish employees were factory workers. Meanwhile, of 8,528 sales clerks at Eaton's in 1937, only 20 were Jewish.[16]

CBC newswriter Larry Zolf recalls that, to pay Eaton's back for not hiring Jews or Slavs, he and a friend named Harold decided to steal wallets from the Winnipeg store. "Eaton's was very nice about it. No charges were laid and the wallets were returned, except for the one Harold's parents had to pay for," says Zolf.

Other Jews decided to boycott Eaton's stores altogether. One of these was Zolf's mother, who continued to patronize a small Jewish department store named Oretski's on Selkirk Avenue, until the quality, convenience, and low price of Eaton's merchandise lured her away. In spite of shopping at Eaton's, she remained superstitious about the store, especially its escalators, and told Zolf that the fate of a female neighbour named Mrs. Greenberg had been sealed when Greenberg took an escalator up "and never came back."

Curiously, while such figures as Supreme Court of Canada Justice Bora Laskin's wife, Peggy, could not get a job as a beautician at Eaton's in the 1930s because, it was explained to her, Eaton's didn't employ Jews, as far back as the 1920s Eaton's was donating sums in excess of $13,000 to Jewish charities, including the Montreal Hadassah. And in a speech he made in 1898, Timothy advised his buyers that the key to success was to be "as straight and clear as the Jews they buy from."[17]

In the early 1940s, meanwhile, Flora McCrea Eaton, the wife of Timothy's son, John Craig, raised money for the Canadian Council of Christians and Jews. At one point, she sent out one hundred letters to her friends, requesting a ten-dollar donation from each. She received ninety-six positive responses.

Catholic charities also received generous amounts of Eaton's money – an irony, since Catholics, especially of the Irish stripe, were at least historically the bitter adversaries of Irish Protestants like the Eatons. Meanwhile, Eaton's prejudice against Englishmen working in the company bordered on the comedic. At the turn of the twentieth century, due to Eaton's Irish tribalism, the London Buying Office was almost exclusively populated by Irish employees. Around this time, during a tour of the office, Timothy spotted a slim, bespectacled employee, pouring over his notes at his desk. Turning to his companion, Timothy said, "Who's that?"

"That's Portlock, sir. He's English," the companion replied.

"Fire him," Timothy purportedly said. As evidence that Timothy's bark was always worse than his bite, in the end, Portlock was not only allowed to maintain his job, but became one of Eaton's most trusted and valued employees, joining the store as an office boy in 1905, and retiring as head of Eaton's European buying operations in 1951.

■

Seemingly bulletproof, Eaton's reputation grew rather than diminished throughout the 1940s and 1950s. Formal application forms, introduced in the early 1940s, contained what by today's standards appear to be unreasonably personal questions concerning religious affiliations, disabilities, and level of alcohol consumption.

Dress codes, meanwhile, remained stringent. In the store's early years, women's skirts were never to rise so high that ankles were visible. Sleeves were never to rise above the elbows. After an increasing number of female employees sacrificed the hems of their skirts to greasy bicycle gears, they were finally allowed to shorten them. Until the 1960s, colours were confined to black, navy, or what was described in brochures as "nigger brown." Ornate jewellery was discouraged, as well as flowers in the hair or fancy straps across the shoes. Blouses were not to be made of any flimsy fabric that might cause men's eyes to drift. Men were restricted to wearing navy-blue suits and white patternless shirts.

Norma Rooke, who worked in the drapery section of the Winnipeg store in the 1940s, recalls that the dress code in winter was black and in summer was pure white. If a woman was going out for the evening

"Silly Sue" – part of an Eaton's training film
showing the dos and don'ts of female sales-clerking

Eaton's imposed strict dress codes on its employees – especially females. No shoes with straps, no flowers in their hair, no fancy jewellery. Bright lipstick and nail polish were also out of the question.

straight from work, wearing a coloured or figured dress, she had to obtain a special pass from the employment office and wear a long-sleeved black smock over the outfit. "I remember one time I had bought a dress with the midriff that had a small stripe of pale, pale blue and a small stripe of pale pink, and the floorwalker made me put my smock on," she says.[18]

Charlotte Lepp, a sales clerk in the Winnipeg store, wore a nurse's uniform to sell baby clothes. The line between make-believe nurse and sales clerk became even blurrier when, as part of her job, Lepp was required to weigh and measure babies in order to discern their appropriate clothing sizes.

It was only with the explosion of psychedelic colours in the late 1960s that then-president John David Eaton circulated a memo advising that female employees could wear coloured clothes. But saleswomen could have lived without at least one mandatory accessory – the Eaton's nameplate – whose pin snagged and frayed the fabric of their clothes.

In addition to rigid dress codes, staff members were expected to show initiative when dealing with customers. Each employee's performance was evaluated using detailed Productivity Summaries, as well as a monthly table of Sales to Date.

Management's comments on employee evaluations ran the gamut. One typical example from 1964 said: "Mrs. ——— is a perfectionist. Gives excellent service to customers. Is a much-needed type of clerk. Will try to improve sales." At the other end of the spectrum, another evaluation said, "Spends approximately 65% of time adjusting desk. Have transferred to expense."[19]

When necessary, verbal warnings were given, allowing employees the chance to shape up. If employees failed to do so, they were given warning slips. One employee had a "poor attitude and lack of interest in stock & sales." He was terminated seven months later, after an internal investigation. Another employee was assessed as having a "very disturbing influence in Department – would not re-hire."[20]

Some employees needed prodding, were deemed not aggressive enough, didn't close sales fast enough, or just lacked that intangible quality called "hustle." Other staff members were adduced as needing more confidence. Salesgirls, meanwhile, could be chided for being "a bit impatient with customers."[21]

Should employees fail to improve the quality of their salesmanship, they were relieved of their jobs, and then required to attend "exit interviews."

There, employees obtained their Leaving Slips from the Personnel Office. Aware that every employee was a potential customer, personnel made every effort to assure that the parting was as amicable as possible.

In Timothy's day, employees worked alongside management to realize the dream of providing reasonably priced, good-quality merchandise to customers, who weren't just buying houses, but "castles," and weren't buying clothes, but "fashions." That psychology began to change after the Second World War, when speed and convenience became the paramount prerequisites of successful shopping.

With their emergence in the 1950s, the self-service approach in stores such as Kresge, Zeller's, and Loblaws began slowly but steadily to lure away Eaton's customers. The most audacious of the new arrivals was Sayvette, whose slogans "Complete Satisfaction or Your Money Refunded" and "Your Money Back at Once If You're Not Satisfied for Any Reason," closely mirrored Timothy Eaton's motto: "Goods Satisfactory or Your Money Refunded." Sayvette also boasted that it was open six nights a week until 10:00 p.m.

Eaton's was forced to enact a drastic change in store policy to keep up with the competition. A new motto, "Eaton's Will Not Be Undersold," soon appeared. Eaton's staff members struggled to cater to a more mobile, and – as a result of radio and television advertising – a more cynical customer base, one that had come to see merchandise as disposable and self-service as superior to the human touch.

In a radical departure from Timothy's edict against employing university graduates, in the late 1950s and early 1960s Eaton's actively began to recruit graduates, who might bring fresh ideas to the firm. The cult of hipness soon infiltrated the Eaton's empire. Sales staff watched helplessly as, without advance warning, their middle-aged managers were shuffled from one store to the other, or laid off altogether.

Charlotte Lepp recalls the day when university students arrived and were given the authority to sign off on any payments customers made by cheque, as well as to approve any return of merchandise receipts. "Basically, university students walked in and took over the signatures of our old bosses that had been there for years. [Our managers] became inferior people. I know there were suicides and hearts attacks, lots of them. Some were offered early retirement, but they didn't want retirement; they had big families, what was going to happen to their lives now? They didn't know where to go from there."[22]

The downsizing of middle managers also unnerved Lepp's fellow employees, who engaged in intense discussions around the water cooler. "Almost in a sense you felt things around the world were changing: feelings, caring,"[23] says Lepp.

Beginning in the summer of 1964, formal management-training courses were offered in-store to university graduates employed by the company. Management training had previously been informal, and consisted of moving potential managers around different departments to gain experience. Now, established managers instructed management trainees on everything from discipline and security to staff relations and the philosophy of suburban stores.

To encourage staff members to speed up electronic cash-register transactions, Eaton's introduced Harvard psychologist B. F. Skinner's "programmed-learning technique." Skinner had achieved considerable success in teaching pigeons how to play ping-pong with their beaks, rewarding their success with kernels of corn. By October 1963, Skinner had added his programmed-learning system to the regular teaching schedule of Eaton's Staff Training Department at the main store. In preparation for the opening of the Yorkdale store in 1964, over the course of several days, 1,200 employees returned to the Salestronic registers time and time again to try to increase their accuracy and speed. In the case of new employees, the reward was obtaining jobs; in the case of long-term employees, it was keeping them.

If cash registers felled even the hardiest of sales clerks, the implementation of computerized billing pushed many of them over the brink. In February 1965, an *Eaton News Quarterly* article entitled "Mrs. Martin's New Bill" heralded the arrival of the National Cash Register 315, a computer that was optimistically expected to streamline customer-buying summaries.

In preparation for the computer's debut, each Eaton's customer was mailed an eight-digit account card. In the meantime, the computers were programmed to reject any previous cards that differed from the cards bearing eight digits.

On the surface, the system appeared easy. Sales clerks throughout the store were required to input customers' account-card numbers in their cash registers, followed by the department and section numbers in which merchandise had been purchased. At the end of the day, the cash-register tapes were to be removed and fed into large mainframe computers designed to spit out a summary of customers' purchases, as well as the amounts they owed.

The article stressed that failures in the process could only be attributed to those sales clerks who neglected to input the proper code for the section where merchandise was bought. The article warned that a simple transposition of numbers might cause a customer to be billed for lingerie when he in fact bought a hammer. "He would not be happy if he had to try to convince Mrs. Martin of the error,"[24] the article joked.

As it turned out, the joke ended up being on Eaton's. The expression "Shopping is quicker and easier when you carry your Eaton Account Card" turned into a travesty, and made many a sales clerk harken back to Timothy's day, when cash was king.

"Girls would make mistakes on the cash-register tapes; they would reverse the mistakes, and an error would suddenly be listed as a return," says Barbara Redlich, who, after she left Eaton's, ended up working for the Friden Company, which manufactured the National Cash Register 315 computers. She notes, "The customers would get the statements, showing all these mistakes, and would say to themselves, 'If your system is so poor that mistakes show up on your accounts, we'll go to Simpson's, or pay cash.'" Ironically, many of the women Redlich trained to use the registers were the same women who had castigated her for leaving Eaton's in the first place.

To make matters worse, some elderly female employees were put on a quota system, which required them to tally a certain number of entries per day. "It was terrible," says Redlich. "They couldn't keep up and they were severely reprimanded if they couldn't keep up with the quotas. Finally, in desperation, they just deliberately pulled the machines' plugs to disable them." When the computers ended up being disabled more often than they functioned, Eaton's discontinued the quota system altogether.

■

Throughout the 1960s and 1970s, Eaton's boldly built dozens of suburban outlets across the country. At the same time, they also built marquee stores in urban centres. These included the Pacific Centre in Vancouver and the Eaton Centre in Toronto.

Problems arose when both suburban and urban stores carried identical types of merchandise. Suddenly gone was the allure of making a day special by travelling to a big downtown store to shop when the identical merchandise was available a few blocks away in the suburbs.

Store managers were increasingly faced with the challenge of creating innovative marketing strategies to push merchandise. If quotas weren't reached, the blame typically was divided between the managers and the sales force on the floor, who, in turn, blamed the upper management for their lack of vision.

Creating excitement among sales staff about the products they were selling became an uphill battle in the sort of atmosphere in which the quantity sold became as important as – or more important than – the quality of the salesmanship. When motivational exercises alone didn't prove sufficient to raise sales volume, Eaton's hired mystery shoppers to pose as customers and visit stores in order to gauge the sales clerks' skill. Mystery shoppers watched in particular for sales clerks to "add on" to purchases, by suggesting better and bigger merchandise to complement a customer's original purchase.

"At first it was quite a shock, then it became kind of a game," says Kathy Henkinson, of the Abbotsford store, in British Columbia. "Some girls thought they could tell who was the mystery shopper."

"They used to take away my freedom," says Donna York, who worked in the Nanaimo store in the 1970s. "I used to like to have fun with customers." York was working in the Chinaware department one night when she was approached by a mystery shopper, who bought a magnet in the shape of a cat. "It was late, so I chatted with the woman a little bit; it was very pleasant. Next thing I know, I'm called into the manager's office and told I failed on my job because I didn't try to add on to the magnet. So I said to them, 'Next time someone asks for a magnet, I'm going to ask if they want a fridge to go with it!'" Unnerved by the experience, York took two days' sick leave. "We were little robots in the end."

The Service Wheel, a concept initiated by then-vice-president Greg Purchase, also generated resentment among sales staff. The cardboard wheel listed step-by-step how customers were to be approached. All sales clerks were advised to be available, and to greet customers with a smile and utter the words "May I suggest . . ." rather than "Can I help you?"

The wheel was kept by the cash registers at the checkout counters, and while it may have proved helpful to new employees, it annoyed those with years of experience in customer relations – sometimes with embarrassing results. "I was concluding this sale with a woman named, of all things, Mrs. Dick, while at the same time trying to make sure I followed all the steps on the wheel," says one employee. "When I was finished, I got so confused, I said, 'May I put your Dick in the bag, Mrs. Bill?' Luckily the customer was elderly and didn't understand what I said."

By the late 1970s, staff morale throughout the company had reached an all-time low. Many veteran employees were laid off to make space for less expensive part-time employees, some of them barely out of their teens. Facing the axe, some frightened senior employees retaliated by committing in-store theft, a situation that saddened even hardened store detectives. "Investigating a co-worker was always the worst part of the job," says Yorkdale store detective Bruno Pupo. Pupo was shocked when he observed a veteran childrenswear employee stealing money from a cash register. "This nice little old lady had been one of our best spotters. She would nail shoplifters right and left and call security to pick them up," he says.

The remainder of Eaton's employees fought hard to protect their stores from thefts. Many helped mount "anti-shrinkage" campaigns, at one point distributing pens that read, "$1 in shrinkage cancels $20 in sales." The campaign foundered, however, when many of the pens were stolen, along with anti-shrinkage paperweights and posters.

Despite the installation of expensive two-way mirrors, satellite balls, and electronic clips that activated store buzzers, customer thefts also increased. Eaton's lost hundreds of thousands of dollars a year. Gang members armed with wire cutters could saw through a rack of clothing and make off with ten or twelve suits in seconds. After they were finished, they disappeared into the crowds that congregated in the malls adjoining the Eaton's stores.

In Winnipeg, native gangs sometimes raced en masse into the Eaton's store, smashing and grabbing as much as they could in the shortest amount of time possible. "One year it got so bad, we had all the security staff stand at the doors and at the escalators just to stop them," says store detective Joan Bogart. "We knew they would take the stolen merchandise back to their reservations and sell it for an inflated price."

Bogart believes the core of the problem rested with the Eaton family's

"The only people who didn't like Peter Glen were those who couldn't look at themselves in the mirror," Jim Matthews says of the marketing guru pictured above.

reluctance to believe that anyone might steal from them. "Security wasn't an important thing to the Eatons. They didn't want to think people would steal until the shrinkage problem got so bad they couldn't ignore it," she says. "Everyone knew the rot at Eaton's started at the top. Everyone asked themselves, 'Who's running the company today?'"

With no Timothy to rally the company's troops, Eaton's imported outside sales consultants, whose specialty was to boost sagging morale among dispirited staff members.

"You know what they say about consultants: It's cheaper than fixing the problem," says Peter Glen, a flamboyantly dressed marketing dynamo whom Eaton's nicknamed "a new breed of retail cat." American by birth, and trained in theatre, Glen visited 90 per cent of Eaton's stores, from Halifax to Nanaimo, throughout the 1970s and 1980s, presenting his popular show entitled "Selling Is Our Business."

Four times a day, Glen enlisted employees to perform skits demonstrating sales situations such as the "Wrong Approach," or "Beating Up on Customers." He transformed Eaton's merchandise departments into avant-garde stages. Switched-on television sets were turned upside down to lure curious customers. One manager organized his employees in a three-week "Do Your Own Thing" display contest, the top prize being a cash bonus of forty-five dollars. Second place was awarded to a sales clerk's Fruit of the Loom tree, which she designed by hanging packets of pantyhose, girdles, and bras from the branches of an artificial tree.

The day before his official visits, Glen slipped into stores and secretly videotaped sales clerks as they handled customer transactions. The following day, he gathered the same employees in a group and dissected their performances, using often brilliantly sardonic, sometimes bullying language. Those who weren't reduced to tears by Glen's searing criticisms usually cried tears of laughter.

Overall, reaction to Glen was mixed, particularly among established employees. "His whole purpose was to shock people," says Fran Alford, a childrenswear buyer.

Buyer Alan Boothe agrees. "One thing I didn't like about Peter was that he would pick on one person. Every meeting you could see someone was going to get it. One time he picked on an elderly mattress-department employee. He was going at the guy pretty hard and the guy just snapped and said, 'Look, Peter, my wife's hairdresser is a lot more manly than you'll ever be.' Well, after that you could hear a pin drop. Peter was undone," Boothe recalls.

On the other hand, Glen had his champions.

"The only people who didn't like Peter Glen were those who couldn't look at themselves in the mirror," says Jim Matthews, who saw Glen as just what was needed to restore Eaton's team spirit through the final quarter of the twentieth century.

In press releases, Glen likened Timothy Eaton to the "first hippie," a bold explorer who strapped on a metaphorical backpack to venture fearlessly into uncharted retail territory. As an outsider, Glen was perhaps more capable than those close to the situation of appreciating that it was the Eatonians' sense of family that kept the store operating for as long as it did, with the Eaton family itself providing the glue.

As Glen sums it up succinctly, "The relationship between Eaton's and its customers became an almost patriotic idea. . . . [The] Bay was a company and Eaton's *was* the Eatons."

CHAPTER 3

Santa and Other Extravaganzas

*Early parades • Parade stories
• Santa and other characters • The ending*

TIMOTHY EATON'S BRAINCHILD, the annual Santa Claus parade, not only constituted the biggest movable billboard in the world, but also cleverly transformed customers into active participants in the store's own advertising.

The first Santa Claus parade took place in Toronto on December 2, 1905. Impatient children, who had lined up on the north side of Front Street, pelted each other with snowballs as they waited for the Eaton's employee dressed as Santa to emerge from Union Station, where a Grand Trunk Railway train had deposited him after his mythical journey from the North Pole.

"Santa's" departure from the railway station was delayed long enough for him to polish off a hearty breakfast of bacon and eggs. With crumbs still gathered in his beard, and a sack of souvenirs slung over his shoulder, he finally climbed on board his horse-drawn truck, seating himself on a red-and-black-painted packing crate, from which he flung candies and nuts to dozens of screaming children running close behind.

As Eaton's parades grew in popularity, teams of carpenters constructed floats of nursery-rhyme figures in a variety of unheated garages across Toronto, starting at the drafty no. 5 Eaton's Garage on Terauley

Street (now Bay Street), followed by the Lansdowne Avenue stables, and finally at the giant service building/warehouse located on the outskirts of the city at the intersection of highways 400 and 401. After they were built, floats might receive as many as 150 gallons of paint apiece.

In the parade's formative years, when traffic travelling down Toronto's dirt roads consisted mostly of horse-drawn carriages and a few motor cars, a number of steps had to be taken to convince city safety officials that parades could take place without incident. An advance team of Eaton's employees walked the parade's routes carrying long poles, which they used to measure the height of low-hanging tree branches and streetcar wires overhead.

Store managers were commandeered to act as parade marshals, to prevent children from running out into traffic or attempting to climb onto floats. Policemen were posted to direct cross-traffic through intersections.

The parade route changed at least ten times over the course of Eaton's sponsorship. Beginning in 1909, Santa disembarked at an elaborately constructed "Royal Court," located in Massey Hall. Assisted by co-workers dressed as fairy-tale figures, he entertained nine thousand screaming children who had gathered to greet him.

After 1917, Santa's destination became the Eaton's store itself. Any employee who assumed the role of Santa had to face the daunting task of hoisting his padded belly up a fire ladder from the float to the store's second-floor Eaton's Toyland window, located above Albert Street. More often than not, as "Santa" stumbled, frequently cursing, through the window, he was resuscitated by swigs of "Seagram's medicine," provided by sympathetic store managers.

First aid didn't always reach Santa in time. After one particularly frigid parade, amid a cacophony of bells and whistles, a blue-tinged Santa had to be carried by stretcher from his sleigh into the building. On a stretcher next to him lay his "helper," who, as a result of blowing into an alphorn for most of the parade in sub-zero temperatures, could no longer produce sound nor remove his immobilized lips from the horn's mouthpiece.

Undoubtedly, Santa's most spectacular entrance took place in 1915, when he personally piloted a biplane to an airstrip just north of Eglinton Avenue. Shortly after the plane wobbled to a stop, a slim Santa disappeared into a waiting limousine, which had curtains drawn

The Christmas rush, 1904

Santa Claus in Eaton's Toyland, Queen Street store, Toronto, 1904

Real reindeer were imported for the 1913 Santa Claus Parade.

Christmas Parade, 1918, Toronto

Jack Brockie was the mastermind behind the Santa Claus Parade and events held in the Eaton Auditorium.

across its windows. After a short drive, a substantially fatter Santa emerged from the same limousine and climbed on board his band-wagon float, which was designed to resemble an ancient Norse warship, festooned with a row of shields and banners along the sides, and a grotesque walrus head bearing a golden crown nailed to its front.

In 1928, Special Events Manager Jack Brockie assumed creative control of the parade, giving it the infrastructure that it badly needed to grow. Drawing on his training as a designer, as well as his service in an artillery battery during the First World War, Brockie controlled every facet of the parade's organization, including deciding where each of the eventually eight-hundred-plus participants would stand in relation to the other. In later years, Brockie introduced formal parade themes such as "The Cat in the Hat" or "Jack and the Beanstalk."

Less than twenty-four hours after each parade ended, Brockie gathered together participants and critically dissected the parade, using slides produced by store photographer Harold Hundert. "It was a pretty intimidating experience," says Jim Matthews, who points out that attendees often sank down in their seats to avoid being called upon by Brockie to explain their parade "performances." Matthews says, "Brockie would use this pointer and point at various people on the screen and say, 'Well, what was going on here?' It was brutal!"

Beginning in the early 1950s, Harold Hundert began splicing together sixteen-millimetre films he shot of the parade, afterwards adding music. To capture the parade's continuity, he set up three cameras along the route. After editing the films, Hundert personally screened them for free at schools and churches throughout Toronto, while simultaneously distributing them for a fee to countries such as England, Germany, and even Cuba.

Well over half a million residents, including out-of-towners, lined the downtown Toronto streets to watch the parade. Radio stations, such as CKEY, broadcast a month-long series of shows, charting Santa's journey from the North Pole. Live coverage of the parade was televised nationally on the CBC, CTV, and, later still, on the Global TV networks.

The CBS network in the United States originally purchased fifteen-minute excerpts of the parade in the 1950s, but in response to overwhelming public demand, ultimately ended up broadcasting the parade in its entirety, one week after it took place in Toronto. An impressive roster of celebrities hosted the American version of the parade, including Dick Clark and Arthur Godfrey, who managed to leave a lasting impression with his foul mouth and abusive personality.

Representatives of Macy's department store in New York credited Eaton's with pioneering the parade idea. One year, Macy's invited Eaton's parade organizers to watch the Macy's parade in person. The Macy's parade, which first began in 1925, debuted oversized rubberized helium-filled balloons of cartoon characters, such as Felix the Cat and Donald Duck, in 1927. Eaton's ordered smaller versions of the same sort of balloons used in the Macy's parade, but abandoned the idea after most of them were burst by children throwing rocks.

"A successful parade must flow," Brockie told Canadian Business magazine in a November 1955 interview. "If there's a break in the parade, you're sunk."[1] To best showcase their distinctiveness, floats were spaced at least ten feet apart. The spaces, Brockie reasoned, gave children time to ask their parents questions about individual floats.

Brockie's inventiveness was evident in his schedule for the 1930 parade, which featured a Christmas-tree float surrounded by nineteen bells; a clown; a giant Felix the Cat, followed by a Grand Marshal; wooden soldiers; a Highlanders' band; and a grasshopper.

To draw the community even more tightly into the festivities, Brockie made sure to invite high-school bands to participate, in addition to perennial favourites such as the Forty-eighth Highlanders. "High" might have been an apt word to describe at least some of the Highlanders, who were alleged to have secret flasks of rum in their brass instruments, from which they took swigs in between blows. To avoid having music clash, Brockie instructed the various groups of musicians to play at staggered intervals.

In addition to organizing Toronto's parade, Brockie also acted as a consultant to the Winnipeg parade, which ran from 1906 until 1962. Winnipeg's parade featured original floats built from scratch, usually

constructed in a partially unheated two-thousand-square-foot warehouse on the banks of the Red River.

When Alfred Judt began working as the head carpenter on Winnipeg's
Santa Claus parade in 1955, there were only eight other carpenters in
the construction department. After each parade ended, those materials
not recycled were burned on the banks of the river. Giant papier-

*Santa, getting ready to mount the stairs to Eaton's Montreal store's
"Toyville," 1951. After making it up the steps, Santas were often
revived by a shot of "Seagram's medicine."*

Give a parade, and they will come. Christmas Parade, Montreal, 1945.

mâché heads, meanwhile, were stored side by side in deep eight-foot-long boxes.

Beginning in spring, Judt and his fellow carpenters worked steadily, perfecting floats in time for the fall parade. The carpenters did not relax until after the last float was returned to the warehouse at the end of each parade, usually around 3 p.m. Ninety-proof libations capped off most post-parade celebrations, resulting in at least one amusing incident. As Judt was locking up the warehouse after the conclusion of a parade, he noticed that one of his carpenters had disappeared. After searching through all the heated areas of the warehouse, he was about to give up, when he heard a snuffling noise emanating from one of the boxes containing the papier mâché heads. "I pulled up the top flap and a guy was tipped inside there head first between these giant heads, snoring. He must have just passed out in the box that way," he says.

In 1967, Winnipeg's Santa Claus parade was cancelled, with most people choosing to escape the sub-zero temperatures by watching the Toronto parade on television in the comfort and warmth of their living rooms.

The Montreal parade, which debuted in 1925, took place one week after Toronto's, and used the same floats as theirs. As soon as the Toronto parade ended, the floats were transported to Union Station, where they were loaded onto covered boxcars for their trip to Montreal. Freshly laundered costumes were also packed into hampers and placed on the same boxcars as the floats.

To appease French protesters, who complained about the importation of original floats from Toronto, the construction of Montreal's large Santa Claus float was entrusted to a Montreal artist. The first float consisted of a large whale, painted grey, with a long, upturned tail on which was rigged a golden chair for Santa Claus to sit in.

A contingent of Toronto's Parade designers, including Head Designer Reg Collins, travelled to Montreal in 1925 to kick off the parade. Collins was pleased to note that the spectators at the Montreal parade seemed even more "lively and receptive" than those in Toronto. Even the police seemed to throw themselves into the fun. Brockie noted in *Canadian Business* magazine that "French Canadians treat the event as a carnival, where here it's just a parade."[2]

The popularity of Montreal's parade made it even sadder when, on November 22, 1968, Eaton's Montreal store manager Pierre Witmeur permanently cancelled the parade after he received FLQ bomb threats. A search of the store revealed four sticks of dynamite wired to a clock in the main-floor jewellery department; they were defused by bomb-squad personnel.

In the early hours of the same day, a bomb had exploded in some public lockers in the basement of the store, injuring two members of the nighttime cleaning staff. Two thousand dollars' worth of damage occurred to the basement ceiling, as well as to the escalator leading from the basement to the main floor. As a protective measure, wooden shutters were placed across the store's display windows.

Witmeur finally decided to end the parade after talking with Montreal safety officials. "I talked to the Chief of Police, and he said, 'We cannot be held responsible for the protection of the population,' so I made the decision to end it."

The cancellation of Montreal's parade so soon before it was to occur meant that hundreds of marchers had to stay home and watch the Toronto parade on television. A ten-year-old boy, who had been attempting for six years to participate in the parade and had finally been given a role, showed up in tears at the store's Public Relations department. In a gesture of consolation, management officials gave him the three-dollar fee he would have earned as a participant.

By contrast, Toronto's Santa Claus parade became bigger and more sophisticated as the years passed. To aid them in keeping tabs on possible trouble, parade officials resorted to communicating through walkie-talkies.

A St. John's medical team rode in a special vehicle at the rear of the parade. Despite the medical team's presence, at least two Santas expired while en route. In an attempt to avoid newspaper headlines that read "SANTA DIES," Eaton's kept a spare Santa, either inside the float, or nearby in an accompanying car. These spare Santas came in particularly handy whenever the effort of simulating gaiety forced a few Santas to snap emotionally. One year, medical teams were called on to help an overly refreshed Santa off his float when he began shouting "Merry Christmas, you little bastards" at the bright-eyed children cheering him from the sidewalks.

Once all the official civic permissions were obtained, Eaton's distributed press releases to various media outlets, outlining the parade route and announcing which celebrities would be appearing. One year's parade featured Toronto's "Tiny Perfect Mayor," David Crombie, wearing a frilly baby bonnet and sucking on a pacifier, being pushed down the streets in a baby carriage.

Despite the best efforts of organizers over the years, a few incidents succeeded in interrupting the parade's seamless flow. In the 1930s, the Fairy Queen float lost a large swatch of brightly coloured feathers when its top skimmed a Yonge Street railway arch. Drawing up behind, a Mr. Jackson of Eaton's Hardware department, better known as Santa, was too busy shouting "Ho, Ho, Ho" to notice a low-hanging branch that, when it connected with his head, rendered him unconscious for several minutes. Once revived, Jackson gamely resumed his ho-ho-ing, though at a more subdued pitch.

As a result of these incidents, the dimensions of floats were restricted to a height of no more than eight feet wide, thirteen feet high, and fifty-two feet long. Each float was pulled by Eaton's own trucks and delivery vans, which were decorated with aprons to hide their wheels.

In later years, floats were either pulled by tractors or powered internally by Volkswagen or motorcycle motors. One year, a float consisted of an enormous cake decorated with dozens of battery-powered candles. When the "cake" stalled at the beginning of the parade, it was rolled over to a car and given a boost before it could continue. Lloyd Robertson, the CTV anchorman who hosted the parade for several years, recalls with amusement the year Elmer the Safety Elephant encountered the same fate.

Openings were crudely sliced out of the front of floats to allow drivers to keep their eyes on the road, a nerve-wracking job, considering the drivers' almost complete lack of peripheral vision. Participants trying to operate back-to-back clown floats navigated by gyroscope. It wasn't unusual to find six men crammed into the bottom half of a giant clown costume, using pulleys to manipulate the top half. Once the parades were filmed, these men were alerted by walkie-talkie when to turn the heads of the clowns towards cameras.

A variety of fabrics covered early floats, which were all designed without the use of blueprints. Large heads for clowns or dogs were typically made from dyed cotton. Every effort was made to construct benign storybook characters that wouldn't give children nightmares after the parade. This objective didn't always succeed, particularly the year when a limp Jack-and-the-Beanstalk figure was draped grotesquely over the end of a cart, as if waiting to be guillotined.

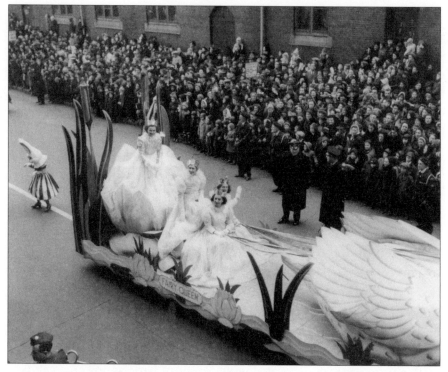

Fairy Queen Float – Christmas Parade, Montreal, November 25, 1944. One year in Toronto a fight broke out when the wrong fashion model tried to board the Fairy Queen float.

Because of its light weight and malleability, papier mâché became the preferred material in constructing float figures, but even it had one serious drawback. When rain or snow fell on them, the comical, over-sized heads became too heavy to balance on parade participants' shoulders, causing those wearing them to bob and weave dangerously into the crowds. "Parade participants were instructed to never remove their heads during a parade, because it might spoil the illusion for the children," says Jim Matthews, who adds, "You'd see people holding onto what was left of their heads, charging through the crowds."

By far the ultimate float for young women was that of the Fairy Queen, who rode on her own ornately decorated float that featured a throne. In 1952, a public-relations nightmare was barely avoided when one of Eaton's models attempted to board the Fairy Queen float by mistake. "It fell to me to let her know as gently as possible that she wasn't going to be the Fairy Queen that year, but just one of her minions," says Jim Matthews, who was acting as a marshal. "Her mother was ready to slug me. That was a great way to start the parade!"

Company employees volunteered to take part in the parade year after year. Model Meg Peck walked the route several times, once dressed as the Queen of Hearts. "They hardly needed to pay us because people were lining up to do it and probably would have done it gratis."

Eaton's dress saleswoman Olive Robinson was 1964's Fairy Queen. She appeared in the parade regularly for forty years as different characters. Among her favourite experiences was playing the Man in the Moon, riding high above a cloud on a float of her own. "It was a panic," she told *Toronto Sunday Sun* columnist Marilyn Linton, recalling that the seat was designed like "a padded outside toilet, and I fell through the hole." Robinson only decided to retire from the job when parade organizers asked her to walk the route wearing a bear's head.[3]

By far the hardest job for parade participants was passing by sick children who were seated in wheelchairs or lying in beds on the curbside, watching the parade. "I'd be singing and feeling wonderful, and suddenly I'd see a small, pale child looking up at me from a hospital bed, all hooked up to tubes, and I'd just lose it," says Maureen Nori, the mother of a parade participant, who was invited to join the parade at the last minute when an extra costume was found in her size.

Early parade marchers were drawn exclusively from the ranks of employees, or local dancing schools. Later, applications were distributed to elementary and high-school students. Depending on their age, fees from three to five dollars were paid to those who participated in the parades.

Each year, there were more people wanting to participate in the parade than there were available spots. "We couldn't keep up with the demand," says Marg Morison, then the Head Costume Creator. "One young boy would phone me every year begging to be part of the parade. When he was finally old enough, I told him he would need to get his parents to take his measurements so a costume could be fitted to him. Soon after he called and said he had gotten a friend to take his measurements and proudly told me he was 162 inches. 'How did you get that measurement?' I asked him. He told me, 'My friend told me to lie on the floor and ran a pencil around my body and came up with a total of 162 inches.'"

Morison's first job at Eaton's was as a parcel-wrapper. Through a combination of brains, initiative, and hard work, she quickly moved up the corporate ladder. In 1944, she was appointed the Head Costume

Creator for the parade, a position which, considering the number of children and adults involved, entailed steady nerves and a diplomat's tact. This diplomacy came in handy, especially when working with the children and grandchildren of the Eaton family itself.

"Marg was a very strict disciplinarian; you couldn't fool around. She had her fingers into everything," says Meg Peck. "She had an uncanny eye for detail and could spot a frayed collar here or an unlaced shoelace there. It was incredible."

"She stomped over and made me spit out my gum," recalls one veteran Eatonian, who once acted as a parade marshal. "She must have been half a mile away and still spotted that gum!"

"It's hard to believe that, in the midst of all the madness surrounding the parade, Marg still had to make sure none of the children wandered off. I don't know how she did it," says Peck.

"I lost lots of costume parts over the years, but I never lost a child," Morison smiles.

As Christmas approached, "Auntie Marg," as Morison was affectionately nicknamed, lent her mellifluous voice to radio shows that featured Christmas carols, interrupted by news bulletins charting Santa's progress from the North Pole.

Morison came by her empathy for parade participants honestly by having participated in the parades herself. In 1924 she debuted as an Indian maiden. The role required her to sit cross-legged on a travois – a sledge originally designed by the Plains Indians, consisting of a net-covered platform dragged along the ground by two shafts of wood – throughout the entire parade. "I was wearing a white leather suit sent down from the Winnipeg store," says Morison. "The head of the delivery department rode a horse in front and kept turning around to say, 'Are you all right, Marg?' By the time the parade was over, two men had to grab me under both armpits to lift me off the contraption. It took two days to get my legs straight again." Morison's last parade appearance was as the back end of an undulating caterpillar.

———■———

Shortly after dawn broke on parade day, parents would deliver eight-hundred-plus children to local churches near the parade's starting point. The boys went to one church, the girls to another. Once at their

Male parade participants preferred having greasepaint applied by pretty female make-up artists, rather than by male make-up artists – as pictured here, 1968.

respective churches, children registered, obtained numbers, and set off to find the costumes that corresponded with their numbers.

In the months leading up to parade day, Morison enlisted a team of Eaton's seamstresses to transform her clothing designs into costumes. It was not unusual for over ten thousand yards of fabric to be used in one year. Costumes were not custom-made, but were made in advance and then fitted to each child. When children didn't like their costumes, they frequently burst into tears. "Most little girls wanted to be either a princess or a fairy," says Morison. "I'll never forget the year a pretty little girl started wailing as soon as we started putting the fairy costume on her. 'I don't want to be a fairy,' she cried. 'I want to be a little mouse.'"

Female makeup artists applied greasepaint to participants' faces. Drivers were always the first to be made up, many of them bleary-eyed and stubble-chinned from being awake all night trying to jockey their trucks into position. Jack Brockie noted in his diary that the greasepaint only accentuated the drivers' chin stubble, making them resemble greased porcupines. Drivers didn't find the whole experience joyless, however. As Brockie wrote in a diary: "After a while it dawned on the makeup girls and women that the faces in the lineup were vaguely famil-iar and a check-back soon showed that the drivers were retiring to the

rear of the line, wiping off their make-up, and coming back for more –
not the greasepaint, but the girls and the face patting."[4]

At the parade's conclusion, a couple of Eaton's dieticians pushed a
stainless-steel cart out of the Queen Street store to the manager's garage
on Louisa Street, where they served hot chocolate and cookies to parade
participants. Not all dieticians savoured this particular facet of their
jobs. "It was kind of degrading," says dietician Dorothy Ferguson,
"because we were in our white uniforms and we didn't really want to
become part of the parade."

—■—

Santa's post-parade activities were the most taxing of all. As soon as he
stepped through the Toyland window, pandemonium broke loose as
hundreds of overwrought children screamed from behind roped-off areas.

Eaton's Fantasy Train carried children in a circle past specially built
magic castles, elves, and assorted Christmas ornaments, each more
elaborate than the next. Every child received a gift at the ride's conclusion, consisting perhaps of a doll or crayons. Store walls were brightly

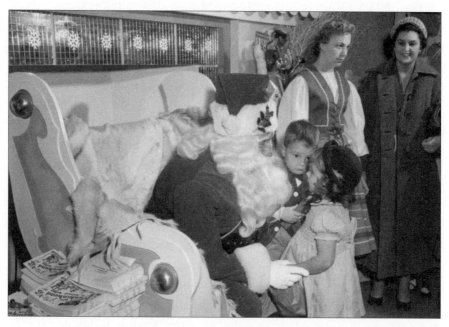

Santa's beards and gloves were disinfected eight times a day –
at least – to ward against runny-nosed kisses and sticky fingers.
Here, Santa greets children in Toronto's Toyland in 1964.

decorated with murals painted by Eaton's design staff. And of course, holding court in the midst of the madness was Santa, still encased in his heavy suit, his face glistening red under the hot overhead lights.

Johnny Patterson, who performed as Santa in the Winnipeg store for over thirty years, recalls that, during lunch breaks inside Santa's special reception area, he would remove his heavy velour outfit and his beard to try to cool off. Once back on his throne, he again braced himself for an onslaught of requests. "All kids were the same," he says. "Lots of them wanted to know why they didn't get the presents they wanted the year before." At its height in the 1950s, Winnipeg's Toyland entertained twelve hundred children in one day.

Most of the tykes remained well-behaved and confined their gift requests to more prosaic items such as dolls or toy trucks; others got more imaginative. Bill Whitely, an Eaton's floorwalker who acted as Santa one year, recalls that one boy asked for his own life-sized fire engine, and, when he sensed he wasn't going to get it, called Santa a "phony," and added for good measure, "I just have to walk into Simpson's to see your double." Prompted, no doubt, by his father, another child requested a bottle of whisky. Marg Morison recalls that a particularly precocious child sneaked around the back of a glass-bowl display that contained a model posing as a mermaid and pinched her sequined buttocks.

Beard-pulling by sticky-fingered children was commonplace, as were runny-nosed kisses. At the prompting of the Health Department, Santa's beards and gloves were disinfected a minimum of eight or nine times a day, an innovation of such magnitude that it was announced in a 1945 edition of the *Globe and Mail*.

Santa learned to turn his head away when particularly persistent children pursed their lips, which may have protected him from germs, but not from the invectives hurled at him by proud parents, who stood fuming outside the roped-off sections of Santa's magic castle. One year, such a large uproar erupted over Santa's refusal to be kissed that he was forced to explain to a *Globe and Mail* reporter that the illusion would be broken if children accidentally tore off his beard with their teeth.

Parents shelled out considerable amounts of money to have photographs taken of their children sitting on Santa's knee. Nevertheless, at least one traumatized parent considered that these photo sessions interfered with the bond Santa should have been forming with her child. Jack Brockie received the following letter of complaint regarding the incident:

Dear Mr. Brockie:
Last week I took my small five-year-old daughter to Eaton's for her first visit to Santa. I chose Eaton's because I have always felt that Eaton's Santa was *the* Santa. [But] what an anticlimactic disappointment this long-anticipated visit turned out to be! [Santa's] one concern, as she approached him eagerly, was that she be in proper position for the concealed camera! As she faced him to speak to him, [he] took her by the shoulders and turned her from him squarely toward the camera! Her long-awaited private conversation never materialized. As she was gently pushed on she turned back and volunteered to Santa that she would like a guitar. "Okay," Santa replied briefly – and that was her first visit to Santa.[5]

Jack Brockie responded to every letter of complaint he received, no matter how frivolous it seemed. In this case, the wounded party received a personal apology from Santa himself.

It was in the evening, however, when most children were home being tucked into bed by their exhausted mothers, that Eaton's Santa sometimes received his most unorthodox and entertaining visitors. Eaton's former chairman, John Craig Eaton, recalls the night Santa Claus was approached by three young women who had obviously been consuming cocktails just prior to their visit.

"Ho ho ho. Come over here girls and sit on Santa's knee," Santa said, according to John Craig. "So one of the girls comes over and sits on Santa's knee, and there's a photographer, and Santa puts his arms around her and says, 'And what would you like for Christmas?' 'Oh Santa, I want a man,' the girl replied. Santa looks at her and says, 'You just wait a half an hour, honey, and I'll get out of my costume and be right with you.'"

All of Eaton's major stores across the country opened their doors to crippled and disadvantaged children one hour before regular opening time. In the Montreal store, costumed staff members pulled wagons full of children with atrophied or amputated limbs towards Santa's throne, located in "Toyville." At the conclusion of the visit, each child received a gift. Eaton's contributed considerable amounts to the cause of crippled

Eaton's opened its doors early in the morning to crippled children.
Here are two children with Punkinhead on Eaton's Toyland train.

children. In 1958, then-president John David Eaton was named the chairman of the capital appeal for the Ontario Society for Crippled Children, for which he raised over four million dollars toward the building of a new Crippled Children's Centre in Toronto.

For Johnny Patterson, one child in particular stands out from the rest. "She was brought in by herself. She was eight years old and had cancer, and she sat on my knee and asked for the same sorts of things any child would. Two weeks later she was dead. That kind of thing was hard to take." Another Santa remembers placing a small girl in his lap who had legs like "pipe cleaners." She asked if Santa could give her new legs for Christmas, because she had been told he could perform miracles. As soon as the girl was out of view, the employee playing Santa walked into a privately screened area and sobbed.

Those who couldn't visit Santa personally could call him on special Santa hotlines that were connected to all major Eaton's stores, or they could write letters containing requests. Even those addressed to "Santa

Claus, North Pole," were rerouted to Eaton's stores. Letters – from as far away as Australia, Iceland, Africa, and England – arrived in giant mailbags, which were opened by casual workers hired for the season. Each year, a tally was kept of how many letters were received.

In his handwritten notes to children, Santa provided detailed information about his progress to their houses. One example, from the mid-1950s began, "My dear, your letter was the nicest I have ever received and I just had to answer it at once. What a time I had getting down to Toyland this year! Lost on an ice floe finding a baby seal, and ever so many other funny adventures."[6]

It was not unusual for sixty thousand letters to pour into Eaton's in one Christmas shopping season alone. Some cunning children enclosed candy or pennies to bribe Santa; others enclosed street maps showing the exact locations of their houses. Special instructions advised Santa on where he might find snacks to eat, and if the child lived in an apartment, admonitions were given against trying to shimmy down an artificial chimney.

In a letter dated November 15, 1958, a little girl wrote, "Dear Santa, I am sending my order in early this year. Please bring me a high-heeled doll, a real baking set, and high heels for myself, so that I can play house. Trusting you have had your polio needle, as I have had mine."[7] A letter from a young boy, meanwhile, revealed his obvious exasperation with the number of people who showed up at the parade. "Dear Santa Claus: I want a pair of skates. I went to see your parade but I did not see it. I am not going to see a parade any more. Because every body pushed me all over the place. Yours whit love, George."[8]

Those letters deemed special were forwarded to Jack Brockie, and occasionally aid was sent to those whose requests for money or merchandise seemed genuine.

Decorations were not only on display on the interior of Eaton's stores, but also on the exteriors. Each year during the 1950s and 1960s adults and children alike gathered on the street, jostling to view extraordinary Christmas window displays created by designers such as Jack French or Dick Dubord from the Queen Street store and Merchandise Display Manager Ted Konkle and his wife, Eleanor, who worked on the College Street store windows.

In one illuminated window, moveable figures skated figure eights on a Teflon rink; in another, a baby Jesus figure lay in his crèche, surrounded

*Member of
Merchandise
Display
Department at
work, early
1900s*

*Display
Department,
1945. To relieve
boredom at night,
male staff
members made
rude adjustments
to the
mannequins.*

*Christmas
window display,
November 24,
1958*

by the figures of three wise men, their velvet costumes designed to Italian Renaissance exactitude. The figures, modelled in Styrofoam, were moved electronically after heated brass rods were inserted into their bases.

One of the windows the Konkles created depicted the twelve days of Christmas, complete with dozens of papier-mâché cows and birds. "We would start putting the window in at 6:00 p.m. after the store closed and would still be there at 1:00 a.m.," says Ted. Much time was devoted to making sure the basic Styrofoam form was articulated correctly at all the joints so the figures could move properly, and then the papier mâché was placed over them.

To say the Konkles worked in informal surroundings is an under-statement. "Eleanor and I used to laugh ourselves silly when we referred to our 'studio,'" says Konkle, who worked alongside his wife at home so they could be closer to their young children. After they were formed, papier-mâché figures were hung from the house's clothesline, or were propped up to dry in the basement or kitchen. "We remember our son sitting in a high chair pounding Styrofoam with something or other. We were weirdos, let me tell you."

Even the Konkles' neighbours got into the act, some working as seamstresses, others brandishing paint. "It really became a community event," says Eleanor. "It drew the neighbourhood together."

Designers who chose to work in Eaton's studios often endured cramped and badly lit spaces, filled with flammable open cans of lacquer and paint. "Linda Keogh was the damnedest one for leaning over her work table with a cigarette dangling out of her mouth," says merchan-dise display artist Sheila Wherry, who noted that the studio working conditions at Eaton's were not always as safe as they could have been.

Among Linda Keogh and her husband John's more famous creations was a seventeen-foot-long and five-foot-high replica of Buckingham Palace made entirely out of Styrofoam, with more than thirty-five thou-sand tiny one-inch to one-half-inch rectangles of gold mirror glued onto it. The palace, which stood in a corner window of the College Street store, was created in honour of the coronation of Queen Elizabeth II in 1953. For a Queen Street store window, Sheila Wherry created a gold-leaf sculp-ture of Queen Elizabeth, seated on her throne. Similar sculptures also stood in the Winnipeg, Montreal, and Hamilton store windows.

When Eaton's needed to design a signature Christmas toy, it came up with Punkinhead, the Sad Little Bear. As soon as he debuted in 1948,

Display window on coronation of Queen Elizabeth II, June 1953.
The palace is made of golden mirror fragments.

Punkinhead became Eaton's perennial mascot, as well as one of its best-selling toys. He was even given his own movable float in the Santa Claus Parade. Punkinhead, whose distinctive feature was an unruly thatch of blond hair growing in the middle of his head, was created by Winnipeg artist Charles Thorson as a counterpart to Simpson's icon Rudolph the Red-Nosed Reindeer.

Thorson was no stranger to cartoon characters, having also helped create characters such as Bugs Bunny, Elmer Fudd, and Snow White and the Seven Dwarfs for the Disney studios. Children alighting from the Eaton's Fantasy Train received free copies of Punkinhead booklets chronicling the mischievous adventures of the small bear, each story written by Beth Hudson, an employee of Eaton's General Merchandise Office.·

A range of Punkinhead products was quickly marketed, including mugs, baby-bottle warmers, rocking horses, lamps, cups, saucers, and record albums. There were even Punkinhead cookies. Although a Punkinhead bear cost less than $5 when he first appeared in 1948, by the year 2000, a good-quality example sold for over $5,500 U.S. on the eBay auction site.

Punkinhead finger puppets were sold in the magic shop of Eaton's resident magician, Johnny Giordmaine. The ever-jaunty and diminutive

A Punkinhead book

*Johnny Giordmaine in his magic
shop in the Queen Street store*

Giordmaine began working at Eaton's in 1919, and remained for more than thirty years. A favourite of Flora McCrea Eaton's, he often performed at family birthday parties, as well as at the Eaton home on Christmas Day.

Back at the Queen Street store, Giordmaine pulled coins out of the ears of wide-eyed children, or turned green handkerchiefs blue with a single stroke of his hand. "He never talked down to you," says Dr. Robert Fowler, who as a child lined up to see Giordmaine pull doves or rubber chickens out of Chinese silver pans, or live rabbits out of hats. "He communicated the whole mystique of magic. He'd come around his counter and say, 'Come here and I'll show you how to do this trick,' as though it was a state secret, very hush-hush."

Executives also fell victim to Giordmaine's pranks. "We'd be on an elevator, and suddenly hear this damn bird chirping. All these guys in business suits would be looking up at the ceiling, and it would be Giordmaine making the sounds with a little device in his pocket," says George Hudson of the General Merchandise Office.

Staff members understandably became exhausted in the days leading up to Christmas. From the store's earliest days, as a gesture of appreciation, the Eaton family sent each employee a card, bearing a family photograph, a gesture that didn't always inspire admiration from members of the staff.

"We got these dopey Christmas cards from Lady Eaton from this villa in Italy, or Switzerland, or somewhere," remembers Doris Anderson.

Barbara Redlich adds. "Her cards weren't in good taste. They'd say things like 'I'm having a great time in Jerusalem.' They made employees look poorer."

Employees made an extraordinary effort to satisfy customers. In fact, when it came to satisfying customers, it seemed there were no lengths to which an employee wouldn't go, especially at Christmas. When merchandise was defective, it was replaced without question. Some employees took this return policy a step further.

In October 1971, CBC Creative Director George Anthony ordered a pair of Ski-Doos out of the Eaton's catalogue for his children. Soon after they were delivered, Anthony and his wife attempted to assemble the Ski-Doos themselves, an undertaking he characterized in a subsequent letter to Fred Eaton as "mechanical nightmare time." Anthony wrote: "I called Eaton's and explained, quite unemotionally and without exaggerating, that it would take the patience of Job and the strength of Hercules to put the effing things together."

Eaton's got on the case. The same day the company received Anthony's telephone complaint, a student part-time helper assembled another couple of Ski-Doos and sent them to Anthony, alas this time minus the handlebars. In his letter to Fred Eaton, Anthony explained he now had "four inoperable Ski-Doos and Excedrin Headache number 17."

Two days before Christmas, Anthony called Eaton's again. This time he reached Jim Matthews, then manager of the Don Mills, Ontario, store, and explained to him that, if there was a way to get Ski-Doos fully assembled by Christmas Eve, Anthony would pick them up at any Eaton's depot.

Matthews promised to personally deliver the Ski-Doos by Christmas Eve. He turned out to be a man of his word. By the time Anthony arrived home from a dinner party at 11 p.m. on Christmas Eve, he found two Ski-Doos fully assembled and disguised in brown wrapping paper waiting for him in his garage, while the two badly assembled ones had been removed from the premises.[9]

———■———

When Fred Eaton announced, in August 1982, that the company would no longer sponsor the Santa Claus parade, many former participants, particularly grown men, vented their feelings in letters to Toronto's daily newspapers. Others made tearful telephone calls to Eaton's public-relations executives.

Prompted no doubt by their grieving parents, children wore "We Love You, Santa" signs around their necks and carried plastic buckets from house to house in their neighbourhoods, collecting money to donate to the Eaton family to help them keep the parade alive.

A volunteer organization called "Save Our Santa" was formed. Its adult male spokesman, dressed in a green-and-red elf's suit, approached Toronto mayor Art Eggleton and tried to obtain his endorsement for the organization.

In the end, the parade was saved by a conglomerate of local businessmen headed by George Cohon, the president of McDonald's of Canada, and Robert Barboro, Chairman of the Metro Toronto Zoo.

Although Eaton's never publicly disclosed the amount of money it spent on the parades, in 1969 the *Toronto Star* estimated costs to be around $100,000. By 1976, with 1,700 participants and 19 bands, the cost was thought to be as high as $500,000 when factors such as fees to participants and band members and the purchasing of television time were included.

The parade, which was still televised to every major Canadian city, had survived through two world wars and a Depression, but did not survive the economic recession of the early eighties, when Eaton's laid off five hundred of its employees across the country. "All I can say is, at a time when retailers, including Eaton's, have been letting staff go, we don't think this is the time we should be spending that kind of money," said Fred Eaton.[10]

At least some Eaton's employees viewed his explanation with scepticism. "The parade was cheaper than some of the advertising Eaton's bought, which often ran between $65,000 and $70,000. The parade cost only $250,000, a bargain when they had a $50-million advertising budget at their feet," says Michael Brough.

Following Fred Eaton's announcement that Eaton's was no longer sponsoring the parade, Parade Director Doug Laphen immediately laid off six of the company's craftsmen, some of whom had worked for Eaton's for more than thirty years. The traumatized craftsmen reacted to the news by locking themselves behind their workroom door. They had already completed 80 per cent of the construction on twenty-seven floats when the news broke. "It would have been a beautiful parade,"[11] one called out to a *Toronto Star* reporter through the locked door.

In expanding on his reasons for ceasing to subsidize the parade, Fred Eaton explained that the family had grown tired of deflecting criticism levied by various municipal officials that the timing of the parade – variously described as too early in the season, or too late – was off; that it exposed children to bad weather; that it was too close to Remembrance Day; and that it conflicted with sporting events, or interfered with traffic.

In December the parade took place using the floats already constructed by Eaton's carpenters. Most children may have been oblivious to the change in ownership. Adults were not. Santa's arrival was anticlimactic. No longer a member of Eaton's corporate family, now he was just another in a long list of imposters.

CHAPTER 4

Feasts for More Than the Eyes

*Eaton's restaurants • Fashion shows
• Eaton auditorium • Entertainment*

TIMOTHY EATON POSSESSED AN uncanny knack for anticipating what his customers needed and wanted. By installing benches, later to become known as "Ladies' Waiting Areas," throughout his store, he transformed shopping into a leisurely, day-long social activity. Having satisfied his customers' desire for physical comfort, he then set his sights on nourishing their bodies.

In 1891, Timothy installed a sixteen-foot-long counter in the drug department of the Queen Street store, where customers gathered to eat ice-cream sundaes as they discussed the events of the day. Oyster stews were served in the winter. The cream, butter, and eggs used in these dishes were supplied by the cows and chickens inhabiting the eighty-five acres of farmland that Timothy had purchased in Islington and Georgetown, Ontario, as a means of keeping his store stocked with fresh produce.

In 1904 Timothy created a lunchroom called the "Grill Room" on the fifth floor of the store, where hot, nourishing meals were served to more than five thousand customers a day. Men were enticed with juicy porterhouse steaks at fifty cents a pound. For the same price, ladies savoured something called an "Afternoon Shoppers' Dainty Lunch,"

The Grill Room, Eaton's first cafeteria, Queen Street store, Toronto, early 1900s

made up of chicken salad, cake and ice cream, tea or coffee, and bread and butter, all served in an airy, well-ventilated room. With his eye always on the functional over the flamboyant, Timothy made sure that the cost of preparing the restaurant's meals remained low.

After Timothy died in 1907, however, his son and successor Sir John Craig, along with his wife, Flora McCrea, displayed more extravagant tastes. They transformed Timothy's unpretentious Grill Room into an upscale dining establishment, where before long three hundred chefs, cooks, bakers, and waitresses struggled to cater to a veritable deluge of customers, all seeking to be the first to savour the finest in department-store dining. Private and semi-private dining areas were cordoned off. While John Craig managed to lend an air of exclusivity to the restaurant, he also shrewdly tore a page out of Timothy's book by declaring that customers would never have to pay "a cent too much" for their meals.

With the outbreak of the First World War in 1914, food rationing made fresh produce difficult to obtain. Despite this impediment, the Grill Room stayed afloat, albeit barely. By the time Eaton's celebrated its Golden Jubilee in 1919, the restaurant was showing signs of middle age.

Flora McCrea soon complained about the restaurant's decrepit condition to the Eaton's board of directors. Flora recognized that, in the economic upswing that had followed the end of the war, shopping had again become a glamorous day-long excursion, particularly among those eager to resume buying fine European fashions, whose production had been curtailed during the war. The Grill Room, with what Flora in *Memory's Wall*, her 1956 memoirs, called its "railway-station-like" menu selections and "clean and dull" decorations, suddenly looked provincial, even second-rate.

Flora McCrea's negative feelings about the Grill Room had been magnified after touring dining rooms in department stores located overseas. In London, she had lunched in the director's dining room of one department store, making note of the presence of Chippendale furniture, oriental rugs, brocade curtains, and fine silverware. "I realized that I could never ask this group of men to have lunch in our restaurant in Toronto!" she noted.[1]

Shortly after returning home, Flora McCrea prevailed upon members of the board of directors to authorize the design of an altogether new stylish restaurant to replace the Grill Room, but her suggestion was digested like gruel by most of the directors, including then-president Robert Young Eaton, who had succeeded his cousin Sir John Craig Eaton as president after John Craig's untimely death from pneumonia in 1922. It was only after an incensed Flora McCrea threatened to close the restaurant altogether that R. Y. Eaton capitulated and agreed to assist her in developing what famously became known as the "Georgian Room."

Violet Ryley, Eaton's premier dietician

An ingredient even more important than good food was necessary to make the new venture a success. It needed the expertise of a trained dietician. For that, Flora McCrea called upon Violet Ryley.

Ryley, known in her field as the "dean" of Canadian dieticians, graduated from the Lillian Massey Treble School of Household Sciences, associated with the University of Toronto, in 1907. After gaining additional training at the

New York City Hospital and Albany General Hospital, she returned permanently to Canada in 1910, where she organized the University of Toronto's dining hall, better known as Hart House. Newspaper articles of the period referred to her as the highest-paid working woman in Canada.

Ryley's genius for organizing efficient food-service departments probably reached its zenith when she worked as the General Organizing Dietician of the Canadian military hospitals from Halifax to Vancouver during the First World War. In this capacity, she had planned every facet of food preparation, from the buying of state-of-the-art kitchen equipment to choosing the correct serving utensils.

Ryley was renowned for using a stopwatch to estimate the strict preparation times necessary for every dish she included in her three-ring, lined recipe manuals – manuals which would become an essential resource for Eaton's dieticians. On one page of her manual, for example, under the category of Apple Balls, Ryley listed the following: "1 qt. – 10 apples, No. Balls per apple – 12, Time per gal. 20 mi. (this includes peeling time). The time needed to clean 11 quarts of blueberries: 15 minutes."

Each estimated time could be revised to satisfy the feeding of over a thousand people. Ryley also provided detailed instructions concerning how to properly clean cooking surfaces, as well as first-aid tips for when kitchen calamities occurred.

In addition to instructing subordinate dieticians on the correct way to whip up visually attractive multi-course meals using the proper utensils, Ryley's recipe manuals also included handwritten maternal homilies on how a dietician could make herself invaluable to Flora McCrea, whom Ryley considered a personal friend.

"If I were Lady Eaton, What would I Want? Thoughtfulness, Kindness, Charm & Courtesy, Efficiency, Make a Study of Efficiency," Ryley scribbled on a memo she gave to Eaton's dietician, Dorothy Ferguson. In 1948, Ryley hand-picked Ferguson to train Flora McCrea's personal cook at Eaton Hall, in King City, Ontario. Ferguson soon discovered that the assignment required not only brilliant cookery skills, but also impressive diplomatic smarts.

"Basically, I was sent to Eaton Hall to straighten out the chef," says Ferguson. "And the chef wasn't very pleased about it." It didn't take long for Ferguson to deduce that the Irish cook's problem was not a lack of training, but a lack of knowledge of Canadian cuisine. When the chef

Georgian Room kitchen. March 3, 1924

Dietician Kathleen Jeffs

was ultimately fired because of insolence, Ferguson was invited to replace her, an offer she declined in favour of returning to work in the Georgian Room, under the tutelage of Ryley.

In her capacity as general manager of the Georgian Room, Ryley met with architects to ensure that the kitchen was designed efficiently enough that hot dishes would not turn cold by the time waitresses served them to customers. The two-storey-high kitchen, meanwhile, was flooded with light, and was equipped with the company's first stainless-steel countertops.

To assist her in operating the Georgian Room, Ryley chose Kathleen Jeffs, who later served as the Chief Messing Officer and a Wing Commander in the RCAF during the Second World War. Jeffs ultimately earned an OBE from King George V for the five years she devoted to providing a variety of nutritious meals to army mess halls all across North America and Europe, a challenge in light of the heavy rationing that was occurring during the war. Her objective was to try and give a woman's touch to mealtime in the messes. Jeffs was widely credited with being the first dietician to introduce grapefruit juice and orange juice to army breakfast tables.

The opening of the Georgian Room on March 10, 1924, revolutionized the retail shopping experience. Prior to the presence of the Georgian Room, there were few other places in Toronto, besides the King Edward Hotel, where shoppers could enjoy a meal in elegant surroundings. Female customers, even those employed by rival stores, could visit Eaton's not merely to purchase merchandise, but to see – and be seen with – their female friends.

Eaton's restaurant dining had progressed a long way from Timothy's original Grill Room. Customers could now taste a slice of the good life by simply riding an elevator up to the store's ninth-floor lobby, and, after a short walk, stepping into a spacious room boasting twenty-four-foot ceilings, tall windows, and genuine walnut panelling. Chinese wall hangings throughout the room were stitched with proverbs such as "One's fate is from heaven; the source of good-fortune is deep like the sea."

Classical musicians performed in their own gallery, located at one end of the room, as the light from ceiling lamps bounced off cut-crystal chandeliers and danced across Lalique crystal glasses and Limoges china before falling onto the finest in white Irish-linen tablecloths. The sumptuous ambience made customers want to look and feel rich, a mindset that didn't hurt when it came to post-lunch shopping excursions throughout the store.

"I remember my best friend and I dressing up to go there once a week," says Trudie Cray, who began shopping at Eaton's shortly after she arrived in Canada from England in 1935. "The restaurant just lifted you back to a more elegant time and place. After we were finished eating, we'd go shopping, and always spent too much. One time, my friend bought an alligator purse. I think I bought a strange-looking fur hat, with a feather in it, that I probably still have somewhere or other. Half the stuff in my closet was bought at Eaton's."

Dorothy Ferguson's first days working as a trainee in the Georgian Room were fraught with anxieties. Her second day started inauspiciously when she was sent to the butcher shop to pick up chickens. "I'm afraid of chickens," she says, "and I was given a basket of chickens to clean, with their heads and feet still attached. I met people that night and said 'I'm not staying.' I changed my mind when one of the butchers took pity on me and started to cut the chickens' heads and feet off before I got there. Those butchers knew the score, they had gotten pretty used to my type coming around."

Georgian Room, ninth floor, 1939

The aesthetic pleasure of working in the Georgian Room took second place only to the sensual artistry of the food itself. "Our fruit salads had to have fifteen or sixteen fruits in them," says Ferguson. After being sliced, diced, and artistically carved, fruits were then laid atop an almost entire head of crisp, fresh lettuce.

In later years, hand-cut potato balls gave way to the frozen cube-shaped variety, yet in the restaurant's heyday the hand-cut potatoes formed the delicious nucleus of one of the restaurant's most requested items: the chicken pot pie. "There was a real ritual to making a chicken pie," says Eaton's dietician Joan Caruso. "You'd have the fricassee sauce on the bottom and then you'd drop in two ounces of sliced chicken, half light, half dark, two potato balls, and you covered it with the fricassee sauce, and then you'd put the pastry over it."

Dorothy Ferguson remembers referring regularly to Violet Ryley's notes before embarking on the preparation of a dish. "When we were in the prep room, we'd have a bushel of beans and we'd personally count to see how many beans were in the pound, how many servings you'd get from the pound, and how long it took to clip the tops and tails. Nowadays they don't bother."

Dietician Dorothy Ferguson (far left) with guests of Eaton Hall in King City

Joan Caruso

Ferguson explains that Ryley inaugurated the official tasting of all new recipes. "We had a ritual, and it happened at eleven o'clock every morning. We went through and everything in the menu of the day was tasted with the section head. All the salads, all the hot food, was tasted with a chef, who would put it on our spoons," she says.

Once a week, managers were invited to taste-test new recipes. To be used in the restaurant, a dish had to receive a minimum score of 80 per cent for flavour, texture, colour, and appeal at three separate tasting sessions. If the dish rated lower, it was eliminated as a culinary contender.

Shortly after the Georgian Room opened its doors, its dieticians established upper- and lower-floor standards of food classification in order to distinguish between Georgian Room–quality restaurants and the store cafeterias that proliferated as Eaton's tried to cater to more fast-food tastes. Georgian Room recipes, for example, contained 18-per-cent cream and 14-per-cent whipping cream, while cafeteria recipes contained margarine and skimmed milk.

The highest standards of quality were also applied to the Georgian Room's staff. Student dieticians were plucked primarily from the four-year Lillian Massey Treble program in Household Sciences that, beginning in 1902, was offered by the University of Toronto, or from the Home Economics Course offered by the University of Guelph. Eaton's was the only institution next to the University of Alberta that offered a ten-month internship course for dieticians-in-training. If a student passed, she was required to apprentice at Eaton's for a period of two years.

Student dieticians were taught on the job and were evaluated based on personal qualities such as quality and volume of work and their initiative, dependability, self-confidence, appearance, good knowledge, and tasting skills. Each student was shown photographs of how fruit salads or some other dish should be arranged on plates, and were expected to be able to replicate the arrangement in a timely and efficient manner. Recipes were considered top secret, and were kept in a cabinet under lock and key.

Not only were restaurant recipes kept confidential, so were each restaurant's precise records of profits. "You didn't discuss wages or sales outside the store," says Caruso. "Every so often we'd be asked to participate in some form of outside survey, but we were never allowed to reveal the amounts of actual sales we made, just estimates."

Rules governing the disposal of food were brutal in their wastefulness. To protect against spoilage, each scrap of food was thrown into the garbage. "We threw everything away. It was terrible," Ferguson recalls. Despite the rules, whenever she could, she placed leftovers in containers and donated them to the nearby Yonge Street Mission for the homeless.

All restaurant employees were required to wear suits and white gloves to work, even in summer, and white uniforms and aprons on the job. For safety reasons, kitchen staff wore heavy steel-toed shoes around the kitchen. A strict code of courtesy prevailed between management and staff in all Eaton's restaurants. "I worked for seven years before I was addressed by my first name," recalls Caruso.

The Georgian Room featured an executive dining area, often frequented by R. Y. Eaton, and, when he became president, by John David Eaton, the son of Sir John Craig. Dieticians kept detailed notes about how executives liked to have their meals prepared. Many of the executives were also particularly fond of the entertainment that was featured in the restaurant.

Welsh singers dressed in red hunting suits were among the first performers to appear in the Georgian Room in the 1920s. R. Y. Eaton enjoyed them so much that he asked if their show could be played on the radio. Jack Brockie contacted radio station CFCA. On the day scheduled for the radio broadcast, R. Y. confronted Brockie and said, "I don't hear the singers." It turned out that R. Y. had wanted the music piped through the store, not through a radio station, causing Brockie to have to scramble to sort out the situation.[2]

R. Y. Eaton generally did not like the upbeat band music that was played throughout the restaurant in the 1930s and decided to supply his own records, mainly those of gospel singer Marian Anderson. When a couple of clerks grumbled, Jack Brockie quietly arranged to have the original band music reinstated.

As the times changed, the Georgian Room had to change with them. Younger faces and a more fashion-conscious crowd was needed to fill the room in order to ensure its survival. Jack Brockie came up with the perfect solution that, like the Santa Claus parade, made customers active participants in the store's own advertising.

Shortly after 1939, Brockie recognized that a new breed of consumer, known as a "teenager," was beginning to have a direct influence on the colours, cuts, and even brands of fashion merchandise Eaton's stocked. Catering to teen desires to acquire cutting-edge clothes, Brockie began staging fashion shows in the Georgian Room featuring live models, usually the teenagers themselves, wearing their own home-made fashions or designs they created but which Eaton's manufactured itself.

On August 18, 1943, an event called "Sew to Show" was mounted in the Georgian Room. In the words of an Eaton's press release, "Two dozen laughing-eyed schoolgirls elved through patterns and fabrics in Eaton's Piece Good Dept. to help pick outfits for school and we made them up exactly as they suggested. You'll see them modeled on our revolving stage, for each smiling dummy doubles for the junior grader who chooses her clothes and whose name she carries."[3]

Every Saturday morning, high-school students between fifteen and eighteen years of age, handpicked by Brockie on the basis of their scholastic achievement, met at the Georgian Room or in other areas of the Eaton's store to discuss fashion trends, as well as to fill out surveys and questionnaires in which they listed the kinds of fashion merchandise they wished to see Eaton's sell in the coming months. Female students were called Junior Councillors. Male students were given the more authoritative title of Junior Executives. Each group had its own formal by-laws and agendas.

In return for soliciting their opinions about fashions, Eaton's offered students a few hours of in-store work every Friday afternoon or Saturday morning. Students were also invited to participate in charity fundraising activities throughout their communities, ranging from entertaining sick children in hospitals to submitting entries in arts-and-crafts contests, each activity designed to enhance feelings of civic awareness. Fun-fair lotteries featured prizes such as three-skin mink neckpieces, ironing boards, or, during one extraordinary year, thirty bags of insulation, as well as one ton of Coca-Cola. Many of Eaton's Junior Councillors and Executives ultimately became leaders in their communities. Two of the more famous former members in Manitoba were former premier Gary Filmon and actor Len Cariou. Toronto boasted Lloyd Axworthy, as well as Eaton's Vice-President of Corporate Public Relations, Sigi Brough.

"They wanted only the best, most social and outgoing students from each high school," says Evelyn Hannon, the mother of CFRB radio host Erica Ehm, who served on the Junior Council in her hometown of Montreal. "We were given a special navy-blue blazer with the Junior Council crest sewn on it to go with grey skirts and a pin identifying us as Junior Council members. The whole experience was quite extraordinary. I really benefited from that year and met gorgeous people who are now leaders in the community."

Teen catalogue cover, 1944

Georgian Room Fashion Show, 1940

At its height in the mid-1950s, Junior Council and Junior Executive groups operated in six major cities across Canada, including Calgary, Edmonton, Winnipeg, Toronto, Hamilton, and Montreal. To augment its Junior Council, in 1965 the Winnipeg store inaugurated a Hi-Set Fashion Club for teenage girls aged thirteen to nineteen. In exchange for receiving beauty information and meeting fashion personalities, Hi-Set girls were encouraged to entice their friends to shop at the store. The highest symbol of success a Junior Councillor or Executive could earn was a triangular pendant in the shape of an A, signifying the word Achievement.

Though he was never a Junior Executive, Burton Lorne Cummings, the fourteen-year-old son of Rhoda Cummings of the Winnipeg store's Wages Office, was embraced as a member of Eaton's extended family. In March 1962, Cummings made Eatonians proud by winning an engraved trophy for playing his own piano composition in a musical competition that was held for amateur entertainers on local television station CJAY. Cummings's success was written up in Eaton's *Contacts* magazine, which speculated about whether the store had a great jazz pianist or bandleader in the making. The answer came a handful of years later when Cummings skyrocketed to fame as the leader of the rock group The Guess Who.

Inspired by the tips he gained from young voices, Brockie began to stage increasingly sophisticated fashion shows, or "Mannequin's Parades" as they were then referred to, in the Georgian Room, featuring such renowned European designers as Pierre Cardin and Pierre Balmain. Santa Claus Head Costume creator, Marg Morison,

Dora Matthews

or Dora Matthews, Eaton's Fashion Co-ordinator, usually hosted these shows. Horace Lapp, famous for having provided piano accompaniment to the films of Buster Keaton and Laurel and Hardy, played live at these events. Before long, women scrambled to buy tickets to fashion shows as avidly as men bought tickets to Grey Cup games. One particularly memorable show featured a mink dress worth fifty thousand dollars that was once worn by Ginger Rogers in the film *Lady in the Dark*.

Originally, models were plucked from the ranks of store employees, later from agencies operating out of New York. One year, Jack Brockie invited top New York model Martha Heatherington to display a thirty-thousand-dollar sable coat. Instead of being able to relax and enjoy the show, Brockie spent most of his time trying to prevent the head of the fur department, a Mr. McGee, from fainting as he watched Heatherington drag the coat down the full length of the runway.

Former fashion model Cathy Fisher recalls the crush of people, especially Eaton's executives, who gathered around tables in the Georgian Room to admire more than just the fashions. "I noticed one guy in particular who came every day for lunch. He turned out to be Ken Thomson [later to become better known as Lord Thomson of Fleet, and owner of Simpson's], who ultimately married one of Eaton's most popular models, Marilyn Levis."

Fisher laughs when remembering one man who came regularly to the shows and read a newspaper. "I said to myself, 'Nobody's going to open

Fashion mavens Doreen Day and Dora Matthews, October 12, 1946

a newspaper while I'm modelling clothes.'" After a few days, Fisher finally approached the man and attempted to pitch to him a mix-and-match outfit, calling over her shoulder as she walked away, "Be sure to tell your friends to come."

"When I chatted to the hostess afterwards, she said, 'You had quite a conversation with John David Eaton,'" recalls Fisher, who had no idea the man reading the newspaper was the president of the store. "The next day John David returned, this time along with three or four other men," she laughs.

Eaton's kept abreast of the latest fashions. Throughout the 1950s, once a month on a Thursday night, the Georgian Room was reserved for meetings of the Eaton's Careers Club, hosted by then-public-relations-executive Barbara Duckworth. Four hundred and fifty people attended each one of these sessions, to trade ideas about fashion. A club also operated out of the Montreal restaurant, and the two clubs compared notes about which fashions were the most sought after.

Eaton's only truly secured its place in the fashion pantheon, however, when its fashion maven, Doreen Day, was elected in the late 1950s as Regional Head of the powerful Fashion Group, a non-profit organization comprised of fashion representatives from prestigious department stores around the world, as well as from fashion magazines such as *Vogue, Harper's Bazaar,* and *Mademoiselle.* Headquartered in New

York, the Fashion Group forecast fashion trends in addition to hosting educational, cultural, and community activities to assist fashion buyers in their pursuit of cutting-edge styles.

———■———

The Georgian Room was one of two art deco restaurants Eaton's built during the 1920s. The second was the Montreal store's magnificent ninth-floor restaurant. On January 26, 1926, Kathleen Jeffs supervised the grand opening of the restaurant. Its long, narrow shape was designed by famed French architect Jacques Carlu to resemble the French luxury ocean liner the *Île de France*. "A lot of restaurants were named after ships, because elegant travel was done in those days," says Dorothy Ferguson. No extravagance was spared in appealing to customers' aesthetic sensibilities.

When the restaurant first opened in 1926, a customer could order from the bilingual menu a three-course luncheon that included fruit cocktail, filet mignon, buttered squash, hot gingerbread or apple pie, muffins, and tea or coffee, for only one dollar.

As with the Georgian Room, the Montreal restaurant was reached by a bank of elevators. These elevators opened onto a lobby, which ran parallel to both Victoria and University streets. Walls covered with pink and grey fabric lined the route leading to the main foyer, situated on the St. Catherine Street side of the store. There, large windows offered a panoramic view of the city.

Architects and designers considered the restaurant an art deco masterpiece, easily the crown jewel among Montreal department-store restaurants. As in the foyer, the walls of the restaurant were covered with a horizontally striped French fabric in grey and pink. Artificial light streaming from a series of circular domes embedded in the ceiling suffused the room in a shimmering glow.

The most breathtaking features of the room, however, consisted of two huge alabaster vases of Belgian black marble, as well as forty-five-foot-tall wall fountains of black marble, above which hung two murals hand-painted by Jacques Carlu's wife, Natacha, in black, silver, grey, and pink.

Soothing music floated out of radios concealed behind metal grilles. The music lent atmosphere to the fashion shows, which were staged on raised platforms located at each end of the room. The platforms were illuminated by concealed electric spotlights, which highlighted the models' clothes.

In the 1950s, the Montreal restaurant still served upwards of eight hundred lunches a day. Dinners were served on Thursday and Friday nights, when the store was open until 10:00 p.m. As late as the 1980s, the restaurant was still turning an average profit of $1.3 million a year. A documentary produced in the late 1990s by French-Canadian film-maker Catherine Martin, entitled *The Ladies of the Ninth Floor*, high-lighted the close relationships formed between waitresses and their regular female customers. At its height, the restaurant operated as a safe and hospitable place for single females to dine. Whether they were rich or merely comfortable, every customer was shown the same degree of deference on the part of the serving staff.

The number of Eaton's restaurants over the years kept pace with the number of stores eventually built. Every Eaton's customer had his favourite restaurant. In 1911, Winnipeg's Grill Room was opened. The restaurant served rich chicken pot pies, rolled asparagus sandwiches, and homemade cakes and pies. Vancouver boasted the Marine Room,

Ninth-floor restaurant, Montreal

with its scenic view of Vancouver Bay, and the equally impressive Alhambra Room, decorated with dramatic Moorish sculptures.

In addition to its famed Grill Room restaurant, the Winnipeg store also had, at 220 feet, the longest meat counter in North America. Meanwhile, its bakery, which operated twenty-two hours a day, delivered thirteen varieties of bread within a hundred-mile radius. It also supplied the widest variety of wedding and other special-occasion cakes. The basement of the store even featured a delicatessen, which carried foods from various cultures, including Ukrainian, Icelandic, French, and Jewish, as well as fifty varieties of locally made sausage.

As with Eaton's employees across the country, Winnipeg employees' service was exemplary. On one occasion, a couple new to the Winnipeg area ordered a gourmet lasagna to be delivered to their home for a party, but they were told the store was out of stock. When they opened their front door that night, they found an Eaton's employee cradling a steaming dish of lasagna, which he served up, along with his profuse apologies. It was only when the wife returned the dish to the store the next day that she discovered that her delivery man had been none other than the store's Operating Manager, Alan Finnbogason.[4]

———◼———

Upon its opening in 1931, Eaton's Round Room, located in the College Street Store in Toronto, proved to be another masterpiece of Art Deco elegance and glamour. Flora McCrea Eaton had again called upon the genius of Jacques Carlu, and this time he created a dome-shaped room within a square. At each corner of the room were window recesses, where elegantly dressed diners retired to sip non-alcoholic beverages as they listened to music piped in through a speaker concealed in the chandelier in the centre of the room.

Concealed lighting fixtures cast the room in a dreamy, otherworldly glow, an effect enhanced in the centre of the room by the presence of an illuminated glass water fountain. Gazing down on diners throughout the room were life-sized marble statues, while hand-painted wall murals depicted mythological figures, such as Diana of the Hunt.

As with Eaton's other top-quality restaurants, only the finest in silverware was used. Beverages were served in Fostoria glass goblets, while tea and coffee were sipped from Royal Worcester china.

Helen Buik, yet another dietician trained by Violet Ryley, managed the Round Room restaurant. Buik began her relationship with Eaton's food services in 1929, ultimately becoming the Supervisor of Restaurants for the entire T. Eaton Company.

Buik had served as a Messing Officer in the Second World War. Originally posted in Yorkshire, England, she returned to Canada to succeed Kathleen Jeffs as Chief RCAF Messing Officer. At the conclusion of the war in 1945, Buik was awarded an MBE in honour of her war work.

That the Round Room managed to come into existence at all was a miracle, considering the tortured path the College Street store itself took to completion. To further enhance his reputation as an empire builder, rather than just a merchant, as his father had been content to be, in 1910 President John Craig Eaton envisaged the College Street store as the Taj Mahal of department stores. Original plans had it phallically soaring to a height of thirty-seven storeys, rivalling another cultural landmark, the Empire State Building. John Craig purchased in advance an entire

Round Room, College Street store

Manitoba limestone quarry to ensure that there would be enough stone to complete the construction.

Once construction finally commenced in 1928, however, a series of mind-boggling calamities nearly capsized the project, not the least being the discovery that the structure was being built on a gradient. "Because it was built on a gradient, shoppers had to step up and down, on and off two different levels," says Fred Eaton. "It broke the flow of the store. It just didn't work."

Complicating matters even further was the presence of quicksand beneath the building, surrounding the area where Taddle Creek ran under the store. Several contractors went bankrupt in their efforts to locate bedrock.

When construction of the store had begun in 1928, the one thing that seemed stable was the economy. By the time the store was opened to the public in 1930, the Depression had seriously eroded its profit-making capacity. The few well-heeled customers who visited to buy home furnishings were practically pounced on by salesmen desperate to earn a commission.

The chilling lack of customer traffic posed special problems for the opulent Round Room. Once again, Jack Brockie's magic touch came to the rescue. Before long, he devised a way to maximize the potential of the expensive new restaurant.

And so, thanks to Brockie, the Eaton Auditorium was born on March 26, 1931. Designed in art deco style by Jacques Carlu, the auditorium featured pale gold Fabrikoid-panelled walls, interspersed with bands of bird's-eye maple. Chairs were also upholstered in Fabrikoid. Oblongs of translucent glass light fixtures were embedded in both the walls and ceiling. These lights could be dimmed to make the stage lights appear even brighter.

By far the most magnificent feature built into the room was the Casavant organ, which boasted 5,804 pipes, as

Dietician Helen Buik

The Eaton Auditorium, College Street store

well as stops used to produce harp and chime effects. The organ was designed and built by Casavant Frères of St. Hyacinthe, Quebec, using Sir Ernest MacMillan as a consultant.

Brockie's first formidable project was to make the auditorium available daily to various civic or entertainment groups, which wanted to make use of it for a reasonable fee. These groups included the Boy Scouts, the Audubon Society, the Eaton Operatic Society, and the Kiwanis Music Festival.

After failing to make a profit for over six months, Brockie realized that other sorts of events had to be added to enable the hall to earn sufficient money to survive. With this knowledge, he opened up the hall to evening concerts, with audience members later visiting the Round Room for hors d'oeuvres or fruit punch. Formal dress was *de rigueur*. To make the events seem even more exclusive, Brockie erected a six-foot-high temporary screen on the first floor, which effectively created an artificial aisle that led directly to the elevators.

The Hamburg Trio is recorded as the first musical group to play at the auditorium. Shortly afterwards, a talent-booker named Colin Tait was hired to lure more marquee-name performers. Sergei Rachmaninov soon agreed to perform, and turned out to be somewhat of a character. Moments before he was scheduled to leave his dressing room to take to the stage, he drew Brockic aside and whispered, "Young man, this is the first clean dressing room I've had on this tour."[5] Told that a newlywed had come all the way from Kingston on his honeymoon to see him, Rachmaninov replied, "Damn fool. He should be home in bed."[6]

Other concerts were performed by luminaries such as violinist Efrem Zimbalist, Sr., diva Kirsten Flagstad, and gospel singer Marian Anderson, who admired the auditorium's atmosphere so much that she performed there more than eighteen times over the course of her career.

As soon as their trains pulled in to Union Station, all out-of-town performers were chauffeured to the College Street store a few blocks away. Jack Brockie or Colin Tait always accompanied them on the trip.

In the 1930s, Antoine de Paris, self-described hair "sculptor" to the stars, was invited to demonstrate his skills at a special on-stage "performance" at the auditorium. Jack Brockie would not soon forget de Paris's arrival at Union Station. Dressed in mauve evening clothes accented by glass-heeled shoes and two French poodles, also dyed mauve to match his ensemble, de Paris strode through the train station, as white-toga-clad maidens scattered gardenias beneath his feet. Monsieur de Paris would later open his own salon at the Eaton's College Street store.

Trained as a sculptor, de Paris had turned to hair when he discovered it was more profitable. Society women of Toronto soon gladly paid up to twenty-five dollars apiece for just a brief consultation with de Paris, who ultimately designed the "Powder blended to Milady's skin type" that sold throughout the store.

Among the most popular performers to appear at the auditorium were tap-dancer Margarita Cansino, later known as Rita Hayworth; Maurice Chevalier; baritone Nelson Eddy; and Martha Raye, who as a teenaged performer travelled everywhere with her mother. Eaton's Merchandise Display artist Sheila Wherry accompanied Mrs. Raye on a tour of Toronto, where Raye fretted over her daughter's future safety in show business. "She was one of the loneliest women I've ever met," recalls Wherry.

Audience members gather at the intermission for
refreshments in Eaton Auditorium Foyer, 1930.

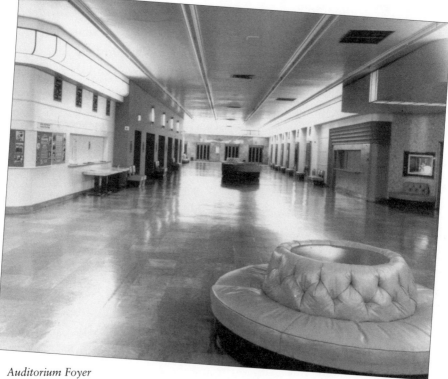

Auditorium Foyer

Of all the performers to appear at the auditorium, Oscar Levant was perhaps the hardest to handle. Shortly before he was scheduled to appear in the late 1930s, Levant suddenly cancelled due to fears that he would be drafted if he left the United States. Brockie had been advised that the one thing Levant was most nervous of was a lawsuit, so, to compel Levant to appear, Brockie wrote him a letter offering him an alternative concert date, and informed him that, if he didn't come, Brockie would sue. Under pressure, Levant capitulated and came to Toronto, though in retrospect talent-booker Colin Tait wished he hadn't.

Tait met Levant, who was accompanied by his manager, at Union Station. The three men proceeded to the Royal York's Venetian Room for breakfast, at Tait's expense. When Levant's manager left to make a phone call, Levant sidled over to Tait and, pointing towards his manager, said, "Let's go. That man makes me nervous." And so began one of the most eccentric treks of Colin Tait's life, even by celebrity standards.

Tait soon found himself walking Levant up Yonge Street, with Levant stopping at every Honey Dew restaurant for coffee, crossing through traffic to avoid a police station, then crossing again to avoid a beggar. When the two men finally arrived at the College Street store, Levant stopped to examine a poster placed outside the building, advertising the names of performers that were appearing in the Master Concert Series of which he was a part. Suddenly, saying that he did not feel he measured up to the other names listed on the poster, Levant announced that he was backing out of his evening performance. Several pep talks later, Tait finally convinced a still-reluctant Levant to perform.

That night, as the auditorium audience applauded softly, Levant walked out to his piano, sat down, and stroked the keys a few times. Suddenly, he stood up and announced to the audience, "When you've got to go, you've got to go," striding offstage, ending the performance before it began. In an interview conducted with him in 1968, Colin Tait recalled it as the worst day he had ever spent in his job at the auditorium.[7]

Tait had better luck with Lucille Manners, known as "Miss Manners." The columnist and social critic had loosened a dental cap by eating tough steak shortly before her appearance. To rectify the situation, Tait chewed some gum and offered it to her. Though the gum kept the cap in, it also caused great pain. Finally, during intermission, Tait and an Eaton's dental nurse who was sitting in the audience rushed up to the nurse's office to obtain some dental cement, which they used to glue in Manners's cap successfully.[8]

For sheer general popularity, however, no auditorium event of the 1930s rivalled the display of the Colleen Moore dollhouse, then valued at an astounding $425,000. The house was displayed during the height of the Depression and became one of the most popular charitable events ever held in Eaton's Auditorium. Money raised from the exhibition went to the Ontario Society for Crippled Children.

Born in 1900 in Port Huron, Michigan, Colleen Moore grew up to become the famous bob-haired "girl-next-door" star of many of D. W. Griffith's silent films. In 1933 she co-starred with Spencer Tracy in her most famous film, *The Power and the Glory*.

Assisted by seven hundred workman, artists, and craftsmen, Moore's father, set designer Harold Grieve, constructed the eleven-room fairy castle, which boasted genuine electric lightbulbs the size of wheat kernels; running water; and a fifteen-inch-high working cathedral organ, which, through an elaborate electrical system, played by remote control. Chandeliers hanging throughout the dollhouse sparkled with genuine diamonds, emeralds, rubies, and sapphires. Alabaster nightingales sang in a garden room. Solid-gold guppies filled a fountain, while ivory horses drew Cinderella's coach. The house was only on tour once before being donated to the Chicago Museum of Science and Nature, where it currently remains.

A lecture series inaugurated at the auditorium attracted a number of famous speakers over the decades. On December 6, 1932, Amelia Earhart delivered a speech exhorting young women to take up flying as a career. Earhart had also come to Toronto to promote a line of women's air-flight clothing she had designed, which Jack Brockie decided to publicize in a most unorthodox way. Preceding Earhart's appearance, in one of his most innovative publicity ploys, Jack Brockie outfitted Marg Morison in a one-piece leather aviatrix suit and dropped her by cables from the Eaton Auditorium rafters in a miniature plane, as she sang "High, High Up in the Sky."

On December 12, 1945, twelve-year-old Glenn Gould, whose only previous appearance in the auditorium had been as an usher, performed on the Casavant organ. Newspapers of the day hailed Gould's performance as a work of genius. Gould would later record most of his albums in the auditorium, whose acoustics he considered second to none.

Even children's parties were held in the auditorium, including those for Florence Mary and for Evelyn Beatrice Eaton. For Florence Mary Eaton's party, a circus theme featured two merry-go-rounds, including one encircling the fountain of the Round Room. Circus acts from New York entertained the children in attendance. At the conclusion of the party, four thousand balloons were dropped from a giant drum suspended from the ceiling.

In the 1960s, fashion shows attracted huge crowds to the auditorium. Among the famous models who consented to appear was Britain's Jean Shrimpton. Marg Morison had met a mildly dyspeptic Shrimpton at Malton Airport. "Without her makeup, she was a mousy, plain-looking little thing that wouldn't attract the attention of a fly," says Morison. "And then she put on her makeup and fancy clothes, and she was just this supernaturally beautiful creature." With Morison hovering in the wings, Shrimpton embarked on what was her catwalk debut.

Despite high expectations, twenty-five-year-old Shrimpton's performance remained memorable primarily for its missteps: SHRIMP FREEZES headlines screamed following the event. Far from being the swan Eaton's had hoped for, Shrimpton acted more like a frightened puppy, dashing out on stage and scratching her nose before finally stopping cold and staring at the audience in an attack of stage fright.

At a press conference following the event, a sullen Shrimpton reminded reporters, gathered at the Sutton Place Hotel to interview her, that her background consisted of posing for magazine photos, for which she earned approximately seventy-five thousand a year, and not for performing in live shows. "I kept telling the people at Eaton's that, but they just said they didn't mind," she stated. Proclaiming "I have no talent. All I have is a photogenic face,"[9] Shrimpton confessed that her favourite activity was lying in bed, which she went on to prove when she failed to appear at any social events scheduled for the evening, choosing instead to remain in her hotel room reading a book.

Eaton's had better luck on August 25, 1967, with the giggly and affable seventeen-year-old model Twiggy, whose boyish figure and huge blue eyes had catapulted her to superstardom overnight. A convoy of Eaton's representatives, composed of Marg Morison, Barbara

*"How do you like looking like a broomhandle?" an audience member in
Eaton Auditorium asked Twiggy during her visit in 1967. Left to right: Twiggy,
Beryl Kelly (Scudelleri), and Justin de Villeneuve, Twiggy's boyfriend and manager*

Duckworth, and Eaton's photographer Norm Scudelleri, picked up
Twiggy and her boyfriend/manager Justin de Villeneuve in a limousine
from the airport and delivered the two to the Royal York Hotel, where
they had a suite reserved for the day.

After charming crowds during a noontime press conference at the
hotel, Twiggy next went to Eaton's Auditorium, where CHUM radio host
Bob McAdorey interviewed her before an audience of more than one
hundred screaming teenage girls, who wanted answers to such burning
questions of the day as how long it took Twiggy to apply six layers of
false eyelashes, as well as what kinds of food she ate. "How do you
enjoy looking like a broom handle?" one of the few male adults in the
audience shouted, a question which the ninety-pound Twiggy deflected
by insisting that she ate hearty meals three times a day. On that very day,
for lunch, she had consumed a cheeseburger with french fries, as well as
waffles with syrup.

"Twiggy was a sweet kid," says Scudelleri, who drove Twiggy and Justin back to the airport after their appearance. "We stopped to have a hamburger on the way to the airport, so I know she was telling the truth about eating."

Six-foot-tall Russian fashion model Verushka also made a memorable appearance at the auditorium, this time in March 1967. "I had Verushka walking in an electric-blue bathing suit under a loose jacket of metal, leading two Russian wolfhounds with cornflower-blue leashes. There were flowers around their necks, and, of course, she just loped down the runway," recalls Ted Konkle. "She told me it was the best show she had ever been in," he adds.

I had Verushka walking in an electric-blue bathing suit under a loose jacket of metal," says Ted Konkle of Verushka, pictured here with Public-Relations Executive Barb Duckworth in March 1967.

Verushka's borzois were not the first animals featured in a Georgian Room fashion show. For an Easter-themed show one year, dozens of young rabbits were let loose on stage, and instantly began copulating. One year, a wallaby was brought in for an event. Soon after its arrival, organizers realized they had not set aside adequate space for it to stay overnight. To the rescue came Marg Morison. She took the creature home, where it soon made itself comfortable drinking milk out of saucers and scarfing down freshly baked bran muffins, spitting raisins out on the floor.

Canadian models remained a consistently good draw at the auditorium. As with the Georgian Room, events such as these were usually hosted by Marg Morison or Dora Matthews, and would usually feature live piano music by Horace Lapp.

Marg Morison took this wallaby home. It liked to eat bran muffins, but spit out the raisins.

"You always felt cherished and cared-for at Eaton's," says Joan Sutton, who later became a columnist. She recalls auditioning in the auditorium in front of Morison and Dora Matthews who, along with a fashion buyer, sat in the dark scribbling notes. As she attempted to execute flawless five-point turns, Sutton remained very conscious of the group whispering in the background.

Like many before her, Sutton remembers Marg Morison as a tough taskmistress, who demanded that her girls wear hats and gloves to work. Lateness was forbidden. Sutton wrote of Morison in a March 3, 1974, *Toronto Sun* feature entitled "Together Now – Toronto's Glamour Greats":

> She was "Mother Morison" to all her models. She kept an eye on our romances, checked our stockings and rumpled collars. She was demanding, tough, an absolute terror, and deep down, incredibly soft. Yes, Marg Morison's name is synonymous with a determined jaw and a twinkling eye. What set that jaw was loyalty: Loyalty to Eaton's, to her teammates and to her own uncompromising set of standards. "Good enough" was never good enough for Marg.[10]

Though she remained childless, Morison confirms her mother-confessor status. "One night, one of my girls came to our house and was knocking on the front door calling up to our bedroom window. She was in tears. Her boyfriend had been killed that night in a car accident, and my husband and I made her some food and let her stay the night with us."

"You knew with Eaton's you were always going to get paid and treated with respect," confirms Jean Macdonald, who modelled for the store in the 1960s. Nevertheless, Macdonald remembers the backstage atmosphere as being an obstacle course of halitosis-breathed hangers-on and half-clothed fellow models.

Most designers were pleasant to work for. There were, however, the exceptions. "I remember when Pucci came backstage and ordered us to take all our underwear off so there wouldn't be a line under our skinny silk dresses. He was such a jerk," says Macdonald. Oscar de la Renta, on the other hand, rated high on the list of models' favourite designers, because of his tact and courtesy. "If Oscar de la Renta had asked us to

Eaton's model
Jean Macdonald, 1960s

Marg Morison and Eaton's models embarking on
modelling tour on Eaton's private plane, ca.1948.
(Photo: courtesy of Marg Morison)

Pierre Cardin lands in Winnipeg, 1969

Designer Pierre Cardin shares an intense one-on-one with
Winnipeg's Lilian Vadeboncoeur, 1960s.

take off our underwear, we would have done it with no problem. He's such a charming man," adds Macdonald.

———■———

By the late 1960s and early 1970s, a large variety of entertainment venues opened throughout Toronto. As a result, Eaton's Auditorium soon lost its ability to attract sufficient crowds to keep it operating in the black. Only the most exclusive of entertainers, or phantasmagorically staged shows, could draw people away from their colour televisions at home.

"As theatrical facilities in Toronto increase, it is possible that the size and style of the Auditorium will no longer be compatible to the demands. Then a plan for its future will have to be considered,"[11] Eaton's president Bob Butler informed the *Toronto Telegram* in July 1975. In light of the competition Eaton's seventh floor faced, Butler was being optimistic.

Beginning in the 1960s, the O'Keefe (now Hummingbird) Centre, the refurbished Royal Alexandra Theatre, and the St. Lawrence Centre opened. All offered populist forms of entertainment that ultimately spelled the end of Eaton's Auditorium's dominance as the place to see and be seen in Toronto.

After the Eaton's College Street Store was acquired by College Park Developers for thirty million dollars in 1977, there were early hopes that the auditorium might be retained as a cultural landmark, since many great artists had staged their first performances there, but these hopes were quickly dashed by the new owners. The developers argued that it would be virtually impossible to attract audience members to the seventh floor without the retail store acting as a lure.

College Park planned to turn the building into a mixture of condominiums and retail spaces. However, the developers were constrained from converting the seventh floor into rented office space by Toronto's City Council, who in 1975 had passed a bylaw under the Ontario Heritage Act designating the floor as having historical value. Permission was thus needed to change any aspect of its internal structure.

Development of the floor was thrown into limbo. As cobwebs formed, an ad hoc Save the Seventh Floor Committee forwarded ideas for restoring the floor to its former glory. One of the group's leaders, architect Jim Reid, even designed a plan that would see the Round Room converted into a 300-seat supper club, with a 150-seat cinema and a foyer that featured a bar. To make their plan seem even more attractive, the committee proffered a list of one hundred performers, including Ginger Rogers, who expressed an interest in performing in the hall. Reid ranked the seventh floor up with other top examples of art deco in North America, such as Radio City Music Hall, and the Rainbow Room, located atop the Rockefeller Center in New York.

Two decades after they began, members of the Save the Seventh Floor Committee continued their battle to restore the floor to its former glory. On March 14, 2001, members of the committee met at a downtown church in Toronto. After delivering a speech that criticized the City of Toronto's obsession with sports over culture, former Aquitaine Records president Eleanor Kodolfsky, ex-wife of record-store owner Sam Sniderman, announced that College Park Developers had finally agreed to fully restore the Round Room and Eaton's Auditorium. In between the applause and cheers, a few audience members quietly expressed concern over the possibility that the restoration might include pop stands and hot-dog vendors' carts.

—■—

Sigi Brough greets Julio Iglesias.

After the auditorium closed in 1976, Eaton's stores across Canada transformed themselves into satellite showcases for touring celebrities. Makeshift stages were erected on sales floors, where celebrities promoted books, records, perfumes, or other products. One of the most popular sites for promoting celebrities was the main floor of Eaton's flagship store in the Toronto Eaton Centre.

Sigi Brough recalls singer Julio Iglesias appearing at the Eaton Centre in the early 1990s. As the sun beat down on his head through the giant sunroof, Iglesias continued to sign albums thrust at him by his enthralled female admirers. Before long, pearl-sized beads of sweat flowed slowly down his face. "Mr. Iglesias, do you need to wipe your forehead?" asked Brough, offering him a hanky. "Thank you *bella*," Iglesias replied, patting his face, then returned the damp hanky to Brough.

"Suddenly I noticed movement out of the corner of my eye, and I saw this woman at the side of the stage jumping up and down and screaming. I thought maybe she was having a heart attack, so I hurried over to see what the problem was and she points at the hanky in my hand and says, 'I'll give you $400 for that,'" laughs Brough.

Other celebrities, including Jimmy Carter and Céline Dion, appeared at Eaton's to promote their products. Possibly the most memorable public-relations extravaganza, however, was Elizabeth Taylor's 1997 appearance on the third floor of Vancouver's Pacific Centre to promote her perfume, "White Diamonds."

More than six thousand fans, mostly female, and one male Elizabeth Taylor impersonator dressed in black sequins with a black feather boa, crowded together elbow-to-elbow into the sweltering heat of the floor. Additional air conditioning in the room came from small hand-held fans designed by Sigi Brough, featuring a photograph of Taylor above the phrase, "I'm an Elizabeth Taylor fan."

Shortly before Taylor took to the stage, a bomb threat was phoned in to the store, prompting Taylor's former-Mossad bodyguards to scan the bottom of the makeshift stage with hand-held bomb detectors. Twenty minutes later, after the all-clear was given, Taylor hobbled out, dressed completely in white. Her equally white Maltese terrier, Sugar, scurried to the edge of the stage before returning to the safety of Taylor's generous lap. Earlier in the day, Brough had ordered a basket filled with treats specifically for Sugar.

Taylor's twenty-minute appearance, during which she answered questions from audience members, ensured record-breaking sales of her perfume. Shortly after she left, members of the media interviewed the next best thing to Taylor herself, the female impersonator, who, in his spare time, worked at a B.C. television station.

Other celebrities to pass through Eaton's during its final years included Farrah Fawcett, Vanna White, Ivana Trump, and Claudia Schiffer. However, for all intents and purposes, Taylor's appearance remained one of Eaton's last gasps at mounting celebrity extravaganzas. As the years passed, the allure of Eaton's as a place to spend the day evaporated, a victim of recurrent economic malaise and its own unshakeable image as a store that catered exclusively to middle-aged tastes. As hard as they tried, Jack Brockie's successors could not replicate his magic.

Beginning in the mid-1970s, Eaton's restaurants had suffered the same diminution in popularity. Seemingly overnight, the public's desire for elegant dining was replaced by a fast-food mentality. Dieticians were the first to notice the change. "We were told flat out that we were expected to make a profit," recalls Joan Caruso, who by the early 1990s had risen to become the Head of Food Services for all Eaton's stores.

"They weren't chefs, they were management people. It affected the quality of the food."

"The men took away our jobs," Dorothy Ferguson adds bluntly of the number crunchers who took over the management of the company's restaurants in the 1980s.

Before she progressed to bigger and better things, Joan Caruso's first job at Eaton's was as a dietician in the Beanery, a cafeteria located behind the Queen Street store in downtown Toronto. For twenty-five cents, factory workers could buy turkey dinners that included refreshments and dessert. "A conveyor belt ran through the cafeteria. You never knew when a parcel from another department might accidentally slip through," Caruso laughs.

By the time her forty years with the company came to an end in 1995, Caruso was fed up with what she saw as the dismaying erosion in the standards of food preparation, especially when it came to ingredients. "There was no longer the famous fruit salad; they thought the lettuce was too extravagant. That salad had been a signature item. And the potato balls we used in the chicken pies, which we had made by hand, were now bought in bulk," she says.

The upkeep of many of the restaurants went downhill as well. The last renovation to the Georgian Room occurred in 1960, when a new stainless-steel stove was installed. "They simply didn't renovate," says Caruso. "And gradually the restaurants became shabby."

The Montreal restaurant was remodelled in 1981, an

Out with the old. The remains of Eaton's Queen Street store, 1976 event Eaton's celebrated by having its waitresses dress in early-twentieth-century clothing. Nevertheless, by 1999 Montrealers had once and for all dismissed the restaurant as an anachronism, catering almost exclusively to elderly Anglophone women obsessed with trying to resurrect the past. Ironically, unlike the Georgian Room, which was demolished along with Toronto's Queen Street store in 1976 to make room for the Eaton Centre, the Montreal Restaurant survived. In 2000, the city designated it as a historical landmark.

When she left Eaton's for good, Joan Caruso represented one of the last of Eaton's highly trained dieticians. The parting was bittersweet. "I worked for Eaton's," she says, "but my co-workers were Eaton's to me, not the 'boys' – and this is where my loyalty went."

CHAPTER 5

The Wish Book

*Eaton's catalogue • Beginnings • Influence of catalogue
• Design and advertising • Decline*

W HEN WILLIAM WARDILL ISN'T using divining rods to locate old
Indian burial grounds, he's writing poetry, much of it in praise
of the store that provided gramophone records and books for his
parents, and, for him, the promise of affordable toys at Christmas.

From 1951 through 1984, Wardill did what his father did before
him: operated Eatonia, Saskatchewan's mail-order house, from what
had originally been a farmhouse post office before the CNR rail line was
built. Seventy-five per cent of the merchandise sent COD through
Eatonia came from the Eaton's catalogue.

"People bought everything from wedding rings to houses through
the Eaton's catalogue," says Wardill. "And they bought houses until
long after the Second World War."

Situated 160 miles southwest of Saskatoon, Eaton Township, nicknamed the "Oasis of the Prairies," originally served as a turnaround
point for the Canadian Northern Railway, which eventually amalgamated with the CNR. Because its name was so similar to the neighbour-
ing town of Eston, in 1921 the name of Eaton Township was formally
changed to Eatonia. Before long, because the township's name was like

*First post office (now
Dawn Realty) in Eatonia,
Saskatchewan, 1919.
Seventy per cent of the mail
orders were for Eaton's cat-
alogue merchandise.*

*William Wardill, postmaster,
Eatonia, Saskatchewan*

Mail-order receipt sent to customer
announcing that requested merchandise
was out of stock and would be sent as
soon as it became available, 1897.

the store, it helped to attract even more new immigrants anxious to set down roots and build houses for their growing families.

More than one million immigrants had already journeyed to Western Canada between 1896 and 1914. Mennonites, Ukrainians, Icelanders, and Russian Jews settled around Winnipeg. Jews gravitated primarily to urban centres, where they opened small shops, while the other groups concentrated mainly on farming.

Dotted liberally throughout the prairies today are the picturesque houses that immigrants purchased from the Eaton's catalogue – many of them equipped with full verandas, back porches, kitchens, dining rooms, even parlours. In 1910, for $945 a man could have the all the lumber for his dream home delivered to his local train station from Eaton's. Blueprints cost an additional $2.50, a price that was reduced to $1.00 when Special Building catalogues appeared in 1915. So efficient was Eaton's catalogue service that one ecstatic customer was moved to exclaim: "Eaton's catalogue is as much a Western institution as the wheat itself."[1]

But Eaton's service didn't stop there. Buried in shallow pockets of prairie soil are remnants of the variety of teacups, salt shakers, china, and pots and pans available through the catalogue. Hoes and garden rakes helped homesteaders plant seeds. Railways transported eggs and live chickens. And for those who could afford it, there were the latest state-of-the-art indoor bathroom fixtures. Prior to retiring for the night, a lucky family might now forgo the muddy-footed trek to an outdoor loo in favour of using the more convenient indoor kind – that is, if they could figure out exactly *how* to use it. In 1903, this challenge seems to have eluded new buyers Mack and Elizabeth Krebs. In a letter to their son, they wrote:

> We went to Eaton's for one of those new bathrooms. It took two plumbers to get it fixed up in shape. On one side of the room is a big long something like a pig trough – only you get in and wash all over. Then on the other side of the room is a little white thing called a sink. Here is where you wash your face. But just listen to this! Over in yonder corner we really got something. In this thing you put one foot in and wash it clean, then you push a handle and get fresh water for the other foot. Two lids came with it, but we can't get no use for them in the bathroom. So, I use one for a bread board. The other has a hole in it so we just put Grandpa's picture in it. Eaton's are awfully nice people to trade with, they sent us a roll of white writing paper with the outfit. We don't write much so I use it to wrap Pa's lunch in. So long Son, Your Ma.[2]

All things considered, the Krebs still made out better than an Eaton's customer in Quebec, who complained bitterly when the standing bath he received had a hole in it. Eaton's sent the customer two more baths, which he deemed equally defective. Eventually Eaton's had to explain to the customer that the "defect" was actually the drain. In the end, the man was allowed to keep all three baths.

For soldiers returning from serving overseas in the First World War, Eaton's houses often represented the first security they had ever known. Many of these soldiers had become acquainted with the catalogues when they found half-charred copies of them scattered on the floor of bombed-out buildings throughout Europe, their pages still folded back to reveal the page from which the last wave of departing soldiers had ordered their merchandise. The "Wish Book," as it became known, allowed them to dream of a way out of the nightmare around them.

One of these soldiers was Charles Heurick. While serving in the trenches in France, Heurick noticed that several of his fellow soldiers were sporting "little timepieces" on their wrists, bestowed upon them by grateful towns and communities back home. One day, during a break in the fighting, Heurick asked one of his buddies if he thought Eaton's would send him a wristwatch COD.

"Why certainly they'd send you one COD. You just write and ask them,"[3] the friend replied.

A few weeks later, while standing ankle-deep in the muddy fields of St. Éloi, Heurick received a small parcel from an army mail messenger. Inside was the little silver wristwatch. The watch was exactly as it had been pictured in the catalogue – with one remarkable exception. On its back was engraved Heurick's name, platoon, and regiment number, at no additional cost.

Heurick wore the watch for the duration of his war service and continued to wear it for another thirty years after he returned to Northern Ontario, where he lived alone in a log cabin, hunting and trapping to keep himself alive. After wearing it for so many years, Heurick looked upon the watch not merely as a good-luck piece, but also as an emotional life-preserver.

"Most of the time I had only my little wristwatch for company. It gradually became sort of an obsession with me," he wrote in a letter addressed to Eaton's in January 1939, adding:

> During the long winter nights especially, when I'd glance at the time, the little face brought back such queer memories. You know, the way a perfume, or maybe a song, will bring back certain memories you'd never have thought of having had if not been for some such prompting. It was the same with the little wristwatch. The time came when I could almost imagine it was living; did it not have a little face, and did it not have two little hands. Then, for some unknown reason, I got the idea that my luck would take a turn for the worse if we ever parted. There was no reason to think this way, but somehow or other I couldn't help it.[4]

When Heurick ultimately lost the watch years later while moose hunting, he feared that his luck had taken a permanent downturn. In his devastation, he confided to Eaton's that he had relied on the watch more than he even would a wife, concluding his letter despairingly, "There never was a wife as reliable as my little watch."[5]

In the late 1960s, a serendipitous meeting reminded an Eaton's employee of the international reach of Eaton's catalogue during the Second World War as well. While touring the Tower of London with

Drivers looked upon their horses as friends.
Horses and drivers lined up outside Moncton store.

his wife, one-time Moncton catalogue employee Larry Hutchinson was approached by a British man curious about the light meter Hutchinson was using to take pictures. "Your accent sounds American," the man said.

Hutchinson corrected him. "No, it's Canadian."

"Where are you from?" the man asked.

"New Brunswick," Hutchinson replied.

"I spent two of the happiest months of my life in Moncton," the man said, identifying himself as a former RAF pilot who had undertaken his flight training in the early 1940s at an abandoned airstrip not far from Moncton's catalogue distribution centre. Pointing toward Hutchinson, the man said excitedly to his wife, "There was a store there, I'd buy things and they would ship them to England. Remember the parcels I used to ship back home, this is the man who got them for me."

News of the catalogue's benefits swiftly spread into even the remotest regions of Canada. Customers appreciated not only the extraordinary variety of goods they could order, but also the usefulness of the catalogues themselves. Catalogues served a variety of purposes. Amateur hockey goalies used the heavy volumes for knee and shin pads. When heated, catalogues served as decent bed-warmers. One customer even made papier mâché jewellery by rolling small strips of catalogue pages in glue. And – of particular relevance to families like the aforementioned Krebses – catalogues also made excellent toilet paper.

In 1913, a mail-order distribution warehouse stocked with heavy merchandise was opened in Saskatoon. A similar type of warehouse was established in Regina in 1917. By 1920, Eaton's operated mail-order distribution centres in Winnipeg, Toronto, and Moncton. Winnipeg served regions extending as far west as British Columbia. The Ontario centre catered to regions as far east as Quebec, while Moncton's encompassed the Maritime provinces. Eaton's mail-order operation become so vital to Canada's economy that it was hard to remember that its origins had stemmed from a simple idea of Timothy Eaton's.

———■———

In the fall of 1884, Timothy Eaton's staff members distributed his small pink catalogues by hand to visitors attending the Toronto Industrial Exposition, later named the Canadian National Exhibition. Inside were textual descriptions of products ranging from children's cashmere hose to corsets, and from cotton sheets to hemp carpets.

The first primitive mail-order "department," which was formed in 1885, was no more than a small raised gallery located approximately eight steps up from the main floor of the store at 190 Yonge Street. The first female employee, Emily Cowley, joined the firm as a clerk in 1885, when she was only sixteen years old. Prior to being accepted for paid employment, Cowley completed a six-month training course. Her starting salary was $2.50 a week, a sum that was raised to $3.00 when she was accepted for permanent employment. Sensing her skills lay somewhere other than in sales, Timothy placed a pencil and paper in front of Cowley and asked her to write her name. When she finished, he examined her penmanship and, satisfied with what he saw, took her to the second floor, where he instructed her to start addressing envelopes containing handbills announcing the opening of his new mail-order department.[6]

Cowley was also made responsible for clipping samples from bolts of fabric that were stacked on the shop floor and pinning these fabric samples to each separate catalogue. Since the first catalogue contained only textual descriptions of merchandise, these small samples of dress materials and ribbon enabled customers to feel the quality of the merchandise being offered.

Before long, a second woman was hired to join the mail-order team. Alli Arnold, whom Timothy ultimately nicknamed "the Mother of the Mail Order,"[7] was employed to keep the ledger books in the mail-order department, as well as to act as a buyer for customers who ordered in-store from the catalogue. It wasn't long before Arnold became so busy listing a record of each purchase in the ledger book that Miss Cowley was promoted to take Arnold's place as a buyer on the floor, while another girl was hired to collect fabric samples.

In addition to possessing a strong work ethic, mail-order girls were expected to exhibit sound judgment in matters of dress, and to be able to determine what qualities and types of merchandise people required in various regions of Canada. Customers often assisted buyers in the most extraordinary ways. Some sent in pencil tracings of their shoes, or of their bare feet, in an attempt to ensure that footwear fit. Dress fabrics, meanwhile, varied according to the climate of the region in Canada in which the customer lived.

In the store's early years, orders were processed by Arnold, Cowley, and the sample girl at a crudely built twelve-foot-long counter made from old packing cases. At one end of the counter the three women itemized the orders, then after wrapping them with sturdy brown paper and twine, carried them to the back of the store. If parcel-wrappers miscalculated and used too much twine, they were expected to either re-use it or reimburse the store for the wasted stock, although on at least one occasion, when spotting a young female employee buying a spool of twine from another employee, a gallant Timothy Eaton personally

Horse-drawn rigs

Cash office, Queen Street store, early 1900s

stepped in and let her have it for free. Once securely fastened, customers' packages were loaded onto horse-drawn carriages and taken either to the train station for shipping, or to their homes in the city.

Inside 190 Yonge Street, customers who lined up six-deep at counters to examine in-store merchandise collided with those customers who were dashing in to select merchandise from the catalogue. Electric generators controlled the flickering carbon-arc lamps on each floor and powering the giant overhead fans, which often circulated air so violently that light merchandise and papers were blown off tables. Electricity also activated the bells that rang to signal the opening and closing of the store, lunch-hour shifts, and other events that occurred amid the whirl of commerce. Once sales were finalized, sales slips, along with cash, were placed in narrow metal cylinders and whisked to a central office through octopus-like hydraulic tubes. Once they received the slips and cash, boys and girls hurriedly made change, placed it in the canisters, along with the sales slips, and sent it back to the sales clerks.

Twenty-one-year-old Frank Beecroft was soon assigned to supervise the hurricane of orders that arrived daily by mail. To his chagrin, he discovered that, despite her best efforts, Arnold had not kept formal books, but had simply opened mail-orders, removed the enclosed cash, and

1902 Eaton's catalogue cover

Eaton's first
catalogue, 1882

Eaton's catalogue
cover from the
1920s

placed the cash in a cash box, then filled each order personally. Beecroft quickly arranged a more efficient bookkeeping system, whereby orders were stamped with a number as soon as they came in.

Beecroft then turned his attention to distributing advertising hand-bills to potential customers. He effectively organized groups of young girls to fold up ads and place them in envelopes to be mailed. In conjunction with the catalogues, advertising quickly became an invaluable tool for the company. Prior to 1901, when he placed his first full-page ad in the *Toronto Star*, Timothy Eaton was content to simply display a few posters in the windows of 190 Yonge Street to interest passersby and allow his catalogues do the talking for him. Eaton's would eventually hold an 11.7-per-cent interest in the *Star*, where an ad entitled "Eaton's Daily Store News" appeared regularly on the back page. These regular ads were cancelled only in 1911, when Timothy's son, John Craig, protested the paper's stand on the Canada–U.S. Reciprocity Bill.

Before long, customers' demands for Eaton's merchandise outdistanced anything even Timothy could dream of. Correspondingly, working conditions within the store reached pandemonium pitch, with sales clerks, buyers, floorwalkers, and parcel-wrappers all crashing into each other in confined spaces.

With fresh and flirtatious young girls on the scene, it was perhaps inevitable that Frank Beecroft was required to add one more duty to his administrative work – that of referee for budding office romances. Beecroft's first project involved none other than John Craig Eaton.

Handsome and high-spirited, John Craig began his apprenticeship in the mail-order department of the store, where, Beecroft recalled, he liked to "joke and be silly with the girls."[8] One summer a fellow employee named Miss Peurgesou decided to invite ten boys and ten girls to visit her father's fruit farm in Mimico. All the store's employees had bicycles, but John Craig dazzled the girls in particular by owning the then-Jaguar of transportation vehicles – a horse and buggy.

The boys were asked to pick their partners from among the girls and pair up. Once the selection was completed, a "nice little girl" named Gertie Cook approached Beecroft, greatly distressed because both Beecroft's son Billy and John Craig Eaton had asked to escort her to Miss Peurgesou's farm. Gertie did not want to refuse John, but she also didn't want to hurt Billy. Beecroft advised her to tell John Craig that Billy had asked her first, and that she should abide by whatever John

Craig decided. Beecroft later noted in his journals that John Craig took news of a competitor bravely, and gallantly told Gertie to go to the fruit farm with Billy, while he would ask another girl. Ironically, not long after, Gertie and Billy ran off and got married, and unexpectedly left Toronto for good.[9]

Despite innocently romantic diversions such as this, relations between male and female employees were frequently less than harmonious. Several department managers complained that there were so many buyers dashing throughout the store to fill the catalogue orders, which had been received both by mail and in person, that they were now crashing into those customers who were leisurely browsing through the in-store merchandise.

Relations between staff members became so tense that store manager Harry McGee eventually set aside a special stockroom just for buyers. Each buyer was assigned a desk, with strict instructions from McGee that all drawers were to be locked using one key, with a duplicate key from each desk to be left at the Private Office.

Rules within the mail-order department remained strict. Passes were mandatory for any employee leaving the department, and no gum-chewing was allowed, even in the washrooms. In spite of his efforts to instill discipline, however, McGee didn't quite succeed in quelling tensions between the sexes.

In a letter he wrote to Eaton's management in 1963, a stock-taker named Robert McQuarrie recalled the situation with disgust: "A more unsatisfactory state of things could not be imagined, girls talking and gossiping, sitting down behind counters, in each other's departments, lazy, saucy, impudent, coming in and out at all hours."[10]

Timothy Eaton often scolded his employees when he caught them making mistakes, but, as Emily Cowley noted, "his kind heart soon took over and when a girl burst into tears after a scolding, he would pat her on the head or shoulder and tell her not to cry – just to be more careful and not to make so many mistakes another time." One day, while Timothy was showing visitors through the store, Cowley took a telephone message for him and received the highest accolade accorded a female of that day – a pat on the head from Timothy – followed by the compliment, "This is our little personage."[11]

Male employees didn't find Timothy's management style so endearing. Frederick William Story, who was hired in 1891 to manage the

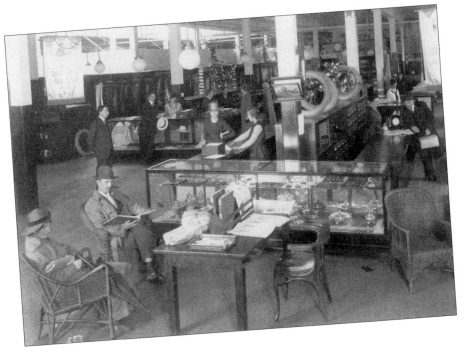

Mail Order Reception Room. Fifth floor, Mail Order building, Toronto

Order Turrets, 1918

delivery system as well as to buy Timothy's horses, recollected that Timothy would fire a man instantly for any cause. "The man had absolutely no chance to give his side," said Story. "He was told, 'You're fired. Go and get your money.'" Story recalled that Timothy was very against Labour Day, and would fire anyone who looked out the window after the parade. "Any interest in anything like a union or collective bargaining was cause for instant dismissal,"[12] he recalled.

Indeed, even in the earliest days of the mail order, Timothy did everything he could to derail union uprisings. In 1901, a strike by the printers' union threatened to compromise the timely distribution of Eaton's catalogues. Dozens of unionized printers marched up Yonge Street past the store carrying placards that read: "Don't Buy at Eaton's." Timothy's response was swift and merciless. "Buy some presses," he told an employee named Lowry, "and find some typesetters and men to run them."[13]

Lowry quickly rounded up some non-unionized typesetters. Soon after, as added insurance against the possibility that the non-unionized typesetters might join the striking printers in sympathy, Timothy purchased a complete electrotyping plant from the Ostrander Company of Chicago, whose experts taught Eaton's staff members how to run the electrotype machines efficiently. Though some staffers complained about the indignity of having their faces smudged with black lead as they electrotype-set the catalogues, the scheme worked, and much to the distress of the unionized printers, the catalogues were distributed on time.

As the catalogues grew in size from eight to forty to one hundred pages, orders poured in, requiring increasingly efficient methods to fill them. In 1909, the Mail Order department, now on Louisa Street in Toronto, acquired its own stock of merchandise, which was divided into separate departments, each overseen by its own manager and staff. In 1907, the Winnipeg store had already reserved three upper floors for light mail-order purchases.

The eighth floor of the Winnipeg store featured an area nicknamed "The Cage," where each day, as soon as the thousands of letters arrived, teams of young women sorted them into bundles of twenty-five before running them through an opener. After bundles of letters were opened, they were rebundled and passed along to a different group of girls, who opened the orders, checked the value of the orders against the amount of cash enclosed, and passed the orders along to cashiers, who detached the cash and sent the money to the banks. The orders were forwarded to the appropriate departments for processing.

Before long, a particular species known as "parcel girls" evolved. These women spent their entire day wrapping yards of paper and yarn around hundreds of packages, then placing the packages on conveyor belts that ran underneath their tables to the mail department.

In his job delivering invoices from one department to another at Eaton's, Tom Pezzack recalls that, when Sir John Craig was president, he saw to it that merchandise was arranged in large squares in each department, with four aisles leading to the middle, where a parcel girl stood working. "John Craig used to walk down in front of our General Office and across the aisle where there were two enclosures for parcelling. He always had a pretty girl there. Every once in a while – and it soon became general knowledge – some pretty girl would be asked to come to visit Sir John in his office. Let's just say he was liberal in his outlook and lavish with his gifts."

Margaret Gair was sixteen years old when she was hired to work as a parcel girl in the Winnipeg store. Her job required her to wear black satin smocks and walk around with metal clippers, which she used to cut ribbon, hooked to her fingers at all times. Giving paper or twine to someone without permission remained a serious offence. "We had a place in the tunnel leading to the mail-order area, where phone in orders were sent from. I remember standing in front of these big pigeonholes. People would place things in the holes and we would pull them out, wrap them, and make sure the route number was placed on them. It was fun," she says.

Once orders were filled and wrapped, order forms were sliced up and forwarded to postal department workers. These workers then typed the destinations of each parcel onto Eaton's signature red, white, and blue delivery labels. Every order in the system had to be stamped with a series number that identified it.

In the postal department, hundreds of large bags hung like gaping mouths from wall hooks waiting to receive packages. Like an air traffic controller, a man stood in a centrally located watchtower, personally making a final check of each parcel's destination before dropping it down a chute towards the appropriate bag.

Mail chutes also constituted the final destination for parcels in Eaton's Montreal store. There, a steady stream of parcels was carried towards the postal department by a network of movable belts situated near the basement ceiling. Often the belts ground to a loud halt when parcels were piled so high they jammed against the ceiling. As soon as parcels reached them, Transfer Shipping Department staff, nicknamed the "Wizards of Routes," glanced at the addresses, carefully wrote the correct route number on each package, and then dropped them down the appropriate chutes to the bags below. Bags were then carried to the loading platform, sometimes as late as eleven at night. By seven o'clock the next morning, all parcels deposited on the loading platform the night before were lifted onto horse-drawn carriages for delivery.

Delivery horses received the utmost care from Eaton's staff members. Indeed, Eaton's horses regularly won top prizes at the CNE and Royal Winter Fair. And no president loved horses more than R. Y. Eaton, the

Central Dispatch, 1959 – "The Wizards of Routes"

company's third president, who, some employees joked, put as much energy toward drafting detailed instructions on the care and feeding of horses as he did toward the care and feeding of his own staff.

The stalls, located on the fifth floor of Eaton's Albert Street building in Toronto, across from Eaton's main store, were scrubbed and disinfected each morning. A special hospital ward was built, containing thirteen box stalls, where a horse showing the least signs of indisposition received quick treatment. As a result of all this loving care, the sickness rate among Eaton's horses remained low, with one painful exception. In 1925, an epidemic of pink eye swept through the Hayter Street stables, where all of Eaton's horses had been moved in the early 1920s. A large tent was erected across part of College Street, where approximately one hundred fifty horses were put down, much to the distress of R. Y.

For more than fifty years, up until the 1930s, horses delivered merchandise from all major Eaton's stores across Canada and, as a result, became quite beloved. Children on delivery routes fed them apples. More industrious individuals collected the manure for use as fertilizer in gardens.

The aroma of fresh manure in Toronto could become pungent. In 1891, John Jones, then Street Commissioner at Toronto's City Hall, wrote Timothy Eaton to complain. On March 23, 1891, Timothy fired back one of his trademark acerbic replies:

> Dear Sir: In reply to yours of the 2nd Re. Complaints from Orde St. The charge you make is admitted and I beg to say that according as the snow melts away the manure is scraped off the street every day and if you get the sun to shine steadily for three days there will no further cause of complaint, and you can assure any person making complaints that the manure is scraped off every day it is soft . . . [We] thank you for your prompt attention and only wish we could get you to be as prompt and careful and watchful in clearing away the rubbish on James St. We tried to get you to do so but we had to get carts and draw it ourselves. Yours truly, TE.[14]

Customers greeted Eaton's horses by their first names, while the horses automatically stopped when arriving at the houses of regular customers. As a driver dashed from house to house on foot to deliver three

*Horse stable, Toronto, 1919. Children would feed
apples to horses while they were on their deliveries.*

or four parcels at a time, his horse automatically moved up the street to
follow him. Drivers who fell asleep from the long hours on the job were
led home by their horses.

Winnipeg delivery driver John English recalls that the trust between
a customer and her delivery man could become deep. "If she was away
when a delivery was scheduled, she would leave the order coupon with
the required cash on the kitchen table – often beside a freshly baked
pie," he says. After eating some pie, drivers would glue the order coupon
into a special book and stuff the cash into their pants pockets.

The Winnipeg horse stalls were situated on the first four floors of a
six-storey building at Hargrave Street and St. Mary Avenue. Ramps
allowed the horses to ascend or descend from floor to floor. It was rare
for a horse to forget at the end of the delivery day exactly which stall
was his. Later the horses were moved to barns located on the Pembina
Highway.

By 1936, Eaton's horses were retired in favour of the famous red-
white-and-blue-coloured delivery trucks, designed by R. Y. Eaton. The

horses were brought out of retirement one last time during the Second World War, because of gas and rubber rationing, which drastically reduced the number of cars and trucks allowed on the roads.

During the Second World War, women took the places of the male drivers who had entered the military. Winnipeg driver Ann Atkin was renowned for being able to carry one hundred pounds of sugar without breaking into a sweat. "There were no elevators in those days, so if you had, say, a twelve-bottle carton of Pepsi, you were pretty much pooped by the time you'd climbed up five flights of stairs," she says. Deliveries of more numerous smaller items were even more exhausting because of the number of times Atkin had to climb stairs to complete the order.

When the Second World War ended, Atkin was transferred to a telephone order desk, where she had to wear a dress and work for a fraction of the salary she had received as a delivery person. But she retained no hard feelings. "It made me mad to lose my job to a man," she says, "but that's the way it was back then. I knew I was lucky just to have a job."

Atkin may ultimately have been luckier than she thought. By the late 1970s, delivery drivers' jobs had become increasingly dangerous. After a Winnipeg driver was robbed and mugged, locked strongboxes were installed in the vans, where drivers placed any money they collected. Keys to the boxes were located in the store's delivery office. As Winnipeg driver Steven Kiz recalls, "Gone were the days when the driver was like a travelling bank. [The] good old days of safely carrying large sums of money and leaving your van unattended and unlocked came to an end."

—■—

Eaton's catalogues unquestionably helped to open up Canada – especially, thanks to the railroad, Western Canada. By 1914, a specialty department was set up in the Winnipeg store devoted solely to processing orders from the catalogue's western division. On hand to create the catalogue's artwork was Frederick Brigden, who was renowned for nurturing some of the greatest names in Canadian graphic art. One of these was Charles Comfort, who worked on Eaton's catalogue. Years after he left Brigden's, Comfort achieved fame as perhaps Canada's greatest war artist, in addition to acting as director of the National Gallery of Canada. Disney artist Charles Thorson also got his start at Brigden's.

Fred Brigden regularly advised and consulted with merchandise buyers about how to enhance their products' visual marketability. As fast as buyers talked, Brigden drew, sometimes right in the departments themselves. After the drawings were completed, they were line-engraved on glass plates and prepared for printing. Fred Brigden soon established one of the biggest and most successful engraving plants in Manitoba.

Brigden's studio was a godsend to Winnipeg's buyers. Because the catalogues were printed in Toronto, Eaton's buyers had been forced to remain there for protracted periods of time to supervise the illustrations they had selected for inclusion in the Winnipeg catalogue's pages. By moving his business west, Brigden now afforded Western buyers more time to evaluate the needs of their particular regions and less time travelling to Toronto to supervise artwork.

The establishment of cross-country mail-order extension offices, where merchandise advertised in the catalogue was stocked, further enhanced the ability of Eaton's to deliver merchandise to customers as quickly as possible. The first order office was established in Oakville, Ontario, in 1916, and by 1928 several more small outlets had been opened in towns and villages across the country. Mail-order extension offices truly proliferated after 1928, when Eaton's bought twenty-one small department stores in Ontario and Montreal that had formerly been owned by the Canadian Department Stores Limited chain.

Order offices provided customers with the opportunity to come and meet Eaton's company representatives face to face to discuss the relative merits of catalogue merchandise. Snags only developed in the plan when order offices sprang up at the rear of Eaton's retail outlets. It didn't take long for customers to bypass in-store merchandise for similar, lower-priced merchandise available through the mail-order office at the back of the store. The situation infuriated store managers, who saw mail-order offices as directly competing with their stores. To try to alleviate the problem, Eaton's offered a 10-per-cent bonus to salesgirls who, upon finding a store item was not available, referred customers to the catalogue in the order department at the rear of the store.

By 1943, customers visiting the Winnipeg store's mail-order show-room could enjoy the luxury of sitting in spring-seated and washable swivel chairs. Customers were encouraged either to bring in their orders or to consult catalogues, which had been placed on special modern slab tables that sat atop tapered stands. Once the customers chose the merchandise they wished to see, clerks retrieved it from the various departments and assembled it on pyramid-style bunks for customers to pick up and examine. Payment was made at special cash wickets.

Truckers who placed orders were always served first. As soon as the truckers placed their orders in a specially reserved section designated by red flags, squads of sales clerks fanned out to find the merchandise as quickly as possible and deposited it either at the main-floor trucking depot for pick-up at an arranged time, or at various truck depots across the city.

———■———

Eaton's went on to publish five basic catalogues out of Toronto each year, in both French and English. Rather than being a literal translation from the English, the French version of the catalogue was more inter-pretive in nature, and it was often a challenge for the French copy-writers to fit their text into the same amount of space allotted to the English text. Descriptions frequently suffered as a result. Boys' jeans, for example, were touted as being "Wanted by buckaroos!" This was translated into French as "Tenue de cowboy." Translations from French to English were equally strange. Negligée-clad women, pictured as enjoying, in French, "La Vie en Rose," fell off their pedestals in the less sexy English version, where they were hailed as "In the Pink."[15]

In spite of these problems, at least one Quebec resident proclaimed the French edition of the Eaton's catalogue a "masterpiece." In a letter addressed to Eaton's management, customer Eugène Brochm wrote:

[The] point I wish mostly to insist upon is the high quality of French used everywhere in this *album* as the French call it. One would never think it is a translation, but the result of an idea created in a French mind and worded by a purist. Not only the technical vocabulary is appropriate but the choice of expressions, the variety of descriptions and the syntax are a revelation . . . [I] do not think we have in our French province of Quebec anything that can compare.[16]

Language problems may have been surmounted in the catalogues, but trying to unite the fashion sensibilities of Eastern and Western

Canada was like trying to unite oil and water. Where, in Quebec, the watchword was élan, the watchword in Winnipeg or Saskatoon was practicality. In a 1969 edition of Winnipeg's *Eaton Quarterly*, author Fredele Maynard wrote of the 1928 catalogue's western fashions: "Even moderately frivolous garments are recommended in terms which emphasize feel, not look. [Perhaps] in the big department stores of Montreal and Toronto smart shoppers asked 'What does Chanel say?' On the prairies, the lead question was likelier to be 'do the merino combinations have a closed or open crotch?' "[17]

The exposure of excess female flesh in the Western editions of Eaton's catalogues could enrage puritanical shoppers. A woman from Lloydminster, Saskatchewan, was outraged that Eaton's artists glorified immodest dress, consisting of "low necks and shoes with very little leather."

In Eastern Canada, a distressed catalogue shopper disparaged Eaton's for selling shorts to women. She wrote,

> I noticed in the paper that a woman was fined in Eastern Canada for wearing shorts in her backyard hanging out her clothes, men said she was too immodest to be seen outside her door in shorts & yet Eaton Co. advertise in Sales Summer Cat White shorts for women . . . [S]lacks are also forbidden by Gods laws for women read Deut 2.2 Chapter – 5 verse. . . . [A] woman shall not wear that which pertaineth unto a man Deut 22:5.[18]

Clearly frustrated by the image of affluence Eaton's continued to project during the Great Depression, a customer named G. A. Sims composed a searing page-by-page analysis of Eaton's Spring and Summer 1937 catalogue, eviscerating the scantily clad men, women, and children frolicking for the camera on the catalogue pages. No amount of propaganda was going to convince Sims that better economic times were just around the corner. As a result, he proceeded to unravel Eaton's version of the National Dream seam by seam, beginning with fashions worn by Canadian girls. Sims wrote:

> [We] would like however to remark, in passing, that nothing is too good for our Canadian girls, and furthermore, you get what you pay for, and that certain garment marked a 1.00 will outwear

half a dozen similar articles marketed at 39 cents, don't matter how much you sit on it. [O]n page 73 we come across chubby little boys in their nighties and underware [sic], four of them sitting in a row, evidently waiting for Santa Claus, and all smiling, and it is refreshing to see that the one who wears the cheaper suit is smiling just as hard as the one garbed in the more expensive article. This is true democracy and such a spirit of fair play we expected from our Canadian boys. [T]alk about action on page 75. It is hard to imagine that those young men may at some future date become sit down strikers. The page is so full of action that after studying it we dropped our pen and took a run around the block. [O]n page 76 the children are a little larger and look more sophisticated, the kind who would ask a perfect stranger for a nickel for the show, changing the request in later years for a cup of coffee.[19]

Sims was not alone in criticizing the catalogue's candy-floss hyper-realism. Critics claimed that Eaton's catalogues did not merely fail to respond to the economic realities of the day, but pulled the gabardine over customers' eyes by promoting strictly Anglo-Saxon standards of style and beauty. It is true that, until its last decade of existence, the catalogue rarely included models of foreign extraction, or mixed race. In fact, the summer catalogue for 1975 contains no non-white models at all.

Fredele Maynard noted that in 1928 Eaton's seemed "spectacularly unaware of large elements in its cultural heritage," adding that "an 'Eskimo' doll is a run-of-the mill doll in, of all things, a clown suit with pom-poms and ruff at the neck." Indian crafts, meanwhile, featured "tie-holders, score pad covers and cushion tops all decorated with the identical silhouette of a feathered chieftain (circa Tecumseh)."[20]

If Maynard had cast her eyes back to even earlier catalogues, she would have noted the presence of "nigger" dolls on sale for twenty cents, alongside the popular German-manufactured Eaton Beauty Dolls, which initially sold for a dollar, and remained not only one of Eaton's best-selling dolls, but a valuable collector's item. The ivory-faced Eaton Beauty Doll represented Eaton's ideal of feminine beauty. To own her was to become part of a national sorority. Indeed, her pre-eminent status among dolls was compromised only briefly in the 1930s by the emergence of the Shirley Temple Doll, equally cute, but considerably more dimpled than her Eaton Beauty Doll competitor.

The *Northern Miner* of June 1937 upped the ante in cultural insensitivity with its claim that Indian girls were increasingly seeking out Eaton's catalogues so they could gaze "with envious eyes at the fashionable outfits of their white city sisters."[21]

The generic reference to "Indian girls" was particularly stinging, considering that the CNR railway, which enabled Eaton's mail-order merchandise to be delivered coast to coast faster and more efficiently, could only be completed by appropriating vast tracks of Indian land once owned by Canada's Cree, Blackfoot, and Métis.

As its catalogue business grew, Eaton's did not merely alienate members of cultural minorities or managers of small Eaton's stores with mail-order extension offices in their backs, it also devastated the economic health of the owners of small, independent shops, particularly those located on railway lines. Filled with the scent of pipe tobacco, hay, and fresh manure, these shops had always cultivated a family atmosphere, and existed as meeting places for local farmers. Once rural dwellers heard about the seemingly limitless selection of goods available through the Eaton's catalogue, however, they began bypassing the pleasures of social shopping. Fortunately, the clashes between small shop owners and Eaton's never erupted into violence, as did clashes in the United States when, for instance, Sears Roebuck's mail-order distribution offices were literally burned to the ground by local merchants.

One of the victimized shopowners was a Timothy Eaton wannabe who had always kept one step ahead of bankruptcy by buying and selling small shops along each stretch of newly built railway line. His final stop was in Winnipeg, where he opened a shop that included a post office in the back. Among the items available for customers' perusal was the Eaton's catalogue. The man's son recalls:

> I remember when it first dawned on Dad what was happening. You see, you didn't send money through the mail to Eaton's. They didn't want money. Postal orders. That's what they wanted. It was down there in black and white. I think it said 'Send No Cash.' So these people would come in to Dad's store and he'd see them going down to the back to the wicket and he knew darn well that they were buying postal orders in his own store to send off to

Winnipeg. To buy things that were on sale not 10 or 20 feet from them, right in Dad's general store.[22]

Not even the prospect of experiencing delays in the delivery of merchandise could dampen catalogue customers' enthusiasm. One shopkeeper became so infuriated that he wrapped an iron a customer had just purchased in his store and placed it on a shelf, telling the customer to return in two days to pick it up. The message didn't penetrate. Two days later, the customer returned to order a garden hoe from the catalogue.

The extended credit lines that customers had once enjoyed in small shops also became a casualty of Timothy's one-low-price policy, which he achieved thanks to the bulk manufacturing and purchasing power his company possessed, as well as the Goods Satisfactory or Money Refunded policy he introduced in 1870. Timothy's son John Craig Eaton sweetened the pot even more in 1918 by guaranteeing free delivery on orders of five dollars or more. Before long, the amount was reduced to two dollars. Eventually, Eaton's promised to reimburse customers for all the costs they incurred in having to return unsatisfactory merchandise.

Those customers who didn't pay their bills promptly, however, received several warning letters from Eaton's, each one less friendly than the next. If customers were particularly recalcitrant about paying, their names were kept on file and money was demanded from them in advance for any future purchases. One customer from Campbellford, Ontario, didn't take it kindly when Eaton's accused her of not paying for her merchandise. In a November 25, 1930, letter addressed "To the Eatons Please," she wrote:

Dear Sirs –,
I have received many letters from yous. We have had quite a bit of trouble with yous. I am *certain* and <u>sure sure sure</u> that I paid it. I can take my oathe that I paid it. We got the cheque and a letter sent back to us saying that you got the money. I am sick and tired getting your letters. I am very, very, very, very sure I sent you the money. I am <u>SURE</u> I sent you the money, I am sure. P.S. I am sure.[23]

Perhaps those who suffered the most from Eaton's monopoly on bulk manufacturing and shipping were individual craftsmen, especially furniture-makers, who were unable to build tables, chairs, and sideboards fast

Lilian Vadeboncoeur, 1945. Winnipeg's Research Bureau.

enough to beat the number manufactured in Timothy's factories. It didn't help that Eaton's furniture designers were among the best in the world.

Merchandise sold under the Eaton's label, meanwhile, was tested to make sure its catalogue descriptions were accurate. Hyperbolic adjectives such as "fabulous" and "amazing" were forbidden. Furs seemed at least one exception, with dyed skunk transformed into "Alaska Sable," and hare dyed a shade touted as "Imperial Mink."

In 1907, John Craig Eaton established the first research bureau ever maintained by a Canadian retail organization. Housed originally in the mail-order building on Louisa Street in Toronto, Research Bureau staff examined merchandise using a variety of instruments, in order to ensure that it possessed uniformity in size and construction.

Six months after the research bureau opened, Engineer E. J. Tyrrell supervised the opening of a chemical-testing laboratory. There, he inspected products purchased from all parts of the world to ensure that they lived up to their descriptions. Fabrics were stretched, rubbed, and faded by a special machine, then subjected to dyes and chemicals. A novel machine, nicknamed a "Fadometer," simulated sunlight and determined the fadability of colours. Chemists even coated their arms with suntan lotion and stuck them inside the Fadometer to see how effective the lotion was.

In the 1940s, Lilian Vadeboncoeur, who was one of the few women in her day to obtain her Bachelor of Science degree from the University of Winnipeg, tested paints and examined fabrics in the textile lab of Winnipeg's research bureau. "If the label said 100 per cent cotton, it had to test out," she says.

Vadeboncoeur also used a special machine to count the number of threads in nylon stockings to discover why they had run, and "candled" eggs that farmers had brought in for sale by shining lights behind them to make sure they hadn't been fertilized.

—■—

As buyers' fashion tastes became more sophisticated, the inclusion of sketches of sexy women, not just throughout the catalogue but in newspaper ads, became invaluable.

A successful candidate, notes Fredele Maynard, was expected to have "smooth skin; sparkling eyes; fluid lips; well-balanced, regular features; a good smile; and, most important of all, the ability to retain a certain expression for several minutes."

Some models viewed posing for the catalogue as a stepping stone to Hollywood stardom. High-fashion models – or those who looked "as if they might choke on a lettuce leaf," in Maynard's words – were shunned in favour of ordinary girls with "pleasantly rounded bosoms, legs, and derrières." But the results often backfired. As Maynard noted:

The women in the flat, stylized illustrations are decidedly on the heavy

Eaton's early models, such as this one, were taken from the ranks of the employees. Many harboured dreams of stardom from appearing in Eaton's catalogue.

Catalogue production, 1967

side, but the heaviness is without any suggestion of sensuous ripeness. They are quite breastless, these large bovine females – and no wonder. The corset page reveals horrifying Glex O Steel casings "Strongly boned throughout to hold and give the figure a straight line" . . . For women whose figures resist equalizing, there is a rubber reducing brassiere. Legs, revealed to just knee level, are sexless as sausages.[24]

"Modelling didn't exactly require a lot of brain work," says Jean Arnistie. Arnistie was a nineteen-year-old graduate of teacher's college when she and two girlfriends applied for summer jobs at Eaton's in the summer of 1949. One girlfriend was offered a job as an elevator operator, the second was hired to train employees, while Jean was given the biggest plum of all, the opportunity to pose as a sketch model for Eaton's newspaper advertisements. Despite the introduction of photography in Eaton's advertising in the late 1930s, sketches were still regarded as an effective advertising tool, especially when depicting intimate apparel. "It was a tremendous boost to my ego," Arnistie admits. At five foot five, she was considered too short for the job, but was advised by the art department to lie and say she was five foot seven.

Conforming to the modesty of the time, Arnistie wore undergarments she modelled on the outside of her regular clothing. As the sketch artist worked, Arnistie held poses for up to three-quarters of an hour at a time. "I had to hold my hand in a certain position, as long as I never looked like I was holding either a shot glass or a cigarette," she laughs.

When the time came for Arnistie to eat, she was escorted to the cafeteria by an Eaton's watchdog, who monitored what she ate to ensure it did not exceed a prescribed calorie limit. Arnistie states, "I was allowed raisin bread and always only 2-per-cent milk. My weight was never to fluctuate beyond 111 to 117 pounds."

As soon as the workday ended, Arnistie, accompanied by the head of the art department, escaped to jazz clubs, where she promptly violated at least one of Eaton's ten commandments by indulging in high-calorie alcoholic drinks.

Child models of the thirties and forties, chosen for their Shirley Temple cuteness quotient, made popular photographic models for catalogues. Since Toronto had no modelling agencies in the 1930s, Marg Morison often scouted models from among shoppers' children.

"I could only have been about five years old at the time, but I remember Marg approaching my mother and saying something like, 'What lovely little girls. Would they like to model for Eaton's?'" says Marilyn Elhart, who, along with her twin sister, Jacqueline, gained celebrity recognition among Eaton's customers as the "Wilkins Twins." "Streetcars

"The Wilkins Twins," Marilyn Elhart and her sister Jacqueline.
Marilyn would attend Eaton's final auction.

and cars would literally stop when their drivers saw us," Elhart recalls. "My sister and I dressed exactly alike and we were the cutest little things you ever saw in your life."

For close to a decade, barely a week went by without Elhart and her sister being called out of class to the principal's office and informed that they were needed on a photo shoot. "The principal was under my mother's thumb," says Elhart, who felt that she and her sister's high profile – being featured in one of the most-read books in Canada – isolated them from other children.

"We would go into the store at night after it had closed, for fittings," Elhart recalls. "Mrs. Morison always walked around with a slate in her hand, and a big hat on her head. To me she always looked very efficient."

While waiting for their outfits to be brought to them, Elhart and her sister roamed through the dark store. Their favourite activity was examining the bones of their feet in a foot X-ray machine. "I must have kept my foot in there for endless lengths of time. It's a wonder I didn't suffer radiation poisoning," she says now. Indeed, years later the X-ray machines were removed from Eaton's and other shoe stores when a study revealed that their radiation levels were grossly above normal.

Elhart found the atmosphere in the Eaton's store respectful and considerate, in contrast to the scene she encountered at Pringle and Booth's photography studio, Pringle and Booth being the company that shot almost all the Eaton's catalogue artwork. "Jacqueline and I would have to sit in Pringle and Booth's studios for hours. We were hot, and it always smelled like orange peels. Afterwards, we had to wait around to see if the pictures were right. I remember that older models used to wander around with no clothes on; it was quite disturbing for a little kid."

Generally a catalogue cover shot netted the Wilkins twins twenty-five dollars each. And Elhart believes that Eaton's may have sold clothes designed and sewn for her and her sister by her mother, though her mother had never told her that she was providing the store with these items. "One time I noticed that, under our picture, the caption said, 'The dresses the girls are wearing are available.' I was shocked when I saw that," she admits.

Much to their mother's chagrin, the Wilkins twins' modelling careers ended abruptly when they reached their teens. "We were my mother's little pieces of gold; we were her chance for success, but that all fell apart. I mean, who wants gangly teenage girls? They're not cute," she says.

By 1976, Eaton's catalogue would also outgrow its appeal. Due in part to increased competition, the influx of cultural minorities to Canada, and the rise in suburban shopping centres, the Eaton's catalogue gradually ceased to have the relevance it had once had. In the years before the final catalogue was printed, Eaton's was caught in a struggle to satisfy its older customers, while catering to its younger customers' desire for a speedy turnover in one-of-a-kind fashions. By its final years, the "Wish Book" had become the "Wish We Could Book," and not even serious surgery could save it.

CHAPTER 6

Closing the Book

The closure of the Eaton's catalogue

A GRIM-FACED, SIXTY-YEAR-OLD Eaton's catalogue employee stared out the glass doors of the Winnipeg Eaton's catalogue building, an envelope containing his severance papers tucked under one arm. Scores of other laid-off employees filed past him and onto the street. When the last employee had left, the man finally departed, trailed by a reporter, who wanted to know what it felt like to have little hope of finding another job. "That's a dumb question. It's lousy. It's like being on a ship in the middle of the ocean and getting a note from the captain that says the ship's sinking and that there's no room for you in the life boat,"[1] the man replied. A woman waved her manila envelope in the air and joked bravely, "Our graduation papers."[2] With the exception of those executives in the know, most Eatonians reacted with shock to the announcement that production on Eaton's ninety-two-year-old catalogue was ending. Some employees heard the news over the television. Sixty-seven-year-old David Kendrick, an Eatonian for several decades, pitied some of the others. "I feel sorry for the younger guys who'll wind up without jobs," he said.

To the general public, the decision to end the catalogue appeared hasty. In reality, the catalogue's final act began – ironically – on February 14, 1975, when the American retailer J. C. Penney decided against subsidizing Eaton's catalogue as a joint venture. At least a few Eaton's employees sensed trouble even before the Penney announcement.

Charles Kadin, a catalogue typography manager, recalls being flabbergasted by a speech given in 1974 by Eaton president Bob Butler, at which, instead of focusing on how to increase catalogue sales, Butler spoke primarily about the benefits of the soon-to-be-built Eaton Centre. "That was the last straw," says Kadin. "Butler didn't sound like a man with a vision for the catalogue, instead it was like, 'What catalogue?'"

The reality was that, shortly after the 1920s, Eaton's catalogue began slowly but surely to bleed money, and the reason was ridiculously simple: as more and more families acquired cars, rural dwellers preferred to drive into city centres to shop, especially for big-ticket items. Customers wanted to examine merchandise before buying it.

The rise in popularity of suburban discount stores in the 1950s, beginning with Kresge, further eroded Eaton's catalogue profits. Then Simpson's joined the stampede toward the suburbs by opening a store in the Cedarbrae Mall in Scarborough, Ontario, in 1960.

Eaton's countered the move to the suburbs by building the single-storey Don Mills store in 1962. According to company architect, Hank Hankinson, the Don Mills store was built so quickly that quality

Gordon Ford, Manfred Buehner, and Brian Jupe of the Eaton's catalogue art department

material was sacrificed for speed. "It was the cheapest store we ever built. The foundations were so shallow they wouldn't accept another floor," says Hankinson.

While suburban stores ultimately became highly profitable, their convenience also spelled doom for the Eaton's catalogue, eliminating the need for customers to shop over the phone. By the time the last Eaton's catalogue appeared, 60 per cent of suburban customers throughout Canada lived within a thirty-minute drive of an Eaton's store.

Possibly the greatest damage to Eaton's catalogue business, however, came when customers discovered that, for sheer variety of selection and quality, in-store merchandise far surpassed the goods sold through the catalogues. Photographic reproductions also had their limitations. The most common complaint was that the colour depicted in the catalogue did not match the actual colour of the merchandise. As a result, catalogue return rates were astronomical. "We knew the financial numbers were not sustainable. As hard as we tried, consumers weren't shopping through catalogues. It was more satisfying to shop at suburban stores. Many clothes were hard to fit if bought through catalogues," admits Fred Andrews, a manager with the Winnipeg store.

When all the negatives of producing the catalogue finally outweighed the positives, on the morning of Wednesday, January 14, 1976, Eaton's president and CEO Earl Orser officially announced to the press the end of the company's catalogue operation, with the last date for placing orders set for April 4, 1976. Orser explained that the high costs of producing the four-hundred-page catalogues had driven up the company's losses to seventeen million dollars a year. J. C. Penney was out of the picture, and there was no hope of a white knight appearing to save it. Orser expressed confidence that catalogue customers would switch their allegiance to Eaton's suburban stores.

Less than two weeks before Orser's announcement, store managers from across the country had gathered at a Holiday Inn in Toronto. There they received pre-written scripts to read aloud to employees on the day of the official announcement. The carefully worded scripts were designed to assure employees that every effort would be made either to bump them to other jobs within the company or, with the assistance of Manpower, to find positions for them elsewhere. Sixteen weeks' notice was provided to allow staff to look for work, with time allotted for them to attend job interviews.

A group of upper managers and executives had spent many months hammering out the catalogue-closure plans at a series of secret locations throughout Toronto, the covert project resembling something out of a James Bond movie. Catalogue Advertising Manager Manfred Buehner, one of those involved in the planning, recalls that one dingy meeting room had bare concrete walls, with only a single light bulb dangling from the ceiling. To add to the feeling of skullduggery, Buehner and his fellow planners were required to call a security guard to escort them up and down the building's single elevator.

In June 1975, Buehner decided to resynchronize computers to print out smaller catalogues, particularly in October. "In October, the engravers' union threatened to strike," he says. "The company was worried about sabotage by union members at the printers if they got wind of the catalogue closure. They were afraid people would go crazy."

In Toronto, fears of assaults, bombings, or kidnappings by disgruntled staff members reached such a crescendo that protecting the physical safety of senior managers became paramount. Security devices were installed in some managers' homes. A supplementary security office with its own telephone number was temporarily established for managers in case they saw unusual activities around their homes.

Eight-by-ten-inch manila envelopes were distributed to managers, marked ominously "Personal Profile. To be opened only by the [name of employee] or, in the case of an emergency, a Police Officer." Inside, cards outlined to already nervous managers the types of retaliation against them that might be carried out by catalogue staff. Managers were encouraged to delist their telephone numbers, keep their garage doors locked, and place deadbolts on their doors. Families were advised to insert code words into conversations to alert each other to danger.

To the relief of many managers, catalogue staff reacted with sadness rather than rage. Just prior to Orser's official announcement to the press, Toronto catalogue staff members assembled in a large room in an Eaton's-owned building on Terauley Street, where Catalogue Supervising Manager Al Kelley announced the closure. Kelley, who had undergone a knee operation mere days before the announcement, hobbled onto the scene on crutches. As he stepped up to the podium to announce the closing, he dropped one crutch and nearly stumbled face forward onto the floor.

Personalized severance packages were distributed right on the scene. Full pension privileges were to be retained. Early retirement provisions were also included. Those who were eligible received an employee-purchase allowance for life, and group life insurance on a diminishing balance over ten years. For those not entitled to early retirement, the group life-insurance plan was extended six months from the date of termination, and sickness income coverage was extended, without cost, to the employee. Meanwhile, personal purchase allowances were to extend until December 1976. Manpower representatives were on the premises, as well as advisors from the provincial Ministry of Labour. Most employees left the way they had come – stunned.

"We were in shock," says copywriter James Adams. "Most of us returned to our desks, but there was nothing left to do. People started making phone calls right away, looking for work."

"We hired security people and nurses to be there when the announcement was made, in case people collapsed," says Manfred Buehner. "It was an awful day. One person had a heart attack and died shortly after. One woman died six weeks later. Everyone was affected mentally. The company hired psychologists to train staff in how to prepare for a new job. Many staff members were overheard lamenting that they should have been informed sooner, so they could have worked harder."

Winnipeg's catalogue employees were to suffer an equally devastating blow. To mitigate some of the suffering, managers were told to pack their shaving kits and report to the Charter House Hotel, located behind the Winnipeg store, where, in meetings lasting through the night of January 13, they were coached on how to conduct exit interviews with the employees who were to be terminated the next day. "We were given packages explaining how much severance employees were entitled to. A lot of employees were let go. But a lot were absorbed into the retail section. We spent three-quarters of an hour with each person. There were a lot of tears. For a lot of people, it was their whole life," says John Mainella, then Group Merchandising Manager.

One unsuspecting victim of the putsch was Dave McFetridge, then Order Filling Manager for the Winnipeg store. News of the closure came just two and a half years short of his normal retirement age. "Looking back, I should have realized that there was some kind of change occurring. Normally, we planned the budget for the next year. In 1975 we didn't do that. I wondered what was going to happen. I was offered a reasonable deal for early retirement, but there were no openings of jobs for my skills at that time."

Greg Purchase, then vice-president of Eaton's Western division, told *Winnipeg Tribune* columnist Harry L. Mardon, "Our major concern in this has been the people. Naturally, there was a lot of shock and disappointment. But the response has been good, as people realize the company is trying its best to be fair."[3] Purchase was pleased by the tremendous response shown to Eaton's former employees by local companies. In all, thirty to forty companies offered positions.

The enthusiasm for Eaton's employees was the same in the Maritimes. "We got a lot of calls by new employers saying what good workers Eaton's employees were," says Bill Lockwood, then General Manager of the Atlantic Provinces catalogue.

In the end, small centres, such as Dauphin, Manitoba, and the city of Moncton, New Brunswick, suffered the most. Dauphin's mail-order centre employed six people, who had to move out of town to find work. People dropped into the centre to ask if it was true first, and then, hearing that it was, asked where they were going to shop. The woman who had managed the centre for twenty-one years told the *Winnipeg Tribune* that her mother and grandmother had both ordered from the catalogue. The centre drew visitors to Dauphin, and they would stay to shop in stores and eat at local restaurants. In Morden, Manitoba, the manager said, "[We] still can't believe it. We don't want it [Eaton's catalogue store] to close, [the] store has been everything in Morden for the last twenty years."[4]

Like Manfred Buehner, Bill Lockwood was informed of plans to close the catalogue in the summer of 1975. Promising to keep the news secret was easier said than endured. Six months of silence forced Lockwood and at least one other colleague to the hospital with severe headaches. "It was a lonely time," he admits.

"I don't know how we kept the news quiet," says Fred Eaton, who also felt the strain. "We didn't know what we were going to do or how we were going to do it. I don't know how you keep a secret of that kind for so long – loyalty, I suppose, must have been the basis of it."

Fred was forced into the awkward position of bluffing to long-time associates and friends about the future of the catalogue. "One of my very best friends in those days was Gordon Fisher of Southam Printers, who printed the catalogues. I remember, when we made the official announcement, he phoned me up and said, 'Fred, why didn't you tell me?' and I said, 'Gordon, we couldn't tell anyone.'"

With the closing of the catalogue, Southam Murray, a division of Southam Printing Ltd., had to lay off hundreds of staff members. Up to then the company had been printing approximately five million copies of Eaton's twice-yearly catalogues, grossing two million dollars a year, plus four smaller supplemental catalogues.

Fred points out that, though it was deceptive, the decision to end the catalogue was deliberately not entered into the minutes of directors' meetings until December 8, 1975, one month before the official announcement. "We didn't want people to say, 'You made the decision months ago.' I wanted to prove that we had not made a decision, that we were examining the possibility but had not made a final decision."

In the days preceding the sad announcement, Bill Lockwood, Fred Eaton, and Earl Orser flew to Fredericton to meet with Acting Premier John Stewart Brooks. "Basically we wanted to gauge his feelings on the announcement," says Lockwood. "The meeting went very well. I was surprised by the outlook of the provincial government. They didn't criticize Eaton's, they just said, 'Business is business; we can't tell you how to run your business.'"

A few days later, Fred Eaton and Greg Purchase flew off to visit Premier Ed Schreyer in Manitoba, where Fred received a slightly more unorthodox response. "He was completely disengaged," Fred says. "He didn't give a damn. All he could say was, 'I'm thinking of retiring and going into the pressed-log business. Do you sell those things?' It was really funny," Fred continues. "I thought, 'Holy Christ!'"

On the day of the announcement, Bill Lockwood and Bill Wilson, then Manager of Corporate and Consumer Affairs of Eaton's head office, met with Moncton's mayor, Gary Wheeler. "The closing of Eaton's catalogue office in Moncton is the most dramatic blow to the city's economy since the Depression,"[5] a stunned Wheeler announced to the media shortly after the meeting concluded. With visible emotion, he estimated that the city would lose eight to ten million dollars annually because of the closure, and that the freight handled by the CNR would be reduced as much as 20 per cent. With no new industries on the horizon, Wheeler looked to Canada Manpower for assistance, though a spokesman for Manpower warned that it would take two or three new industries and a long time to replace the jobs.

Bill Lockwood was moved by the selflessness shown by representatives of Moncton's 607 full-time and 370 part-time catalogue employees.

"We knew Moncton would be the toughest to close, because it had the smallest market," says Lockwood. "There were not a lot of employment opportunities for those who left. It made quite an impact on the city. Winnipeg could stand 1,500 or 2,000 dumped, but here it was a big thing. But people were sympathetic. 'We feel so sorry for *you* because you had to keep it quiet for so long,' they said."

Lockwood credits Earl Orser for ensuring that the proper rehiring strategies, arranged through Manpower, were already in place during the months leading up to the catalogue closure, not only in Moncton, but in Toronto, Winnipeg, and Vancouver. "Earl did a good job," he says.

Vice-President of Merchandising Stan Shortt also credits Orser for handling the situation as adroitly as he could. "By the late seventies, the bedrock of employee relations was weakening," says Shortt. "You'd ask, 'How do we handle this closing with that many people?' Counselling and support networks didn't exist. It was an upsetting time, but considering the fact that nine thousand people were being laid off, it went remarkably smoothly. We only had three or four lawsuits, simply because the closing was conducted so well. There were many millions of dollars of contracts, yet there were only a few lawsuits. Earl Orser was really the brainchild of that."

Those associated with actually designing the catalogues weren't so laudatory. "Orser was well-known as a hatchet man. His mandate was to cut back," says Buehner. "What very few people know is that the last catalogue was the most popular ever – sales went through the roof, it was the best ever in history. The Christmas catalogue of '75 was also very successful. Within two years we could have been breaking even and modernizing systems. We had $440 million in sales in the last year, and they just threw that away. We had a record of every single customer of the catalogue. Store people were never interested in taking advantage of this."

In his 1986 book, *A Store of Memories*, Simpson's president Allan Burton echoes Buehner's opinion. Burton wrote: "They [Eaton's] did about $400 million annually across the country, and lost $18 million a year doing it, while Simpsons-Sears was doing the same volume and making $18 million a year doing it! [The] company had opted for sudden youth by hiring a couple of dozen MBAs and giving early retirement to men of experience, so they found themselves with men of insufficient depth and experience and little loyalty."[6]

As a catalogue manager overseeing a staff of over seventy employees, Charles Kadin had immediately seen problems with the new breed of university-trained applicants he interviewed for jobs. "I would interview copywriters, university graduates, and they couldn't write a sentence, they couldn't even fill in an application form. There was no logical progression in their thought patterns. Their grammar was poor, and their punctuation terrible."

When all the arguments ceased over who or what had caused the catalogue to fail, however, department managers were left to deal with the human fallout. In Toronto, Manfred Buehner and Catalogue Circulation Manager Bill DeFoe provided scraps of work to employees who remained until May 4, the date the last small clearance catalogue was produced. In the meantime, finished artwork and various art supplies were thrown out by the barrelful. Almost nothing was spared. "It was insanity," says George Hudson, then Head of General Merchandising. "Shelves of artwork were just pitched. I grabbed one or two things as remembrances."

DeFoe and Buehner continued to work around the clock. At one point, Fred Eaton commissioned them to complete a Critical Path Flow-Chart to illustrate the entire history of the Eaton's catalogue. When completed and made into a mural, it proved difficult to lift onto the walls of a Bay Street Eaton's boardroom, where Fred had requested that it be placed. "Security had to let us into the building at night, so no one would see us. We had to stand on stepladders and put the chart up with pushpins. After we were finished, I looked at Bill and said, 'Wow, this is beautiful!'" The two men toasted their accomplishment with a shot of Scotch obtained from the well-stocked bar located at the back of the room. Then Buehner began strolling through the room examining the name cards that had been placed on the table in preparation for the next day's board meeting. Buehner noticed one name he didn't recognize, then another. Suddenly, he turned to DeFoe and said, "My God, some of these names don't even ring a bell." "I knew that was symptomatic of the problem," Buehner says today. "Too much deadwood on top."

Meanwhile, the empathetic DeFoe spent much of his time listening patiently to employees' problems and placing phone calls to find them work. "It was not a pretty scene," say Buehner. "There Bill and I were, just sitting on the floor with one secretary to assist us. The Eaton family couldn't have cared less, Fred Eaton never came down to visit us, never. Stan Shortt never came down. They never asked, 'Are they going to be okay? What are they going to do?' When it was time for me to prepare to leave, I met with Stan Shortt, but he just told me to write my own job description."

As upsetting as it must have been for catalogue employees to find their jobs gone, it was equally upsetting for the printers and photographers who worked on the catalogues. Harvey Morris, the president of Pringle and Booth photography studios, shot much of the catalogue's artwork. He refers to January 14, 1976, as "the worst day of my life." In that single day, Morris lost one million dollars a year in guaranteed business, ultimately forcing him to lay off eighteen staff members, "something I had never done before," he says. Like others, Morris had heard rumours of the catalogue's demise for weeks. "We kept asking Bill DeFoe, 'We keep hearing you guys are going out of business, and if you are I want to know about it, because I've got to make a lot of plans.'"

Instead of being able to come clean, DeFoe and Buehner were forced to send Morris to Bermuda for, in Buehner's words, "a bogus photo shoot." Meanwhile, Buehner and his colleagues had to struggle to devise credible excuses to prevent Eaton's buyers from finalizing contracts with suppliers.

Ultimately, Morris received confirmation of the closing after a grotesque comedy of errors. On Monday, January 12, 1976, sacks full of letters promising to pay outstanding balances to Eaton's suppliers were delivered to the offices of Canada Post across the country. That same day, Bill DeFoe flew to Ottawa to alert Liberal Party members of the closure, as well as to extract a promise from the Postmaster General that none of the letters would be delivered to their destinations prior to the formal announcement, scheduled for Wednesday, January 14. To prevent pandemonium, it was of paramount importance that, large or small, no supplier should receive notice of the closure before the company's official announcement.

Then the hammer fell. On Tuesday, January 13, several bags of notices were accidentally delivered to some Quebec suppliers. "For once, Canada Post delivered early," says Buehner ruefully. Within hours, panic erupted amongst the companies in question. Recipients of the letters read them with incredulity, shock, then anger. Soon the media got hold of the story.

Buehner was at home at approximately 5 p.m. on Tuesday, January 13, when he heard news over the radio of Canada Post's delivery of the notices, and he knew instantly that eight months of secret planning had just gone up in smoke. The telephone beside him began ringing. It was Bill DeFoe on the other end of the line, summoning Buehner to the Holiday Inn in downtown Toronto. Buehner lost no time in jumping into his car and speeding down to the hotel. As soon as he arrived in DeFoe's suite, a telephone was thrust in his hand and he was instructed to begin calling as many suppliers as he could to perform damage control and to offer settlement terms.

One of those whom Buehner attempted to telephone was Harvey Morris, who had missed the news because he was attending the Toronto Boat Show. Buehner paged Morris at the show, but missed him by seconds. Morris was already on his way to dine at a downtown restaurant accompanied by his banker. Shortly after the men arrived, a record-breaking snowfall began, rendering the city roads too slick to manoeuvre on safely.

As Morris and his banker were settling down to a cocktail, Buehner and DeFoe were back at the Holiday Inn, still attempting to phone suppliers. At 6:30 p.m. the two men took a break from their phoning long enough to switch on the nightly newscast. There, an elegantly dressed Fred Eaton, attending an official dinner party, was cornered by a reporter in possession of one of the infamous settlement letters that had been sent to suppliers. Confronted with the proof, Fred had no choice but to acknowledge the truth. "We were stunned," says Buehner.

The heavy snowfall in Toronto began to make light fixtures flicker across the city, but the real electrical storms occurred inside. Harvey Morris and his banker had their knives and forks poised to cut into their steaks when the restaurant phone rang. "I'll bet that's for me," Morris joked. "I just had an instinct of what was up," he says today. He was right. Morris's wife was on the line, informing him that Bill DeFoe was looking for him.

By the time Morris returned the call, DeFoe was already attempting to drive thirty miles north of the city centre to cut a deal with Brigden's Printing Studios, located in Richmond Hill. Even so, Buehner instructed Morris to go to Toronto's Holiday Inn to await DeFoe's return.

"For Christ's sake, Manfred, have you looked outside? The snow's four feet deep . . . ! Look, I know you've closed the catalogue, so why don't you just tell me that and we'll be on our way?" Morris recalls saying. Buehner remained non-committal: "Bill DeFoe has to see you tonight," he told Morris again.

With his dinner sitting like a cannonball in his stomach, Morris, along with his banker, slid through the snow to the Holiday Inn. While Morris's banker made a beeline for the hotel bar, Morris proceeded directly to Buehner's room. "I had figured out they were gathering vendors, trying to sign off that night before news officially broke the next day," Morris says. As 11:00 p.m. approached, and DeFoe still hadn't returned from Richmond Hill, a fed-up Morris departed for his photography studio in midtown Toronto, and left instructions for DeFoe to meet him there.

Finally, close to midnight, Morris spotted a pair of headlights bobbing up the hill towards his studio. When Morris opened the door, he confronted a wet and exhausted DeFoe. "Have a drink. You've been driving through some pretty rotten traffic," Morris told him. DeFoe downed a restorative glass of Scotch and recited the same words he had rhymed off several times that day: "As of 2:00 p.m. tomorrow, we stop all catalogue operations."

DeFoe withdrew a form from his briefcase for Morris to sign, promising that Eaton's would pay Pringle and Booth's expenses up until 2:00 p.m. the following day. Pringle and Booth had invoiced Eaton's for cash twice a month and, as of 2:00 p.m. the next day, that revenue was about to dry up. "Luckily, my bank manager heard the whole thing," says Morris. "He was my salvation." Morris refused to sign the document that night, and refused to sign several more revised versions of the document, even as late as August 1976.

In an ironic twist, the next day Morris flew to New York to offer his services to J. C. Penney. Penney, whom Eaton's had hoped would be its catalogue's white knight less than one year earlier, immediately cut a deal to finance Pringle and Booth to cover the period when money was scarce. Before long, Pringle and Booth was doing the J. C. Penney catalogue's photography. "In eighteen months we ended up doing more business than before Eaton's collapsed," Morris says.

Meanwhile, the human drama of the journey toward the closing of the catalogue reached its height in Bill DeFoe. In the months before the announcement, DeFoe developed a twitch on one side of his face. Buehner noted that it occurred intermittently, then gradually worsened.

Rather than see a doctor, as Buehner urged him to do, DeFoe self-diagnosed the problem as a particularly acute attack of Bell's palsy, exacerbated by stress. "Before long it really started to get bad, and Bill looked awful, and finally I said, 'Bill you really should see a doctor about that twitch,' and he kept insisting, 'No, no, it's temporary.'"

It would not be until the catalogue-closing operation was complete that DeFoe would discover that he had not been suffering from Bell's palsy at all, but from a malignant brain tumour, which had grown so large it could not be surgically removed. A few years after the closure of the catalogue, he and Buehner met for drinks at a downtown Toronto hotel, and it was then that Buehner saw the true toll the catalogue fiasco had taken on his friend. "He tried to stand up when we were leaving, and nearly fell forward onto the table," he says. "I asked him if he needed a drive to his home, which was located just around the corner, and he said no. By then he was using a cane. He died shortly afterwards."

To honour his loyal staff, DeFoe had designed a tribute booklet entitled *The Way We Were*, which listed the names, addresses, and photographs of all the employees of his department. Inside the front cover of the booklet, beneath his own picture, DeFoe wrote:

> The closing of the catalogue operation not only marks the end of an era but also the beginning of new careers for us all. Each and every individual in this Department can and should take great pride in the professional and humane way they handled the catalogue termination period. It was extremely difficult for us all to maintain high morale yet this department did – a great tribute to each person. I want to thank you for your tremendous and unforgettable support and wish everyone success in their new endeavours. I hope this photo album will help you all maintain contact with friends and associates.[7]

Less than three months after the catalogue's collapse, Simpson's-Sears began sniffing around Eaton's mailing list of over 2.17 million customers. Rather than sell the list, Eaton's hired a broker to rent customers' names and addresses without permission to junk-mail advertisers, a move for which they were chastised by several consumer advocates.

——■——

As traumatized as Eaton's staff and suppliers were by the death of the catalogue, they were only half the story. The other half were the customers – especially those who lived in rural settings – who woke up to read in their morning newspapers the announcement of the end of a Canadian institution. A veritable blizzard of angry and wistful letters arrived on the desk of Eaton's Communications Director Kay Staib. An eleven-year-old boy from Flin Flon, Manitoba, wrote:

> How do you expect to make up the money you are losing by discontinuing your catalogue? You are going to lose more money than you are already losing. People don't buy your catalogue just to order things from. They also buy it to look at it.[8]

Another customer had an interesting cost-saving tip for management:

> Dear Sir,
> Isn't there some way to cut costs and allow the service to continue? Perhaps, the elimination of fancy carpeting in your sales offices might help.[9]

Meanwhile, a plus-sized customer did not enjoy the prospect of sizing up the competition:

> After reading you were going out of the catalogue business, I poured myself another "Harvey Wallbanger" and shed a few tears. [I] found that Eaton's gave me so much to choose from in the way of clothes, Simpsons do not carry enough variety for the gals like myself that take larger sizes, maybe now I will have to go on a diet for sure.
> [Well] I hope that you will get some idea as to how sorry I am and I imagine thousands of families are that we will no longer be able to shop by catalogue, perhaps it will mean that I might end up with a great deal more money in the bank, but what's money if you are unhappy?[10]

And then, there were the inevitable expressions of grief from customers who had used the catalogue to select everything from bridal dresses to baby clothes. A typical example read:

It was your company who put us on our feet in 1966 and we often say our Thanks to you. We were young married couple with not a penny to our name and Eaton's took a chance on us and gave us a start. We then had a bad need of work clothes and baby things. Without your help then God knows where we would be now. God Bless the many people on your staff. And God Bless the helping hand. You will always be in our hearts.

I feel as if a dear friend is passing away.[11]

Not all of those linked with Eaton's, however, grew misty-eyed at news of the catalogue's demise. Marketing guru Peter Glen said of customers' sentimental letters: "They're too little too late. Let's face it, the catalogue was doing badly, and when customers say, 'Ah, I just miss this so much,' where was their money? [The catalogue] was an archaic, much-too-heavy, big, out-of-date mess. I think all that nostalgia for a few old ladies who want to write in and an eleven-year-old boy is regrettable but basically irrelevant. If we were in the book business we could please that eleven-year-old boy. The catalogue lost money. It is an idea whose time went."

The eleven-year-old boy from Flin Flon, however, was more prescient than anyone thought when he speculated that the store might lose more money by closing the catalogue than by continuing to publish it. In its 1977 fiscal year, Eaton's financial losses mounted, rather than decreasing. In response, Eaton's streamlined its central division's buying habits by laying off more than one hundred employees, while calling upon merchandising managers and store managers to respond to the needs of customers in various regions.

Retail stores stocked shelves with new merchandise, expecting a flood of former catalogue customers. Meanwhile, the company had been busy building stores. An Eaton Centre went up in Waterloo, Ontario, and another in Guelph. More stores were built in Calgary, Edmonton, and Sarnia.

Even before the catalogue closed, in 1973, Eaton's had commissioned the building of Vancouver's Pacific Centre. Mayor Tom Campbell, dressed in an all-white suit, attended the topping-off ceremony, an ancient Scandinavian ritual that involved the placing of a symbolic item, such as a tree, on top of a building. Campbell chose to place the last steel beam on the building's framework. In order to do so, he decided to ride the beam from the reception platform to the site where the beam would be placed. Recalls architect Hank Hankinson, "Unexpectedly, the beam stopped directly atop one of the building's elevator wells. When Campbell looked down, he froze. Several police had to pry him off the beam. As he was dragged, the rust from the beam stained the seat of his pants." It may have been a bad omen, for, while the centre performed brilliantly during its early years, by the mid-1980s it would be reduced to playing catch-up with Sears.

Hank Hankinson, Eaton Company architect who designed the Eaton Centre.

To welcome Eaton's arrival in Vancouver, the Hudson's Bay Company sent the Eaton family two white lovebirds – ostensibly a symbol of peace between the two retail giants. John Craig Eaton toyed with the idea of sending the cage back to Hudson's Bay representatives, along with a note containing the following jocular message: "Thanks for the birds. They were delicious."

—■—

In February of 1977, the eagerly anticipated Toronto's Eaton Centre, designed to be the empire's headquarters, was set in place. The new store stood embedded in half a million yards of a slimy earth nicknamed Dundas Shale. Where Eaton's Queen Street store had been built atop a foundation of strategically laid stones, the Eaton Centre was balanced on a series of concrete footings. When the time came for the footings to be poured, a jaunty John Craig Eaton, wearing a pith helmet inscribed with his name, threw a coin into the footings for good luck. Architect Hank Hankinson and Jack Dohan of Eastern Construction followed suit, and the ceremony was dubbed "Three Coins in the Footing." In a burst of enthusiasm, a rock-sawer, who had been watching the ceremony, jumped down to shake John Craig's hand. "I used to work at Eaton's," he said.

The Eaton Centre received rave reviews from among the 4,500 old and young Eatonians who attended the opening-day ceremonies on

February 10, 1977. Commemorative plates, priced at fifty dollars each, were sold to mark the occasion. Ontario premier Bill Davis delivered a rousing speech, calling the store one of the eight wonders of the retail world. Meanwhile, Toronto mayor David Crombie officially pronounced the store open. Shortly afterwards, thousands of eager shoppers fanned out around gleaming display tables stacked high with merchandise. Still more rode the escalators up to the top floor and slowly worked their way down.

A former College Street store employee who was transferred to work at the centre compared it to walking out of a back alley into a castle. Meanwhile, a long-time customer's assessment was more down-to-earth. "It looks expensive," he said.

The Eaton Centre did not come into being without some human sacrifices. Approximately three hundred, mostly old-time employees were laid off shortly before the store opened. Some female staff members charged that, if not literally fired, older sales staff members were discreetly moved to the back of merchandise departments to make room for younger staff members to sell – particularly high-priced fashion merchandise.

"The minute we opened the Eaton Centre, the fun went out of working there," says Ed Larter, who had worked on maintenance and construction for Eaton's for twenty years, until he was laid off shortly after the Eaton Centre opened. "I came back from my holidays and they handed me a letter detailing severance terms, benefits, and a 25-per-cent purchasing discount for life."

Steering the Eaton Centre down the road of success was manager Jim Robertson. "Jimmy Robertson was a wonderful man," says Fred Eaton. "A good Scottish guy. I remember he said to me one time, 'I'm going to leave Simpson's in my wake,' and he did. He loved that store. It was a speeding bullet. God, it was thrilling. I mean, he'd say, 'I've just done so many dollars yesterday, a new record!' It was wonderful!"

In spite of Fred's enthusiasm, there were some initial marketing missteps. In his book, *Hard Rock Retailing*, Greg Purchase admitted alienating some customers by placing only high-end merchandise at the front of various departments. His remedy was to reverse the display order, moving the high-priced merchandise to the rear of departments and moving the less-expensive merchandise forward, a solution which seemed to work, as profits skyrocketed.

Though supporting management's decision to close the catalogue, Peter Glen nevertheless felt that the Eaton Centre, while it started out as a glittering diamond, degenerated in his words into nothing but a "big Clinique counter." "We all got excited about the Eaton Centre, which was going to be the greatest thing in Europe and Africa and everywhere else, and it isn't and it never was. By that time it was like, 'Let's get rid of the College Street store, and let's have Mr. Purchase have everything cheap' . . . and it never came off . . . it did not work."

"Peter Glen is completely entitled to his opinion, but the store turned out to be the greatest cash box I've ever seen," says Fred Eaton. "It turned out profits. My God, it was a brilliant store. To me it had a soul from the moment it opened. It was there to dominate Toronto's retailing . . . and

It was like a speeding bullet," Fred Eaton says of the Toronto Eaton Centre, built in 1977. "It was there to dominate Toronto's retailing . . . and it did."

it did. It *was* a big Clinique counter, but it was a lot more than that, too."

In Winnipeg, meanwhile, three days after the January 15 announcement, Eaton's informed the press that an ambitious multi-million-dollar development project was under way to transform the Winnipeg Eaton's catalogue building on Donald Street into a retail-shopping, parking, merchandise-mart, and office facility. On November 17, the wrecker's ball began taking its first swing at the old catalogue building. On hand were Fred and George Eaton, as well as Brian Laxdal, Eaton's Senior Vice-President of Winnipeg and Western Stores. The thirty-million-dollar project, to be named Eaton Place, was to open in March 1979.

Rather than dwell on its past, Eaton's now risked its future on expanding, rather than contracting, its operation. What no one anticipated was how persistently the amputated catalogue would pain like a phantom limb.

Eaton's final catalogue

CHAPTER 7

The Maharajas of Eaton's

The lifestyle of buyers • Buyers and natural disasters • Wartime
• Cold War travels • End of an era • Buyers vs. sales

T O SUCCEED, EATON'S BUYERS had to endure weeks away from their families, carry a metaphorical pocket calculator between their ears and a passport the size of a telephone book in their hands, and rely on wits and guile to wrangle the best deal out of shrewd suppliers.

"Buyers were like maharajas," says Ted Gittings, who worked in the accounts department. "People back on the ranch resented them."

"Oh sure, that was very true," says Gene McCarron, a toy buyer. "That was the glorious life. You were considered to be wined and dined by suppliers who got you drunk and just talked you into buying something."

The reality of buying was more sobering. Aside from the requisite after-hours-martini tours, buying trips often consisted of arduous physical excursions against a backdrop of world wars, natural disasters, and political infighting. Shelter might be taken anywhere from the Savoy Hotel to clay huts, while menus might include some unusual dishes. Amid these conditions, buyers were expected to make the best deals possible in the least amount of time. In spite of intense competition, for more than one hundred years, Eaton's name remained an "open sesame" around the world, much respected because its buyers had a reputation for paying bills on time, and in cash.

In 1880, Timothy personally chose his first buyers from among a pool of highly trained department managers, who knew which merchandise moved and which didn't. In an effort to avoid price markups, Eaton's buyers bought directly from the manufacturers themselves, rather than through wholesalers.

Eaton's first overseas buyer was Timothy himself. He began travelling overseas in 1870 and continued to do so off and on for fifteen years. His renowned distaste for dealing with wholesalers at home served him equally well in other countries. Compared with other firms, he got suppliers' goods cheaper, faster, and with less fuss.

In 1893, Eaton's first buying office opened in London, England. By 1898, another office had opened in Paris. Cash up-front was the company's initial policy, and it worked beyond even the founder's wildest dreams. At one of the firm's celebratory dinners, an ecstatic buyer named Ecclestone bragged: "One firm told me that the only fault was that we paid too quickly. I think the buyers all feel the responsibility resting upon them, and realize that 'A penny saved is a penny earned,' and 'A thing well bought is half sold.'"[1]

London buying office

For those earnest young employees who took to heart Timothy's adage that learning is best done from the bottom up, experience could be a cruel teacher. Timothy's hand was not only on the till, but also on the tiller. He could shrewdly spot suppliers who were trying to unload stale-dated merchandise on unseasoned buyers. "Know what to throw over your shoulder,"[2] he'd advise his novice buyers, likening what sellers said to salt. In sometimes folksy, avuncular language, he'd speculate on what he would do, were he sitting in foreign offices himself, hearing an overzealous supplier trying to unload inferior products at inflated prices. "I might have a mind to tell him this," he'd write in his letters, or, "I'd be inclined to tell him that." The letters, which were frequently written over several days, swung wildly between high compliments and stern rebukes.

In a November 17, 1892, letter, Timothy painstakingly itemized his reasons for dispatching a Miss Brown to the London office to straighten out an enthusiastic young buyer named Frank MacMahon, whom he accused, in language that must have made MacMahon wince, of buying "abominable stuff" from unscrupulous London suppliers, who "think, as a rule, they are very smart and have a higher opinion of themselves as regards the class of goods that will sell in Toronto, than I have." The letter continues:

> Miss Brown informs me that she has written to you several times not to send anything more of this kind. Now I say to you, "Don't send us anything more unless you put them on some old ship and Insure them well so that we can sell them to the Insurance Co.," in other words, we don't want any more of them here. . . . [When] you send the goods here the Depts. positively refuse to accept them, and Miss Brown would look a wonderful guy if she would gather all these chiffons, handkerchiefs, Windsor's and such goods around her ears and walk through the store. We wouldn't like to see her do it, would you? [Fancy] yourself in Miss Brown's place for five minutes, opening up a case of goods. In one corner of it is a lot of stuff which the Dept. positively refuses to accept. You are standing looking on. Wouldn't you feel foolish? I won't say how you would feel, you can fancy for yourself.[3]

Timothy greatly respected his female buyers, believing that they possessed an instinct for anticipating lucrative product trends. As early as

1893, Eaton's employed two hundred female buyers. The first recorded female buyer proved her dedication to the company when she combined her first buying trip with her honeymoon. Meanwhile, at a New Year's Eve banquet thrown for the staff in 1898, Timothy bragged about another female buyer, who had slogged knee-deep in mud for more than an hour towards a paper factory in Holyoke, Massachusetts. Factory workers who greeted her tried to shoo her away to their company's retail store, but instantly relented when she uttered the magic word: Eaton's.[4]

The store's overseas buying operation expanded and improved with time. By 1919, when Timothy's son Sir John Craig was president, offices had been opened in Manchester, New York, Zurich, Belfast, Leicester, and Yokohama. Managers native to each respective country were installed in the various foreign offices to spot cutting-edge fashion trends, acquaint visiting buyers with local customs, or serve as interpreters in business negotiations. Buying-office managers also had to ensure that merchandise was paid for quickly and that goods were packed and shipped without incident.

The Manchester office acquired fine cottons and low-price serge and tweeds, as well as earthenware and glassware. Leicester specialized in hosiery and knitted merchandise, such as sweaters. Linens were shipped

Starting for the pyramids. Two female buyers riding camels, ca. 1920.

from Belfast, while Paris served as the headquarters for the latest trends in fashion. The New York office, meanwhile, became a second home to Eaton's buyers, where they could obtain silk, velvet knitwear, footwear, and other clothing.

Eaton's may not have been the biggest or most modern store in the early twentieth century, but its name was one of the most respected. Suppliers vied so aggressively to pitch their merchandise to Eaton's buyers that, by the 1920s, Paris buying-office management hired an English military veteran, his uniform ablaze with rows of medals, to physically restrain them. Some enterprising suppliers tried to slip the veteran a few bills to sweeten their chances of success. Female suppliers, meanwhile, offered dates.

"Eaton's was fair and didn't deal below the table," says fashion buyer Michael Brough. "In the Orient, we were nicknamed the 'Kings of the Big Pencil' because of the volume of purchases we ordered and the speed with which we paid."

In spite of the sometimes exotic temptations around them, Eaton's buyers had to abide by the same Spartan rules laid down by the store's founder:

> Pay for all your own dinners, don't go to suppliers' private homes, pay for everything yourself – Don't leave your order books lying around, don't buy goods after daylight, or on Sunday under any circumstances. Always arrive at a foreign station at least an hour in advance of your departure.[5]

To appreciate the frenetic and punishing schedule buyers were subjected to, one need only examine the 1901 itinerary for Mr. J. A. C. Poole, an early buyer for chinaware, glass, and housewares, who by 1903 had made more than forty-five trips to Europe and the Far East. These journeys, as exciting as they looked on paper, more closely resembled military tours of duty:

J. A. C. Poole:
Left T.O. at 5:30, Monday Feb 11 – sailed on SS *Commonwealth* from Boston – arrived at Liverpool on Friday, February 22nd

Stoke	– 4 days
Kohn	– 2 days

Leipzig	– 7 days
Berlin	– 4½ days
Dresden	– 3 days
Karda (Bohemia)	– 1 day (did not like)
Tepletz	– 2 days
Karlsbad	– 3 days
Nuremberg	– 3½ days
Coburg	– 1 day
Sonneberg	– 5½ days
Stuttgart	– 1½ days "This is a very fine city"
Paris	– 4 days
London	– 5 days
Stoke	– 4 days
London	– 3½ days "We went to the Lyceum to see Ellen Terry and Irving" – arriving at home May 17.[6]

In a schedule even more gruelling than Poole's, one intrepid Winnipeg rug-buyer journeyed by airplane, ship, car, and train, from Beirut to Baghdad and finally to Tehran in search of oriental hand-loomed rugs, which became a highly prized commodity in the affluent 1920s. Parts of his official description of the journey, entitled *Footprints in the Desert Sand*, read like scenes from the film *Raiders of the Lost Ark*.

The buyer began his journey by steamer from Marseilles to Beirut, with a layover in Cairo for two days to see the pyramids. On board the steamer he met "Mohammedan" pilgrims from Africa. Each night at sundown, the pilgrims knelt on prayer rugs, their murmured prayers carried softly on the ocean current. At the end of one prayer session, the buyer respectfully asked if he might photograph one of the pilgrims. After a brief pause, the pilgrim in question replied in English, "How much will you give me?" The startled buyer hesitated, then finally stammered, "Two francs," the poetry of the moment dying faster than the sunlight. "No," the man said. "I am British. I want England money."

With his sense of romanticism stirred but not completely shaken, the buyer disembarked the next morning in Beirut, and immediately departed on a three-hour car trip amid the ten-foot-deep snow banks that covered the Lebanese mountains. To complete his journey to Baghdad, he was next obliged to board a six-wheeled bus that was stocked with enough rations to last seven days. In good weather and dry road conditions, the trip might have taken thirty hours, but with the melted snow, the trip lasted days longer, even with two drivers exchanging driving duties. The journey continued through Ar Rutbah (Rutba Wells) in Iraq, a town filled with marauding tribes of violent thieves. The buyer finally arrived in Baghdad at eleven at night. He was immediately inoculated against the plague.

Despite his exhaustion, the breathtaking beauty of Baghdad's surrounding countryside quickly revived him. "One can no more describe Baghdad than one can catalogue the colours of the sunset, or the shapes of the rising clouds. The colours change with every hour of the day," he wrote, marvelling at how different the country's varied topography was from the flat plains of Manitoba, his native province.

As morning broke, the buyer took the Maude Bridge over the Tigris River, from which he watched men paddling *guffas*, primitive boats resembling the scraped-out rinds of flattened oranges. Afterwards, carrying his own bedding, he boarded a train that carried him 105 miles by night from Baghdad to Khanaqin, where it pulled in at 6:00 a.m. After breakfasting there, the buyer was driven by car to Kermanshah, his vehicle passing caravans of camels carrying barrels of gasoline on their backs: "The fuel for the newest carried by the oldest form of transport," the buyer noted.

Arriving in Hamadan at noon the next day, the buyer lodged with a Persian family in a small four-room house that featured a rug-weaving loom in the family room. Before entering, the buyer had to wait for the woman of the house to cover her face.

From his temporary lodgings, the buyer set off with his camera around his neck to the local river to photograph the colourfully dressed Hamadan women washing clothes on rocks. He emerged unscathed, remarkable considering that mere weeks before, the American Vice-Consul in Tehran had been set upon and killed by the people because he had taken pictures of a funeral procession.

Soon after arriving at his final destination of Tehran the next day, the buyer got down to the hardest part of the trip – haggling with the locals over the price they would accept for their rugs. As the women who made the rugs peeked out between slats cut into the sides of their huts, the Eaton's buyer and local men engaged in prolonged, high-pitched bartering that concluded with a brief handshake, a sip of sweet tea, and a

Women washing clothes in river in Hamadan. The buyer who took the picture was lucky to escape alive, since only weeks before, the American Vice-Consul in Tehran had been beaten to death after photographing a funeral procession.

Rug buyers in Iraq, 1920s

promise that the rugs would be loaded onto trucks and transported to the nearest seaport for delivery.[7]

An Eaton's buyer's gruelling pace had not abated much, in spite of the availability of faster modes of transportation in the decades following Poole's trip. "The travelling was very bad for family life," says Eaton's buyer Alan Boothe, who travelled up to six to eight weeks at a time in the 1960s and 1970s. Once he returned home, he tried to release some of his pent-up tension by coaching his son's hockey team.

An average buying trip for Gene McCarron, meanwhile, lasted three months. McCarron remembers flying directly from Toronto to Vancouver, on to Tokyo, then to Hong Kong, and finally to Taipei. He says, "I had appointments booked for the day after I arrived, even though I felt like a zombie. It took me two days to remember who I was." Rather than choosing to party at night, McCarron retired to his hotel room to recover from the strain of adapting to a foreign culture.

"I would say, on balance, that buying was harder for women, not so much for men," says Fran Alford, a knitwear buyer in the 1970s, who was only willing to travel for long periods if her husband accompanied her. "Men could be away for months at a time. That was just a more accepted thing," she says. As soon as she completed her visits to various suppliers' offices, Alford would eat dinner, and then return to her hotel room to complete the tedious paperwork that accompanied each purchase.

Another female buyer, Janet Law Dickie, also found the travelling daunting. Dickie began her career first as a wage administrator, then later as a senior sales representative, at the downtown Vancouver store. At only twenty-six years of age she became Eaton's national buyer of glass and crystal. Until she married and gave birth to her first child, Dickie travelled an average of three weeks at a time to factories in countries such as Germany, Italy, Hungary, Yugoslavia, Sweden, Denmark, Spain, and even China.

On her first trip to a factory in Hungary, Dickie, accompanied by Frankfurt Buying Office Head Heinz Boehlke, met with suppliers at 9:30 a.m. around a huge boardroom table. "All these men of about fifty were sitting around the table just staring at me. They were all Party members who spoke German to Heinz," Dickie recalls. "They poured brandy and told me to drink it. Then the suppliers and buyers began directing their comments to Heinz, because he was a man and because he spoke German. But Heinz said, 'Gentlemen, the lady makes the deci-sions, I take the notes.' I almost cried when he said that. Until then I felt completely out of my depth."

By contrast, many male buyers expressed surprise that they seemed to fall into buying jobs while pursuing other positions at the store. Lloyd Bull, for example, started out as the pharmacist at the Queen Street store, before being tapped as a buyer of women's fashions. Fred Andrews, of the Winnipeg store, began making horse harnesses in 1938, before grad-uating in the 1940s to becoming a menswear buyer. Both men eventually became store managers, a position rarely offered to women.

Nevertheless, just as it was in Timothy's days, women buyers were as ferocious as men, if not more so. "You might have to work a little harder than the guy next door, but you could definitely move up," says Beryl Scudelleri, who, after obtaining her B.A. from Queen's University, began working as a retail sales clerk in the Business Girls' Shop of the Queen Street store in Toronto.

Scudelleri travelled throughout Europe and the Far East, purchasing children's wear. And she learned early to travel light, restricting her luggage to one purse and one suitcase. "The key to a good buyer is to be able to go through a line and be able to decide quickly," she says. "You'd say, 'I want this, this, and this.' You had to have a certain eye for what was saleable and what the customer wanted."

In the Far East it wouldn't be unusual for Scudelleri to pick up kids' cotton dresses for $1.99 and sell them for ten times as much back home in a Trans-Canada Sale. Knowing exactly what to buy could only be learned on the selling floor of Eaton's stores, where the best buyers, such as Scudelleri, gained their early experience. "The biggest coup a buyer could achieve was signing a hot supplier to an exclusive contract," she says. "That was a feather in your cap if you tied up a line. On the other hand, if you made a boo-boo, it was bye-bye."

The importance of not making a mistake was made clear to Janet Law Dickie, who risked the chop herself when an order went terribly wrong. "I ordered leaded-glass goblets with a carving of a pinwheel in the centre. While talking on the phone to the manufacturers, I realized that all the pin-wheels were being carved counter-clockwise, instead of clockwise, as I had specified. Hundreds of them had already been done. We couldn't change the order, because the factory had almost completed making them."

Dickie points out that one of the major challenges for any buyer was estimating the demand for any one product. "You had to know to purchase just enough and not too much. If an item was selling well, you might order more, then returns might come in and you would be left with a surplus. It was a crapshoot. Other times you'd order a lot and nothing would sell," she says.

"You bought what you thought would sell," agrees Gene McCarron. "One year I bought four or five thousand coffee mugs on a buying trip in the Far East. Right off the bat, the supervisor got his back up. When I came back and said I'd bought all the coffee cups, he said, 'How drunk were you that night?' We had to build in markdowns, but the mugs sold out before Christmas."

———■———

Armed with experience, most Eaton's buyers could survive any political storm. Violent natural and man-made disasters were another challenge altogether. In 1911, James Forster rode a train through a part of China infested with what he identified in his account as tsetse flies (but were probably mosquitoes) carrying the bubonic plague. Forster and his colleagues were forced to stand for hours, as clouds of the deadly insects billowed less than three feet off the ground around their ankles and legs. To protect their skin, the men wore special paper trousers tied to their shoes. Their hands, meanwhile, were protected with paper gloves.[8]

The following year, the *Titanic* set sail from Southampton on its maiden voyage. Several Eaton's buyers, including James Forster and an associate named Mr. Harper, bought tickets to sail on the ship, but arrived at the dock too late to go aboard. The one buyer who was probably congratulating himself on arriving in time to make it on-board – George E. Graham – died when the ship sank. Graham, who was a children's-toy buyer for the Winnipeg store, left behind an infant son and pregnant wife. The Winnipeg store closed for a half-day to mourn his death, with curtains drawn across display windows.

Less than one year later, a second maritime disaster devastated Eaton's buying offices. This time, one of the victims included an Eaton family member. On May 7, 1915, Iris Burnside – the niece of John Craig Eaton – and three of the store's top buyers, G. A. Powell, F. A. McMurtry, and W. MacLean, drowned after the steamer they were travelling on, the *Lusitania*, was torpedoed just off the coast of Ireland.

Josephine Burnside, John Craig Eaton's sister, lost her daughter, Iris, when the Lusitania was torpedoed in 1915.

Shortly after receiving the news, Eaton's employee Tom Somerset joined Iris's devastated mother, John Craig's sister, at the Imperial Hotel in Queenstown, Ireland. Bodies of the victims had been laid out in rows along the hotel's dock, but Iris's body would never be found.

As Tom Somerset and Mrs. Burnside sat in a car, waiting to leave Queenstown, Mrs. Burnside described her and her daughter's experiences during the last moments of the disaster. Burnside told Somerset that she and Iris had been in their stateroom when the torpedo stuck. Shortly after putting on their dressing gowns, Mrs. Burnside and Iris were preparing to leave their room, when MacLean rushed down, closely followed by Powell and McMurtry. Together the men literally propelled the two women up a sloping staircase onto the steamer's slippery and already dangerously listing deck. Somerset recalled in a letter:

> While on deck the men got the two ladies into one of the lifeboats, but apparently the tackle of this boat fouled, and it could not be lowered, so they had to get out. Apparently there was no chance of getting into another boat as they simply stood on deck with others, hoping that the ship would not sink. The unfortunate part of it was that none of them had life belts. She told me that McMurtry left them for a minute, and went to his room to get his life belt, but when he came back he told Mrs. Burnside quietly and in a matter of fact manner that his room was under water. Just like what old Mac would do. Well, they all stood together on the deck. Everybody was quite calm and quiet. Iris seemed to be a brave little girl. Her mother heard her speak to MacLean and say – Mr. MacLean, save mother. Next thing she remembers was a wave coming.[9]

The wave swept both women into a whirlpool of water. Iris disappeared almost immediately. Her mother also submerged, but just as quickly resurfaced in a violent explosion of water. With the assistance of a young man, Mrs. Burnside grabbed onto the keel of a lifeboat, where she dangled for eight hours, exposed to the elements.

A passing minesweeper picked up Mrs. Burnside and transported her to a family-owned hotel in Queenstown, where the owners comforted her as best they could. Somerset wrote:

> What impressed me most, and I think you ought to mention it to Mrs. Powell and Mrs. McMurtry, was her quiet description of how these three men went to their fate like the brave gentlemen they were. They stood as I have told you all together on the deck and then the wave came and they were all parted and Mrs. Burnside never saw any of them after.[10]

Powell's estate was awarded $26,250 by Eaton's, with Powell's sister Mary Jane receiving $1,675. McMurtry's widow and daughter received a settlement of $49,050. The widows of both McMurtry and Powell wrote letters thanking Eaton's executives for their generosity. Mary Powell even went so far as to graciously remark: "I am sure you are aware of the affection Mr. Powell had for his associates and the deep interest he took in the business – and indeed I can understand his loyalty to the T. Eaton company when I am shown personally so much helpful and Christian sympathy by those who were so near to him in his lifetime."[11]

In comparison, settling accounts with Walter MacLean's family members degenerated into a farcical and unseemly grab for John Craig Eaton's millions. John Craig awarded MacLean's widow $20,000 plus all of Walter's money on deposit and his wages up until August 25. Mrs. MacLean received the settlement graciously. In a letter of January 5, 1916, to John Craig, she wrote: "I greatly regret that owing to the shock I have suffered through the loss of my husband in the 'Lusitania' disaster, and the birth of my little boy a fortnight after, I have been in very delicate health since, otherwise I would have written you sooner. . . . [I] greatly appreciate your kindness in making the handsome gift which you have made to me."[12]

MacLean's widowed mother, however, was less appreciative of Eaton's largesse than her daughter-in-law. On August 28, 1916, the senior Mrs. MacLean wrote a letter to John Craig Eaton, claiming that, prior to his untimely death, her son Walter had coaxed her into selling him her small business in exchange for one pound a week in income for life. With Walter gone, she claimed that she now faced poverty, and asked John Craig to please cushion his settlement.

Mrs. MacLean's claim of poverty was quickly echoed by her son, J. Charles MacLean, who wrote his own letter to John Craig Eaton, dated October 19, 1915, in which he requested additional financial restitution for his mother to compensate for Walter's death. He wrote: "The result is that Mother's position financially is far from satisfactory, and she now feels that it was a mistake on her part to give up her business. Of course, if poor Walter lived, and retained your confidence, the position would be different."[13]

Faced with a potential public-relations embarrassment, John Craig dispatched J. McGillvray, then head of the London buying office, to investigate the true financial status of Mrs. MacLean. In a letter dated February 18, 1916, written to Eaton's executive J. J. Vaughan, McGillvray reported that Mrs. MacLean was

[not] in the poor position one of her sons suggests. She sold the business to one of them and is being paid so much a year, and is living as well and comfortably as she ever did. In fact – she is in a position to keep two of her unmarried daughters living at home with her, although they are both capable of earning their own living. The Mother appears to be a clever honest person, but the sons appear to be a very miserable lot, and I believe they would do almost anything to get money . . . They are a type entirely different to the one we had . . . Mrs. MacLean's five sons have incomes from 100 pounds to 500 pounds per annum, and are able to assist their Mother should she at any time require it.[14]

Four months after receiving McGillvray's letter, and on the instructions of John Craig Eaton, J. J. Vaughan dispatched his own letter to Charles MacLean, informing him that Eaton's had conducted a full inquiry into the financial circumstances of his mother and concluded that no further action needed to be taken.

For sheer apocalyptic horror, however, few disasters could rival the Great Kanto Earthquake that hit Yokohama in 1923. It was all the more devastating to Eaton's because Yokohama was the home of one of its most successful foreign buying offices.

Opened in 1919, the Yokohama buying office specialized in embroidered cotton and linen products. Doilies and clothes made on family-owned handlooms provided exotic alternatives to staid knitted wools and flannels. Dyed silk products, including quilted vests and embroidered silk kimonos, were snapped up, in spite of their exorbitant price of $100 apiece. Dyed crepe de Chine was also a popular product, as well as silk, used for lampshades. The Yokohama office also exported Thermos bottles and toys, including porcelain popguns and tea sets.

The tremendous business enjoyed by the Yokohama office came to a horrific halt when the earthquake struck on the morning of September 1, 1923.

A handful of hours before the quake, store manager Mr. Cabeldu arrived at the Eaton's office with silk inspector Mr. Hachizo Yagi to dispatch a number of orders that had arrived from the Toronto and Winnipeg stores. The merchandise had already been packed and loaded onto the SS *Empress of Australia*, which was docked in the harbour.

Shortly before noon, Cabeldu and Yagi left the office and parted ways, Yagi walking toward the nearby Teletype office to place additional orders, Cabeldu disappearing in another direction. The men were barely out of each other's sight when the ground beneath them began rumbling loudly, rose up in the air more than thirty feet, then swayed sickeningly both vertically and horizontally before finally falling back down, lacerated with river-wide fissures.

Across town, Yokohama staff member B. C. Walker huddled in the only room in his house that didn't collapse when the quake struck. Fires raged throughout the city. A giant gale blew embers onto rooftops. The fire engines that hadn't been destroyed rushed to try to save flaming buildings, the clang of their bells rivalled only by the shouts of pain and terror arising from the people trapped beneath wreckage.

To add to the inconceivable bedlam, Japanese vigilantes stabbed, clubbed, and stoned on sight Koreans, who were suspected of poisoning the city's wells. "All Japanese men seemed to be out of their right senses,"[15] B. C. Walker wrote in a letter home, which documented the

Yokohama buying office, 1919

*Yokohama buying office staff, 1922. Mr. Cabeldu, far right, was killed
in the Yokohama earthquake shortly after this photograph was taken.*

horror around him. He noted that, until police reinforcements arrived, it was dangerous for any foreigner to walk the streets alone.

Looters broke into the safes of various businesses. B. C. Walker assigned three Eaton's staff members armed with clubs to protect Eaton's safe, which stood out conspicuously amongst the building's burning embers and other debris. Inside the safe was the history of the Yokohama office's buying operation, including all the financial records and lists of orders. Once he had done this, nourished by two rice balls and a bottle of boiled rainwater, Walker set off to search for his younger brother, who had obtained employment with Eaton's only a month and a half before the quake, as well as to discover the whereabouts of Mr. Cabeldu.

It didn't take long for Walker to find Cabeldu. With his left leg twisted grotesquely beneath his body, one wrist snapped, and his body badly charred, Cabeldu was lying on the sidewalk, where he had landed after jumping from the second-floor window of a barbershop. "[There] was nothing on his body to show that he was killed by the falling debris, so I am afraid that he must have been alive when the flames reached him. We all felt very cut up when we found him in that condition, more especially as we have always found him such a nice man to work for,"[16] Walker wrote.

Proceeding to the *Empress of Australia*, Walker immediately reported Cabeldu's death. He then returned to personally cremate Cabeldu's body where it lay, gathering up the ashes in a sack and burying them on the grounds of the British Consulate. Meanwhile, despite being guarded by staff members, Eaton's safe remained vulnerable to thieves. Days passed without the safe being removed or opened. Before he could find a way to move the safe, Walker was told that, due to health concerns, all British subjects were required to evacuate Yokohama for Kobe. Walker initially refused until he located Mr. Yagi to watch the safe in the absence of other staff members.

Mr. Yagi tried to enlist the help of Japanese authorities in forcing open the safe. When help failed to materialize, Yagi and some Japanese colleagues tried unsuccessfully to force the safe open themselves, using rocks. Just as they were doing so, American seamen walked by, the U.S. navy having been assigned to patrol the city streets to protect against looters. Yagi called out to them: "This was the place of The T. Eaton Co. Limited of Toronto, a great department store in Toronto, Winnipeg, and Montreal of Canada, so I want to break this burnt safe and take out all recorded books."[17] (In a letter Yagi wrote to Eaton's in 1968 describing the disaster, he erred in listing Montreal as a store, when it hadn't been built until 1926.)

Finally persuaded, one sailor pointed his gun at the safe lock and fired. As soon as the door swung open, the late Mr. Cabeldu's brother, who had just arrived in Yokohama, took charge of the books from Mr. Yagi, and hurried to take them to B. C. Walker in Kobe.

Walker was already en route back to Yokohama from Kobe, so the men crossed paths without meeting. Walker discovered upon his return that his own brother had been killed at the Eaton's office, along with twelve other staff members.

For three days, using bared fingers, Walker tried to dig his brother's remains from beneath the collapsed building. By the third day, he fell ill from drinking poorly sanitized water. Forced to give up, he finally returned to Kobe, where he caught up with the late Mr. Cabeldu's widow and collected the badly charred Eaton's books retrieved by Mr. Cabeldu's brother. Walker deposited the books in a vault located in a small room in the Toyo Botan Co. Building nearby. Afterwards, he asked to have 15,000 yen wired from Canada to be given to Mrs. Cabeldu.

Walker was relieved that the order that had been placed on board the SS *Empress of Australia* was already safely on its way to Canada, although he worried that, because many papers had burned in the fires that followed the earthquake, he would not have an accurate account of how many goods had been paid for but not shipped.

Drawing on the discipline his Eaton's training had instilled in him, Walker installed himself in a small house in the suburbs of Yokohama and set about paying now-destitute staff members their September salaries. He then requested copies to be sent to him from Canada of all of the September 1 invoices and packing statements, copies of all silk-shade cards, a list of department heads, and addresses of merchants in China with which Eaton's did business. On top of all that, he also had to deal with a small shipment of buttons and brushes on board the *Empress of Russia*, scheduled to leave on October 10. For B. C. Walker, the comforting rhythm of work sustained him.

— ■ —

Less than twenty years after the Yokohama quake, there was no rest for another Eaton's employee. Eaton's Paris Buying-Office Manager David Biesel, an Englishman, watched nervously during the first week of June 1940 as German troops bore down on the city. Government offices had already closed, as had the venerated Lloyds Bank. Biesel reluctantly closed the Paris office and drove by car to Bordeaux, where he hoped the authorities might let him relocate the office. Throughout the journey, Biesel had to drive around thousands of refugees fleeing Paris on foot. As soon as he arrived in Bordeaux, Biesel attempted to obtain permission from the French police to relocate Eaton's offices. On June 17, however, before he could complete his request, he, like his fellow British subjects, was ordered to evacuate to England.

The Germans occupied Paris on June 14. Displaying quintessential Eatonian bravado, in Biesel's absence a group of French buyers set up an independent company at the height of the Nazi occupation and named it "R. Chavance Company." Not connected in a corporate sense with Eaton's, it served only to protect the Eaton premises against German occupation, as well as to provide income for Paris-based personnel. Though merchandise was scarce, some Eaton's goods were sold through the makeshift office, and as a result the company stayed in business.

———■———

Back home in Canada, Eaton's faced the dilemma of figuring out how to liquidate stock already purchased but not yet sold from countries that were on a friendly basis with Germany. The question of acquiring even more products from German allies was moot. As had happened in the Great War, in the Second World War the Canadian government passed an act which prohibited companies from buying merchandise from any country with even a tangential relationship with Germany.

On September 6, 1940, a memo was circulated to all Eaton's stores by the Merchandise Office, stipulating that products from Germany and Italy would continue to be sold, but only if placed beside similar merchandise from a friendly or neutral country. Despite this memo, Eaton's remained in a quandary. It was illegal to remove country-of-origin labels from merchandise, yet, as of August 1940, Eaton's still had almost 4,000 German, 3,000 Japanese, and 185 Italian pairs of gloves to sell, not to mention 900 pieces of German and Italian jewellery. The store decided to leave it up to the customers to decide which products to buy.

It didn't take long for customers to voice protests once they spotted enemy-made merchandise. In March 1940, an army veteran from the First World War loudly threatened to bring his entire legion in to boycott any product made in Germany. When other customers attempted to buy German merchandise, the man informed them that, every time they did so, they were paying for the bullets that killed innocent women and children. When this failed to achieve the desired results, the man designed his own "Made in Germany" pamphlet and jammed it on top of the offending merchandise. As soon as the store manager ripped up the pamphlet, the man simply replaced it with another, declaring that he would soon return with ten thousand more.

On September 25, 1941, the Department of National Revenue, Canada Customs Division, by an order-in-council, halted the importation into Canada of goods from Japan, the Japanese Empire, and Manchuria. This last move was taken when customers complained of seeing products labelled "Made in Japan."

Japan's entry into the war came as an enormous shock to then-Eaton's president, R. Y. Eaton. Even in the early days of 1940, R. Y. doubted that Japan, which bought four times as many goods from Canada as it sold to Canada, would jeopardize its economic health by severing its Western trade ties. After the fact, he speculated about the high costs Eaton's would incur by having to buy goods manufactured in Canadian factories to replace those previously manufactured in Japan, especially since he suspected that Japanese goods might still remain available in competitors' stores.

The news of Japan's entry into the war turned out to be the second time R. Y. was taken off guard. Like many other North Americans, he had not envisaged that Germany would seek to dominate the world unless they could be certain of complete victory. To show how complacent he had become, as late as 1940, he had written of Germany in a letter: "If running true to form, they are likely soon to nibble off another piece of territory somewhere, and later nibble off some more, but in location and extent not enough for other countries to make an issue of it and thereby risk a World War."[18]

Two years earlier, Eaton's buyers had similarly failed to predict Hitler's maniacal acquisitiveness. In 1938, china and glassware buyer

Louis Keene arrived in Vienna hours after the city had been occupied by German troops. As his plane descended towards the airport, Keene observed through his window that the airfield below was covered with German bombers. Such an atmosphere of pandemonium overtook the airport that officials failed to remember to inspect travellers' tickets or passports, including Keene's. The situation had to be rectified the next day, when Keene returned to the airport to clear his papers.

Once in Vienna, Keene's taxi weaved its way through streets teeming with ecstatic flag-wavers, who sang and marched in celebration of the arrival of German troops. Steel-helmeted sentries, bearing fixed bayonets, guarded the entrance to the Grand Hotel, which, in addition to being Keene's destination, had just been converted into the German army's headquarters. Despite the army's appropriation of the hotel, however, Keene was allowed to stay in comfortable quarters on the fourth floor, which featured a balcony from which, later that day, he could observe "the spectacular arrival of Hitler."[19] Men lining the rooftops of buildings aimed rifles towards the street in case of trouble. Army members converted the hotel dining room into a map room. The use of most telephone and telegraph lines was reserved for members of the military, so Keene had trouble sending messages out of the country. The army had requisitioned most cars. Refugees who tried to leave the country by train were "closely examined to see that they were not taking money or other valuables with them. The soles of their shoes were even slit open and leather luggage cut up to prevent this."[20]

Declaring himself to be unperturbed by the chaos around him, Keene completed his work in Vienna before flying on to Berlin. In Berlin, he proclaimed that he was impressed with "the general fitness of the nation – especially the young soldiers who seemed to be the acme of physical fitness."[21] Keene noted that there wasn't a single visible garbage heap in Berlin, and no starving beggars on the streets.

Mere months prior to Keene's visit, two other Eaton's buyers had visited Berlin, and were equally impressed with what they saw. The April 1938 issue of Winnipeg's in-store magazine, *Contacts*, featured an article entitled "Buyers Abroad,"[22] which documented the unforgettable time enjoyed in Berlin by a Mr. Westman and a Mr. Gray. The men had failed to find hotel accommodation in the city, so decided to stay in the Ambassador's suite of Eaton's Berlin buying office. Relaxing on the balcony adjoining their suite, the two men watched a parade of troops, headed by Adolf Hitler. At the parade's conclusion, Hitler delivered a speech, which was broadcast internationally by radio.

Less than a year following Keene's and Westman and Gray's visit to the city, the Berlin office was closed. L. C. Rideal, the head of the office, joined the British navy as a submarine commander. When the war ended, Rideal became the head of the "Continental Section" of the London office, which did business with all the territories of the former Berlin office until the re-establishment of the T. Eaton Company in Frankfurt in 1957.

Bombs fell close to the London buying office during the Blitz, but the building miraculously emerged intact. While the bombing was at its heaviest, staff members moved temporarily to Ascot. After the war, the London office continued operating, but, as with other European buying offices, with fewer staff members.

———■———

Even after the end of the Second World War, the area covered by Eaton's buying offices continued to be immense. The Paris, Frankfurt, and Florence buying offices serviced all twenty-three countries in continental Europe, as well as Iron Curtain countries such as Czechoslovakia, East Germany, Poland, and Bulgaria.

Buyers expecting to resume unfettered travel from country to country after the war now faced Cold War intransigence on the part of border officials. Customs officers throughout Europe showed a perverse pleasure in ripping up anything not nailed down in train compartments, on the pretext of searching for foreign currency. Border crossings, therefore, remained teeth-grinding endurance tests.

In 1964, carrying stacks of Eaton's buying requisitions, Heinz Boehlke arrived at the Polish border to East Germany. Having been assured beforehand that it would be permissible, he attempted to cross the border at a different border station than the one indicated on his visa. It was already 3:00 a.m. and he was exhausted. The custom officer examined Boehlke's passport and visa, and shook his head. "No good," he said. "You're not supposed to cross here. You must change your visa." Accompanied by two border guards, Boehlke carried two heavy suitcases full of product samples several miles to what was the "correct" border crossing into East Germany.

After spending the night at the East German border station, where he had his visa adjusted, he continued on to Berlin on his way home to Frankfurt. At the checkpoint in Berlin, Boehlke slipped his passport into the assigned chute, where it disappeared, then swiftly reappeared in the company of a policeman, saying the words Boehlke could only dread: "You're missing a visa, go back two stations to Berlin police headquarters." Boehlke refused. "I will sit here with my suitcases. I've been travelling for three weeks in Socialist places and I'm not moving a step further," he said, sitting on a bench. Extracting a promise from Boehlke that he would fly out of West Berlin to Frankfurt without touching foot again in East Germany, the border police officer relented and took him across the line of demarcation through a maze of underground tunnels that opened up into West Berlin. "It just proved there are human beings everywhere in this world," Boehlke says today.

In 1968, it was Boehlke again, accompanied by Canadian china buyer Chris Elson and a third buyer, who negotiated a treacherous road trip through Czechoslovakia shortly after the country was occupied by Soviet troops. As dusk turned to darkness, the three men drove a small car over roads already deeply gutted by Russian tanks. In an effort to

Eaton's buyer Heinz Boehlke at glassware showroom of Hungarian National Export Agency "Ferunion" in Budapest, 1964. Beside him is W. F. Smith, principal buyer for glass and chinaware.

confuse the Red Army, the Czechs had removed all road signs and replaced them with arrows pointing north, upon which were written the words "To Russia." More tanks performed manoeuvres in the forests located on each side of the road. In Liberec, Boehlke marvelled at a tank embedded in the side of a house. Finally, in Slovakia, instead of staying in the mountain resort where they had reserved rooms, the nervous trio crammed into their small car to follow the progress of the Soviet occupation on BBC Radio.

While a buying trip to Eastern Europe in February 1964 may not have posed a physical threat to John Craig Eaton's safety, it certainly tested his patience. The trip began promisingly enough on board a luxurious Caravelle jet. "This was pretty posh stuff for 1964," John Craig says. To prepare for his arrival in chilly Zagreb, Yugoslavia, John Craig had donned calf-high flight boots, lined with lamb's wool, as well as a heavy winter coat. Shortly after landing in Zagreb, John Craig met up at the train station with his travelling companions, sportswear buyer Hannah North and Gerry Redfern of the Frankfurt buying office. Together the three boarded a train heading for Belgrade. "By the time we boarded the train, the sun was going down," says John Craig. "And it was starting

Buyers in Switzerland, 1960s

to get a little chilly in the car. I thought, 'Don't worry, they've had the doors open in these cars. It'll warm up.'"

Instead, after two or three hours, the trio's train compartment was even colder. John Craig gallantly loaned Hannah his boots, while both men draped their coats over her shoulders. "Finally I got sick of this and went in search of the Yugoslav conductor, who I found eating this enormous sausage with a knife and fork. I started to eye this sausage, because by this time it's about eight at night and we have three more hours to go before we get to Belgrade. I'm very, very hungry," recalls John Craig. When the conductor refused to share his sausage with the trio, John Craig returned to his compartment and withdrew a bottle of Scotch from his coat. He and Redfern took turns sipping the Scotch out of the bottle lid. John Craig finally persuaded even the Baptist teetotaller North to take a few swigs.

Hours later, the train finally pulled into the Belgrade station, just in time to catch the tail end of an ice storm. Shortly after leaving the station, John Craig hailed a taxi for the three and instructed the driver to head for their hotel. "A few minutes after we'd taken off, I noticed that the taxi's windshield wipers didn't work. It was like looking at a Monet painting as the scenery went by, but the taxi driver didn't seem to care," he recalls. As soon as the trio arrived at the hotel, they wolfed down sandwiches and hot tea before resting and beginning work the next morning. Two days later, John Craig flew to Rome for more appointments, again bedecked in his flight boots and coat to ward off the cold, but this time the temperature was unexpectedly mild. "I got off the plane, and it was sixty degrees out. People wondered, 'What the hell is with this guy?'" he says.

Eaton's buyers were among the first to resume business with China after U.S. President Richard Nixon's historic visit in 1972. Stan Shortt, Vice-President of Merchandising, was sent on a trip with eighteen other employees in 1978. "We were the first people in Beijing. People hadn't seen anyone from the West. As we walked through the street, several people followed us silently. When we got to Shanghai, the Chinese government put us up in the same hotel suite that Richard Nixon had used."

The fourteen-room suite that had been reserved for Eaton's buyers had a guard posted outside. Shortly after the buyers had settled in, the hotel's maître d' arrived and announced that the catering staff wished to prepare French cuisine for them. "They hadn't been able to cook that for years," says Shortt. When the food arrived, it was accompanied by a string quartet, made up of four professors from Shanghai University. "As they played, tears streamed down their faces," recalls Shortt. "They hadn't been able to play music for so long. The Western music books they had were practically in tatters." When finished, the quartet asked to be paid, not with money, but with Western sheet music.

■

By the early 1960s, with improved communication devices, computers, as well as less-expensive methods of shipping merchandise, the need for foreign-based buying offices gradually diminished. One by one, each buying office was closed. By 1969, all British buying offices had closed, except London. When the London office finally closed for good in 1975, there was an outcry that was heard even beyond Britain's borders.

Once Heinz Boehlke parked his car on a Paris street, leaving an Eaton's bag bearing the store's logo visible through a side window. An Englishman who was passing by saw Boehlke leave his car, and said to him, "Are you from Eaton's? I saw your bag there. How did you dare to close that office?"

In 1975, Boehlke had left his position as head of the Frankfurt buying office to head the Paris office. Then operating as the European headquarters, Paris dealt only with fashion, and Boehlke, whose speciality was glassware and crystal, was viewed as a square peg in a round hole. Concerned that the buying office was bleeding money, one of Boehlke's first steps was to implement budgetary constraints, particularly regarding entertainment expenses incurred by buyers in their wooing of suppliers. Enraged by what they perceived as his parsimony, subordinates sent a devastatingly critical letter, unsigned, to Eaton's head office in Toronto, urging the ousting of Boehlke. Afterwards, the atmosphere inside the Paris office became so poisonous that, on more than one occasion, the war-hardened veteran drove home in tears. In the end, Eaton's head office sided with Boehlke.

Boehlke was used to receiving a warm welcome from his employers. In 1958 he attended a party at Eaton Hall hosted by then-president John David. Upon arriving, he was greeted on the property by a man on horseback who ushered him in as though he were royalty. In Winnipeg, the reception was just as warm. On Boehlke's first trip to the city, Gilbert Eaton, former president John Craig Eaton's son, greeted him in fluent German. "It wasn't the work that almost killed me," Boehlke has said of his years with the firm, "it was the hospitality."

———■———

It was "back at the ranch," to coin a phrase, where the true resentment of department managers toward buyers, or "maharajas," as they were nicknamed, boiled over. When a product failed to catch on with the public, a session of vigorous finger-pointing often commenced. Inevitably the department manager blamed the buyer, the buyer blamed the department manager, and both blamed head office. Meanwhile, sales clerks were often stuck trying to sell the unsellable.

One sales clerk's frustration spilled over in a short article he wrote for a 1937 edition of *Entre Nous*, the Montreal store's staff magazine. The article, clearly directed toward globe-trotting maharajas, was entitled, "If I Were a Buyer":

If I were a buyer, I wouldn't keep so many things to myself. I would tell those who work under me as much as I could about the merchandise I bought. I would realize that most things were bought with the idea of getting them over to the customer, and I would realize that the one big way to do this is to sell the salespeople first. I would be alive to the fact that the people who are selling the goods want to know why they are smart, why they were bought and what types of customer I had in mind when I bought them. When on my buying trips I might even get so enthused about things that I'd dash off a letter to my assistant, and instruct him to read it to the staff. When I returned I'd hold "get-togethers" and show what I had bought and explain all the selling details to the entire department. I'd arrange promotions of new things through departmental displays, windows and advertising. I might even ask the staff to call up some of their customers or mail a card telling them of the fascinating new arrivals.

– Anonymous[23]

The article elicited the following pithy response, obviously from a buyer: "Sounds good – wonder if this anonymous contributor would find time to do *all* of this if he *were* a buyer."

It was sometimes easy for buyers to forget during their travels that everything they bought had eventually to be sold, and that their best friend was the copywriter who was expected to weave gold out of straw.

Janet Law Dickie was one buyer who made sure to devise a program that delineated basic, core, and fringe items. As soon as she knew the image she wanted the product to project, she shared her ideas with the artists and copywriters on staff. She understood that good communication between buyers, artists, and copywriters was essential to moving merchandise, and that advertising copy could make or break a product.

Beginning in the 1940s, on the fifth floor of the Queen Street store, under dripping water coolers in summer and dry space heaters in winter, young copywriters churned out delightful, uplifting copy, geared mostly toward stay-at-home moms, who were largely depicted as balancing Gerber baby bottles in between fretting over important issues, like which colour phone to use to place their orders.

Over the years, the City Advertising Department, as it was known, had its share of unique characters, among them Department Manager Percy Morgan. Originally imported from Ireland to act as riding master at John David Eaton's stables, Morgan evolved into one of the most frequently mimicked of Eaton's managers. "He was a real oddball," says Everette Roseborough, one of Eaton's premier fashion photographers. "The copywriters used to mimic his accent rather mercilessly. We used to call him Mista Mawgan in a very affected way."

Doris Anderson, who worked as a copywriter, remembers seeing Morgan pop his head over the tops of wooden partitions to snoop on staff members, a habit that eventually earned him the nickname "Cyclops." Anderson, who wrote copy for notions, ladies' shoes, lingerie, and eventually fashion copy, remembers that, like some buyers, Cyclops never appreciated the creative processes behind writing good ad copy. "Whenever we saw him go by, we would all start typing like mad, or else he'd think we were just goofing off."

Another employee recalls arriving every morning to see Morgan sitting at his desk, reviewing what appeared to be business material. Closer observation revealed that the "business material" was actually each day's horse-racing forms, which lay propped atop Morgan's desk drawer.

A tale much repeated among Eaton's employees, and perhaps more apocryphal than real, surrounds Cyclops's legendary response to a desperate employee who had lost money in the stock market and threatened

EATON'S

FROM NEW YORK: EXCLUSIVE EDITIONS OF THE YOUNG TYCOON COAT

Eugenie Groh's artwork, 1963

to jump from the ledge of John David Eaton's seventh-floor office window. "For God's sake, don't jump here. Go across the street and jump from Simpson's," Cyclops is reported to have told the distraught employee. The result is not recorded.

Eugenie Groh, a multiple-award-winning artist employed in the 1970s by Montreal's City Advertising Department, recalls that the Eaton family discouraged advertising artwork that leaned toward the avant-garde. One exception to the rule was R. Y. Eaton's eldest son, Jack Eaton, who, in his capacity as the manager of the Montreal store, gave Groh and her colleague Jack Parker a free hand. Featured in the Montreal *Gazette*, their ads still stand out as works of art in themselves. Two-dimensional females jump off the page as glistening sexual beings. Encircled by swirls of sensuous fabric, they have expressions that range from bored to rapturous. With some light pen-feathering, Groh could reveal the texture of a garment more effectively than a colour photograph could. What customers didn't see tantalized them more than what they did see.

——■——

The structure of Eaton's buying offices see-sawed over the years before toppling altogether. Beginning in 1945, Eaton's established a General Merchandise Office, through which staple items could be bought in bulk at a discount and distributed by the company's major stores across Canada. Fashion buying, however, continued to be done through regional buying offices located in each province. Store department managers, who tried to respond to their customers' desires, supervised regional purchasing. If a product didn't sell, the responsibility rested with the department managers.

Beginning in 1968, most of the smaller regional buying offices were either closed or amalgamated into one of the four main buying divisions – Pacific, Western, Central, and Eastern – all operating under the umbrella of the GMO. Once this change was inaugurated, department managers for regional divisions scrambled to satisfy their customers' unique tastes in the face of more economical bulk buying. The question became, How could regional tastes be satisfied, without breaking the bank financially?

On August 10, 1977, Eaton's flip-flopped, deciding that it had to give more flexibility for product buying to department managers, even in the smallest of regions throughout Canada, rather than continue to rely on regional buying-division representatives to make all the purchasing decisions.

A memo specifically added:

Eaton's is well represented in each of the major markets in Canada. Market share and competition vary by region as do customer buying patterns, life-styles, fashion awareness and price emphasis. Strong area management is required to provide the marketing expertise and flexibility required to merchandise all stores to better serve the customers and at the same time expand the Company franchise.[24]

Some buyers vigorously disagreed that intensified regional buying was necessary. "That stuff about what sells in Vancouver won't sell in Toronto was just a bunch of nonsense," says Gene McCarron, who saw the emphasis on regional buying imperilling the bulk purchasing power of central buying. "Maybe some types of sportswear, like downhill skiing equipment, would be unpopular in Winnipeg, not in Vancouver, but overall, 95 per cent of merchandise was universal. It was pure and simple a lack of corporate direction that caused the flip-flopping."

Fred Eaton agrees that the company's indecision about whether to concentrate on regional or centralized buying caused the company to lose ground with loyal customers. "Buying patterns did go back and forth," he admits. "There were two arguments. When I was starting out at Eaton's, I was a buyer of outerwear. We would buy snowsuits for children, then we would go to Montreal and meet with snowsuit makers to make the snowsuit pick up an extra button, until it was a ter-rific snowsuit that we could put on sale. Then, of course, you'd say, 'Who's buying the suit? It never snows in Vancouver; children don't wear snowsuits there. They want something called puddle pants.' The same with Winnipeg; there was always competition between Winnipeg and Toronto. Winnipeg had its own base of manufacturers and supply catalogue. It didn't make sense from a management position to say, 'Let's have two different huge operations doing the same thing.' It's the same as saying, 'Let's let every individual store buy its own stock.' It doesn't work."

"Things really started going out of control with the implementation of regional buying," says McCarron. "It was disasterville. I thought, 'Oh no, here we go!' The suppliers were phoning asking, 'Who are we going to deal with? How are we going to cut a deal?' Every guy wants some-thing different, and you're saying, 'Oh, it's okay, it'll work out,' and all the time you're wondering, 'What will happen to me in the show?'"

A new wrinkle appeared on the scene when regional buyers were no longer asked to spot trends, but to buy merchandise based on the literal amount of shelf space allotted to them. Plan-o-grams, as they were known, were ultimately created for each store department. Gene McCarron, who bought toys, recalls: "You were given so much space for each category of toy. You had to draw it all out, photograph it, and present it to the buyers. They hired me to complete that program. Before that, it had been the buyers' tendency just to buy things and then try to make it fit. The whole Plan-o-gram thing just increased animosity between head office and stores."

As the 1970s drifted into the 1980s, suddenly there were so many Eaton's buyers from various regions that one didn't recognize the other. Says Gene McCarron, "I could be in Europe or the Orient, and I'd meet people and they'd say, 'Where do you work?' And I'd say, 'Eaton's.' And they'd say, 'Really? What department do you work in, because I work at Eaton's too.' It was amazing!"

Then, in 1981, when the regional buying model failed to yield significant profits, Eaton's returned to strictly centralized buying. In 1981, Fred Eaton announced that most regional offices were to close and that all buying would be done in Toronto.

The merging of the Western operation of the company with Ontario's cost as many as three hundred Winnipeg employees their jobs and compromised the goodwill the two regions had shared throughout most of their history. "That was the beginning of the end, when Toronto started calling the shots," says Alan Finnbogason, Operations Manager of the Winnipeg store.

Incredibly, on April 7, 1982, Eaton's Vice-President Greg Purchase tried to compromise between regional and centralized buying by creating fourteen separate regional markets areas, each with its own general manager. Buying, meanwhile, was ultimately to be controlled by one centralized group known as the Central Merchandising Office [CMO]. By using this system, Purchase hoped to place managers closer to their markets, so they could become more sensitive to regional buyers' needs, while a centralized buying group simultaneously took advantage of the benefits of bulk purchasing.

The result was not buying strength, but buying confusion. "The buyers changed constantly," says Kathy Henkinson, a sales clerk at the Abbotsford, B.C., store. "We'd end up with full snowsuits out here. The system was never fine-tuned enough."

"The CMO destroyed everything," says Pierre Witmeur, former

manager of the Montreal store. "You couldn't have centralized buying when it came to fashion, especially in Quebec. I yelled at Greg Purchase about this. He just said wearily, 'I hear you, Pierre.'"

Purchase's announcement caused many Eatonians, especially those employed in Western-based stores, to start looking for the exit sign. The bitterness was particularly acute among Winnipeg employees, who didn't like to be dictated to by higher-ups in Toronto.

"All the decision-making power was taken out of Winnipeg and moved to Toronto. You get a situation like that, and it's got to be bad for the community," said Jim Thomson, who was head of the watch- and jewellery-repair section when he retired.

Janet Law Dickie was one buyer who decided to jump ship. By 1984, lured by the offer of a huge increase in salary at Simpson's, she left Eaton's. Within a year, she regretted her move. "It was dreadful, even though I was being paid a lot more, I realized almost immediately that the atmosphere was backbiting and unprofessional; buyers didn't know what they were doing; there wasn't that family atmosphere that we had at Eaton's. Once, while making a sales presentation to a group at Simpson's, I kept saying 'We at Eaton's.' Even though I'd left, I had the diamond E seared into my forehead."

By the 1980s, instead of being glamorous excursions, buying trips were pedestrian affairs. Five-star-hotel accommodations were no longer offered. Business-class plane tickets were converted to coach. Nevertheless, for all the money that was saved by curtailing buyers' expenditures, increasingly large sums were spent on purchasing brand-name designer-label merchandise, which, because it was available in every other major department-store chain, was difficult to move.

"You couldn't just go to a shirt department, you had to go to Pierre Cardin," explains Michael Brough. "One time Jack Eaton of the Montreal store pulled me aside and asked, 'Do you see any navy blue suits here?' I looked around the floor and replied, 'No.' 'Don't you think they're important?' he added. 'Yes, I do,' I said. Jack definitely had a point. There were no suits on the floor, just high fashion."

By the last decade and a half of Eaton's existence, the halcyon days of travelling to exotic overseas destinations to find one-of-a-kind merchandise had come to an end. Even so, there remained buyers who remembered the sacrifices made by their predecessors.

When nostalgic Timothy Days celebrations were held in 1986, Michael Brough looked at the blown-up pictures of the store's founder and thought, "Can you imagine how long he spent on a steamer to get overseas to buy fabrics? It humbled me. As innovative as you think you are, it's all been done before."

CHAPTER 8

The War Years

First World War • Second World War
• Recognition of returning soldiers

W HEN EATON'S PRESIDENT John David Eaton's son John Craig
Eaton was nine years old, he, along with his younger brother
Fredrik, jumped into their father's Mercury convertible and rode to
Eaton's Queen Street store in Toronto. Joining them was company
physician Dr. Mulligan ("Mull" for short). The group entered the store
off Louisa Street, and then proceeded to the roof, where, as John Craig
recalls, "My father, and 'Mull,' and a couple of other guys began to
raise the flag."

The Union Jack had been lowered to half mast since 1939 in defer-
ence to those Eatonians serving in the Second World War. While watching his father raise the flag, John Craig detected a roaring sound around
him. To investigate its source, he and Fredrik ran to the Yonge Street side
of the roof and peeked over the edge. On the street below, a teeming
mass of ecstatic men and women cheered louder and louder as the flag
rose higher and higher. The date was May 7, 1945, the day all German
armies surrendered: "It was one of my first memories of the store,"
recalls John Craig. "And it was wild!"

Nothing sealed the loyalty of Eatonians to their store more than the
efforts made by John Craig Eaton, R. Y. Eaton, and John David Eaton

on behalf of their employees over the course of two world wars. Eatonians may have served King and country in the wars, but it was the Eaton family who welcomed them with open arms when they came home, and made good on its pledge to return them, if not to their original jobs, then to jobs of equal value.

Prior to serving in the First World War, every employee had his photograph taken by Eaton's and hung on the walls of the Toronto and Winnipeg stores. In all, 3,327 Eatonians enlisted for military service. Of those, 2,200 were from the Toronto stores and factories alone, with 1,101 from the Winnipeg store. By October 1919, 1,375 had resumed work at Eaton's. Some 315 died in action or from injuries sustained in service.[1]

John Craig was at his Muskoka summer home, Ravenscrag, when war was declared. Rushing back to Toronto, he called an emergency meeting of Eaton's board of directors to implement a supplementary payment plan for Eatonians, ensuring that married men who enlisted voluntarily received full pay, while single men who enlisted voluntarily received half-pay for the duration of the war.

First World War veteran Dalton Strype was one of those who most benefited from John Craig's generosity. Strype had first distinguished himself by graduating from officer-training school as a lieutenant, his education having been fully subsidized by the store. He later suffered wounds during action at Vimy Ridge, and was awarded the Military Cross with Bar for bravery by King George V at Buckingham Palace. When Strype returned to Eaton's, after having been promoted to captain, his job was still waiting for him.

Tragically, at the age of fifty-two, Strype had to have both legs amputated, due to a medical condition, forcing him to spend the rest of his life in a wheelchair. Without being asked, Eaton's paid for all of Strype's medical bills, including the cost of both amputations, and for all hospital and nursing fees. When the company collapsed in 1999, Strype's daughter-in-law, Dorothy

When First World War veteran Dalton Strype had to have both legs amputated, Eaton's paid all his medical expenses.

Example of Christmas package sent to Eatonians serving in the Second World War. Many of the same ingredients were in earlier packages.

"Victory" statue being crafted by Eatonian Ivor Lewis (left, wearing glasses) and associates. The statue was designed in Lewis's likeness. 1918.

"Victory" statue stood on steps of City Hall in Toronto to advertise Victory Bonds.

First Victory Bond drive, Toronto's City Hall, 1914

Strype, wrote to the *Toronto Star*, thanking the Eaton family for all the support they had given her father-in-law. "I don't think they realized what a difference they made in people's lives," she says today.

During the First World War, government contracts flooded into Eaton's for the manufacture of everything from uniforms to machine guns, and John Craig Eaton responded, donating all profits from the production of items such as these to the war drive. In addition, he donated one hundred thousand dollars of his own money to the creation of the Eaton Machine Gun Battery, which equipped the army with Vickers-Maxim guns and fifteen armoured cars. The family yacht, named the *Florence*, was also donated to the cause. She ultimately sank off the coast of Trinidad.

In 1915, John Craig was given a knighthood in recognition of his contributions. The investiture took place at Rideau Hall in Ottawa, with HRH the Duke of Connaught, Governor General of Canada, bestowing the honour. John Craig's wife, Flora McCrea Eaton, thenceforth Lady Eaton, watched the ceremony with pride.

Eaton's buying offices in London and Paris served as homes away from home for the troops, who could draw on their savings accounts through special banks on the premises. Men serving in the field, meanwhile, received parcels containing everything from coffee, tea, and chocolate to hand-knitted mittens and socks.

Letters containing the names of specific servicemen to whom parcels were to be sent were circulated from store department to department. Each staff member checked off his or her name and the amount he or she was donating. The average donation per month was approximately twenty cents, comparable to about $3.25 in today's currency.

Using himself as its model, Eaton's personal director, Ivor Lewis, who was a talented artist as well as an actor, sculpted a life-sized replica of a victorious soldier dressed in battle gear, eyes gazing rapturously toward the heavens. The statue was placed in front of Toronto's City Hall as an incentive for people to invest in war bonds. Two duplicates were placed inside the store.

Eaton's in-store magazines breathlessly chronicled soldiers' heroics. An issue of *Flash* included a description of the success achieved on April 23, 1918, by Winnipeg elevator inspector Teddy Grimes, who served on board the Royal Navy vessel, the HMS *Vindictive*. The *Vindictive* had sailed into Zeebrugge Harbour on the Belgian Coast and blown up fortifications on the Mole, a strongpoint in the harbour, where German submarines were docked. When the *Vindictive* was later sunk in battle, Grimes escaped on a small motor craft. Despite his close call, Grimes served on board a series of destroyer flotillas located in the Middle East.[2]

Servicemens' letters were circulated to each department head, often before reaching the desk of John Craig Eaton himself. On October 25, 1915, Staff-Sergeant George Fisher wrote a letter entitled "Somewhere in France," as he sat cross-legged in his tent, which was then being buffeted by gales of wind and rain. Fisher had lit a handful of candles to warm the pot that contained coffee sent in a tuck box by his sergeant's mother, along with some biscuits and fruit. The letter is suffused with the melancholy awareness that such pleasures were only too transitory. Barred from divulging information about military manoeuvres, Fisher nevertheless alluded to the dangers awaiting him when he wrote:

Tonight's the night! And we shall all wear our rose-coloured glasses and everything will take on a gay and festive appearance and everybody merry and bright. We shan't notice the gale, or the rain-soaked canvas, or the rumble of guns; nor give a thought to

the morrow with its rotten old 5:30 a.m. reveille; as Omar says:
– 'What boots it to repeat, how time is slipping underneath our
feet, Unborn To-morrow, and dead Yesterday, Why fret about
them if Today be sweet?'[3]

As Fisher sat writing in his tent, ghostlike troops of Canadian,
English, Scottish, Irish, and Welsh soldiers enveloped in a fog as thick as
soup marched whistling towards their trenches. "Are we downhearted?"
one soldier shouted. "NO!" the group roared. "Splendid is the only
word for them,"[4] Fisher wrote.

To get from one destination to another, Fisher and his fellow soldiers
rode in dilapidated cattle trucks, using bags of tent pegs as pillows.
Breakfast was beef jerky and "cast-iron biscuits washed down with iced
tea." The portion of bottled water not drunk was used for spot showers.
"Our camp is situated on a hill and there isn't a tree within sight, no
shelter at all, and you can imagine the icy blasts uttered as well as felt,"
Fisher explained.[5]

Many servicemen who were wounded in battle recovered in convalescent hospitals in England. While in hospital, servicemen regularly
received letters and packages sent to them by members of the Eaton
Girls' Club. The Eaton Girls' Club, which had functioned primarily as
a recreational program for Eaton's female employees, sprang into
action, raising money to send food and clothing to servicemen stationed
overseas during the First World War.

One Australian soldier spent some of his happiest days recuperating
at the Ontario Military Hospital, located just outside London, where
he played cards sent to him by Eaton Girls' Club members and wrote
letters home using stationery also sent to him by the club. Soon after
being airlifted back to Australia in February 1917, he wrote the hospital staff, offering his thanks. "I have been asked since returning if I had
received good treatment and my reply has been, that, were I a million-
aire, it would be impossible for me to have more than was given to me
by your people."[6]

For John Craig Eaton, the war became even more personal with the
Halifax Explosion that occurred on December 6, 1917. The explosion
would remain the most violent ever, until the bombing of Hiroshima
in 1945.

A French munitions ship, the *Mont Blanc*, had sailed into Halifax Harbour to join a convoy supplying munitions to the Allies in France. On board were tons of explosives, including TNT, picric acid, and gun cotton. At the same time that the *Mont Blanc* was arriving, a Norwegian ship named the *Imo* was setting off to New York to pick up relief supplies for Belgium. In the narrowest region of the harbour, the two ships collided. Their steel bows scraped against each other as they slowly parted, igniting sparks which blew up the contents of the *Mont Blanc*. Halifax's industrial North End was levelled, after which a tidal wave submerged everything in its path, including houses and churches. Fires quickly destroyed what the blast, or the water, didn't.

Over two thousand people died in the Halifax explosion, with nine thousand more wounded, some horribly. Residents were blinded when glass from shattered windows flew into their eyes. The blast's reverberations were heard all the way to Charlottetown.

On December 9, John Craig boarded his personal train the *Eatonia II*, bound for Halifax. Built by the Pullman Company, the *Eatonia II* contained a kitchen stove, a chesterfield, two bedroom chairs, four lounge chairs, a bed, and various light fixtures. It also featured uninterrupted phone service. At each station, a specially fitted roll of wire could be unreeled to attach the car's telephones to land lines. After John Craig's death, such illustrious passengers as Winston Churchill, President Roosevelt, and, in 1939, King George VI and Queen Elizabeth, used the train.

Ten department heads accompanied John Craig on the *Eatonia II*'s journey, separate railway cars carrying two doctors, nurses, and other personnel. One car was loaded with blankets, clothing, and footwear. Victims who approached the train when it arrived in Halifax on the morning of December 12 received supplies. At four in the morning, one man, who had just finished digging the bodies of his wife and four children from the rubble of his home, appeared at the train looking for clothes. "I never saw Sir John cry before," an associate said. "He was almost dead with exhaustion himself, but he spent an hour outfitting that poor, sad man."[7] In all, Eaton's donated $66,000 worth of goods. Afterward John Craig's wife, Flora McCrea, had pins produced, inscribed with the initials E.W.S. (Eaton Welfare Service) on the front, and the back read "Halifax Relief, December, 1917."

Eatonia train. Sir John Craig Eaton transported supplies to victims of the Halifax explosion using this train, 1917. The sight of the wounded was so dramatic, it moved him to tears.

Interior of Eatonia train bedroom showing luxurious fittings.

To mark the signing of the Armistice of the First World War on November 11, 1918, John Craig sounded his store's electronic alarm, which roused people for miles around. "At first we didn't know what it was," recalled one startled customer. Eaton's advertising pages in all major newspapers were devoted to marking the end of the war.

On June 24, 1919, Eaton's employees threw a celebration to thank John Craig, not just for his contributions during the war, but also for deciding to give them Saturday afternoons off year-round, with full Saturdays off in July and August. Together the employees at the event pooled enough money to subsidize an X-ray wing at the Hospital for Sick Children in Sir John Craig's name. A cot, also purchased by the staff and christened the "Sir John Cot," was also donated to the wing.

"I am proud of the employees for doing this themselves," John Craig wrote in a letter to the trustees of the hospital. "It was entirely their own idea and they are paying the cost in full, which amounts to approximately $20,000."[8]

And still the gifts kept coming. To mark Eaton's fiftieth anniversary, on December 8, 1919, Eaton's employees donated a bronze statue of Timothy Eaton, designed by Ivor Lewis, to the Toronto store. A duplicate was given to the Winnipeg store. The statues, depicting Timothy as a magisterial figure, would soon become literal touchstones, with customers rubbing Timothy's shoe for good luck.

On December 20, 1919, Sir John Craig returned the employees' generosity by hosting a dinner on the third floor of the Queen Street store. Fifteen hundred Eatonians, many of them severely injured by poison gas or flying shrapnel, raised their combined voices in rousing renditions of "The Maple Leaf Forever," "The Boys of the Old Brigade," and "Drink to Me Only with Thine Eyes," before speeches began.

One of the first to speak was Toronto mayor T. L. Church, who stirred the assembled with a speech in praise of John Craig Eaton in particular, and the legacy of the Eaton's empire in general. He began by invoking the ghost of the father of all fathers, Timothy, and his wife, Margaret, who, though infirm, had also contributed to the war effort by greeting troops as they returned home. There were few dry eyes as Church intoned:

Timothy Eaton lives in the hearts and minds of every man, woman and child. He was king of this great enterprise; had a kingdom of his own. I wish you returned men could have seen that noble woman, the queen-mother of these boys, Mrs. Timothy Eaton, while you men were away; I have seen her at the depot when returned men were coming home, many without arms or limbs and you have no idea how she worshipped you men, how she thought about you, how she dreamed about you, and how she was with you in spirit while you were over in Flanders and France, fighting in the most terrible war in the world's history. Now, the queen mother is with you, and although the king is dead, there is a King reigning in his stead; I refer to your great host tonight, that beloved man Sir John Eaton.[9]

To honour the dead, Eaton's requisitioned three plaques, one for the Toronto, one for the Winnipeg, and one for the Montreal store. Margaret Eaton officiated at the Toronto unveiling of the plaque honouring the 315 Eatonians killed in the war. The ceremony took place at 5:30 p.m., after all the customers had left the store.

In return for their statue, the Winnipeg store's veterans got together and presented Sir John Craig with an oil painting entitled "Surrender of the German Fleet," by Frank O. Salisbury, which was paid for by donations collected among employees.

There were few paroxysms of grief more acute than those suffered by employees upon hearing of the premature death from pneumonia of Sir John Craig Eaton on March 30, 1922. The entire country was plunged into mourning and expressions of sympathy poured in from coast to coast. Tens of thousands of employees from the Toronto store crowded St. Clair Avenue in front of Timothy Eaton Memorial Church, where the funeral was conducted.

The appointment of R. Y. Eaton as president to succeed his cousin John Craig was met with much objection on the part of the tabloid press, who felt that the R. Y. faction had conspired to steal the presidency from John Craig's more deserving sons. However, rather than being Machiavellian, the board was merely acting on a condition in John Craig's will, stipulating that whichever son succeeded him as president had to be at least twenty-seven years old. When Sir John Craig died, his eldest son, Timothy Craig, was only nineteen, and uninterested in assuming responsibility for the store. John Craig's second-eldest son, John David, was only thirteen. As a result, the only candidate for succession was R. Y.

R. Y. had got his start in the organization by working in European buying offices shortly before the turn of the century, and he knew the retail business well. However, his stern disposition was in direct contrast to that of the affable and charismatic John Craig.

*June 24, 1919, presentation to Sir John Craig Eaton of
X-ray cot for Sick Children's Hospital, in honour of
Saturday half-day holidays and employee benefits.*

*Ivor Lewis and staff made a statue of Timothy Eaton
in 1919 to mark the fiftieth anniversary of the store.*

Taciturn as he might have been, however, during his term as a president from 1922 to 1942, R. Y. expanded the Eaton's empire at an accelerated rate. Among the stores R. Y. opened was the Montreal store in 1926, the Hamilton store in 1927, the Moncton store in 1927, the Halifax store in 1928, and the Toronto College Street store in 1930.

———◼———

Like most war-weary Canadians, including Eatonians, R. Y. denied the threat of a Second World War until the last moment. War would again force the government to forbid trade with any country it viewed as allied with Germany.

One Eatonian will never forget September 3, 1939, the exact day war was declared on Germany by Britain and France. Doreen O'Dell worked in the Winnipeg store children's department. Her husband, Phil, worked in the boy's clothing department. On the morning of September 3, Doreen's mother, Mrs. Caine, who was in England on family business, was instructed to catch the first boat heading for Canada immediately. "It was my mother's misfortune to get a berth on the SS *Athenia*," Doreen recalls. Less than two hundred miles west of the Hebridean coast, a German U-boat torpedoed the liner. Just hours after the incident, Britain and France officially declared war on Germany.

As soon as he heard of the *Athenia*'s fate, Winnipeg Store Manager B. C. Scrivner sent Doreen home from work to await news of her mother. For two days, Doreen and her brother kept vigil by the radio, but it was only on Eaton's wire service that Doreen finally heard her mother's name listed as one of the survivors.

Mrs. Caine had drifted in a lifeboat for seven hours before being rescued by the Swedish luxury liner the *Southern Cross*. Within a day, Caine was transferred to the American freighter the *City of Flint*, which was then sailing for New York City. Because so many of its passengers were Canadians, however, the ship changed course and docked in Halifax, where a Red Cross train met the Canadian survivors of the *Athenia*.

Eaton's Halifax store manager rushed to the dock to meet Mrs. Caine, who emerged from her ordeal covered in deep cuts and bruises from climbing up and down rope ladders; her clothes were soiled with oil and water. The manager took her to his home for the night, and the next day drove her to the Eaton's store, where he helped her choose new

Christmas card sent to staff by
Lady Eaton in 1922, the year of
Sir John Craig Eaton's death.

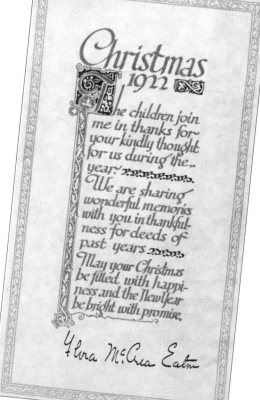

Christmas
1922

The children join
me in thanks for
your kindly thought
for us during the
year. We are sharing
wonderful memories
with you in thankful-
ness for deeds of
past years May your Christmas
be filled with happi-
ness and the New Year
be bright with promise.

Flora McCrea Eaton

clothes, free of charge. Later, he escorted her to the store's beauty salon, where she got her hair styled and set.

"They treated her with outstanding kindness, and, although we had to wait two extra days to see her, we were so grateful for the care and attention she received. All because we were part of the 'Eaton Family,'"[10] says Doreen.

In addition to Mrs. Caine, the list of Eatonians on board the *Athenia* also included Miss Nan Shephard of the Hosiery Department, as well as two employees listed as missing, a Mrs. Annie Waterman and a Mrs. Paul Bishop.

R. Y. Eaton personally attempted to find out the whereabouts of Shephard, Waterman, and Bishop. He telephoned an Eaton's employee in Halifax, who, accompanied by two members of his staff, went down to the dock following the arrival of the *City of Flint* and questioned people for over three hours, but none knew where the three women were.

On October 12, 1939, forced to abandon hope, R. Y. Eaton sent a letter of condolence to the bereaved families. Soon after, he asked if the government was going to seek reparations for the people lost on the ship, but discovered it did not intend to pursue any claims. Individuals were therefore forced to seek reparations, either individually or collectively.

Once war was formally declared by Canada on September 10, 1939, Eaton's actively advocated conscription and, consistent with their position during the First World War, viewed as disloyal any Canadian not willing to volunteer for service.

For several weeks, the Canadian government equivocated about sending troops overseas, a situation that infuriated R. Y., who chalked it up to the government's worry that Francophones, who saw the war as an English–German conflict, would not serve. While it could never be said that French Canadians unanimously supported either the First or Second World War in spirit, they did eventually send troops, most notably after the 1941 bombing of Pearl Harbor, which brought the war tangibly closer to home.

Shortly after the official outbreak of war, J. J. Vaughan, Eaton's treasurer, privately admitted to R. Y. Eaton that he was terrified about Eaton's ability to sustain the same subsidized military payment plan the company had implemented during the First World War. Vaughan noted that the First World War had cost Eaton's approximately $1,000 per man for those who enlisted voluntarily, and $2,200,000 for something over 2,000 men. "The staff is much larger now," noted Vaughan, "and the enlistments are likely to be much more. On the other side our profits – net after taxes, are not as much."[11]

In spite of Vaughan's fears, R. Y. Eaton stipulated that married men serving in the war would receive whatever sums would, in addition to their military pay, bring them up to their original full wages, while single men would receive two-thirds of their wages. In the beginning, there was no guarantee of reinstatement after the war, since the company worried that those who returned physically or mentally unfit might demand reinstatement on the basis of a company promise. In the end, however, almost every Eaton's staff member would be reinstated, due to a government act passed in 1942.

Introduced by King George VI on August 1, 1942, the Reinstatement in Civil Employment Act stipulated that all companies were required to reinstate each discharged member of the military in their previous job, or a position consistent with the one they had held before serving in the war. If employers violated this clause, they had to prove that the employee was physically or mentally incapable of performing work under the employer's service.

To complement the 1942 act, Eaton's directors devised a standard policy to apply to all returning servicemen. The policy required that every Eaton's employee honourably discharged from the navy, army, air force, or merchant marine who desired re-employment by the company was entitled to the same (or an equivalent) position and pay as he had before he left, or the pay that was now being distributed for the same job. If a soldier was handicapped during war service and couldn't qualify immediately for employment, he was asked to seek government training to prepare him for his return.

Eaton's also ensured that servicemen who were undergoing training during the war also received subsidized payments. One of these was Eaton's drapery salesman Reg Collins. Collins recalls what was said to him at the sign-in table in the enlistment office. "The enlistment officer told me, 'When you sign your service document, you're no longer on one side of the table, you're on the other. You won't be Reg Collins any more. You'll be a number. Now you are 219665.'"

During the first few months of his training, Collins, a newlywed with a pregnant wife at home, continued to work at Eaton's College Street store. Each day after leaving work at 3:30, he went directly to Central

Technical School to learn how to assemble aircraft gadgets. Later, he was transferred to the Canadian National Exhibition grounds, where he bunked in a building formerly used to stable cows.

Every morning Collins and his fellow trainees marched in drills, followed by other gruelling exercises. After his training at the CNE, Collins went to St. Thomas, Ontario, to study aircraft mechanics. The building used to house trainees had once been a mental institution. Zigzag bars covered the windows, prompting Collins and his buddies to joke, "When the bars go straight, we'll be getting out."

———■———

In her capacity as honorary president of the Ladies' War Auxiliary, formed in 1939 as a branch of the Eaton Girls' Club, Flora McCrea Eaton raised money for servicemen. After men decided to join the auxiliary, the name Ladies War Auxiliary was changed to the Eaton's Employees' War Auxiliary.

King Karnival held at Flora McCrea Eaton's estate, King City.
Darts were thrown at images of Hitler and Mussolini.

Lady Eaton opened her home, Eaton Hall, to a series of special fundraising and sports events during the war years. One of the more popular games of the day was called "Darts for the Axis," in which darts were thrown at caricatures of Hitler, Mussolini, and Hirohito. Other fundraising events took place in the stores themselves.

Among the most popular fundraising activities for women were "sockey" tournaments, an indoor version of hockey, played with tennis balls and brooms instead of pucks and sticks. The game was so named because newspapermen did not believe it rose to the level of the "manly" sport of hockey. In-store raffles were also held, in which home-baked goods and knitted and hand-sewn garments were distributed as prizes.

There were very few indignities that female civilians wouldn't endure to raise money for the cause. A *Daily Star* article of June 24, 1942, described a carnival held at Casa Loma that included a "ringer" game.

> Blending with the mellow atmosphere of the castle, Eaton girls in vintage clothing, circulated through the crowd spreading good cheer as well as a few packages of nuts, candy and knick-knacks. Girls from the mail order department are planning a "Ringer Girl" game, which will give the customer a chance to try to ring the girl's leg with a hoop. The game is expected to be very popular with the uniformed men.[12]

Lady Eaton emphatically supported the idea of women assuming men's jobs in factories and munitions plants during the war, and donated use of the seventh-floor auditorium of the College Street store as a recruitment centre for the National Selection Services. The need for women workers was so great that the Selection Services even called upon the assistance of married women with children, and established nurseries in factories where the women worked.

The presence of married women working in the stores did not, however, always sit well with single women, who felt that many of the women were merely working as a "hobby," or as a means to supplement their already-healthy bank accounts.

Winnipeg employee Charlotte Lepp, then a single women in her early twenties, would have preferred to see the bulk of married women remain at home during the war. "We were loaded with women that we knew had money stored away for the rest of their lives and were going to work, and if they're keeping work from the young people, that is wrong."[13]

In a January 23, 1943, interview with Lillian Gibbons of the *Winnipeg Free Press*, Lady Eaton responded to the question of whether women would have to leave the company after the war to make room for returning men: "Why should they? They haven't in Russia," she shot back. Her answer was perhaps naive since that is exactly what happened.

The reality was that performing men's jobs provided a mixed blessing for women. While it no doubt gave them their first sense of independent accomplishment, it also reminded them how mundane their previous jobs had been. In spite of Lady Eaton's bravado, most of Eaton's female employees who performed men's jobs during the war either found themselves without jobs or were demoted to poorer-paying positions once the men returned from the service.

A woman who worked in the Winnipeg mail-order division during the 1940s reveals, "I went in with the understanding that I was taking a man's job who had left for the service, and I would be let out, so I knew that was going to happen at the end of the war."[14]

Eatonian males unfit for service also sought ways to help the war effort. A young, newly married man sent a letter offering to provide

Winnipeg delivery drivers planted a victory garden to compensate for the shortage of fresh produce during the Second World War.

in-store music during shopping hours "similar to music being played at American stores like Macy's." Another young man, whose club foot made him unfit for serving in the military, sought work in 1942 as a commercial artist. He had three years of training at the Ontario College of Art, and had worked for a year at the *Evening Telegram*, retouching and drawing cartoons.

Because so many Canadian farmers had gone to war, there was a desperate need to replace them. As a result, the government allowed a certain number of European refugees, including some Germans, into the country to work on farms in the early 1940s. Some of the German refugees attempted to obtain work at Eaton's, but were turned down because of the controversy their presence might stir up. Resentment among Eaton's German, Austrian, and Italian employees, even long-standing ones, ran high. Often friendships were broken, as bitter cultural factionalism set in.

"Enemy Aliens" – as they were officially referred to by the federal government – who had not received naturalization status were dismissed. By law, lists of the names of all German and Italian employees had to be compiled by the company and forwarded to the RCMP. Other employees' activities were monitored through in-store spies. A government proclamation required all aliens to register and report monthly to the RCMP. Any real or perceived Nazi sympathy would result in immediate dismissal and perhaps banishment to one of the internment camps located in every province. On the recommendation of police officials, Eaton's took no action against naturalized German employees unless their conduct created undesirable conditions throughout the store.

Three employees, one a German kitchen worker in Toronto, the other two Austrian-born Montreal factory workers, were discovered to be without naturalization papers. Since they were long-time employees, Eaton's made an exception and told all three to apply to the RCMP for parole before permitting them work again. Twelve German and three Austrian employees in Winnipeg were also told that, once they registered with the RCMP, they could continue to work at Eaton's, with the exception of one, whom the government interned shortly after the declaration of war. The Moncton, Halifax, Sydney, and Glace Bay stores indicated that no un-naturalized foreigners worked for them.

In September 1939, Eaton's risked attracting negative publicity when a thirty-seven-year-old German man named Otto Zwahl was hired to work as a butcher and sausage maker in Toronto's Queen Street store. With manpower being so scarce, it was virtually impossible to find a man of any other nationality who possessed Zwahl's skills.

It wasn't long before the Toronto tabloid *Hush* made note of Zwahl's employment. In an October 7, 1939, story entitled "Eaton's Hires Nazis," the tabloid accused an Eaton's "sausage-maker," clearly a description of Zwahl, of uttering pro-Nazi statements to co-workers. The source of the story was never revealed.

The article so infuriated R. Y. Eaton that he consulted his lawyers about suing the paper for libel, and only dropped the idea when persuaded that libel was not only difficult to prove but that the result would simply increase the circulation of the paper. Instead, Eaton's decided to fire Zwahl, without cause, basing their objection to his continued employment on the international situation regarding the employment of Germans. Since he had assured Eaton's that he was a Canadian citizen before being hired, Zwahl knew that he was being made into a scapegoat so Eaton's could avoid the kind of bad publicity they had received in *Hush*. Zwahl, who had a wife and young son to support, was embittered by the experience.

Barely a month after his termination from Eaton's, still bruised by the *Hush* story, Zwahl wrote a letter of application in response to a blind employment ad that appeared in the *Montreal Star*. He listed Eaton's as his previous place of employment and added that the only reason he was fired was because "as a German born, but since 5 years naturalized Canadian, I had to leave on account of the International situation, though I have never talked or had any arguments about politics. I am referring to this here, because if you Sir have the same opinion, it would save time and disappoint [sic] on both sides."[15]

Unluckily for Zwahl, the blind ad he responded to had been placed by none other than Eaton's itself. As soon as Eaton's received Zwahl's application, they wrote him back, stressing that his dismissal had nothing to do with any prejudice against his nationality. Zwahl didn't buy it, however, and wrote a scathing letter to management insisting that "if I would have been a Nazi sympathizer, I would be in the concentration camp in Kingston, as are many."[16]

The *Hush* story continued to prey on R. Y.'s mind. While dropping the idea of pursuing a legal action, he encouraged government officials to muzzle the tabloids. In a *Toronto Telegram* article, dated

November 6, 1939, Ontario Attorney-General Gordon D. Conant announced that he intended to file injunctions with the province's Supreme Court restraining tabloids of the day, including *Hush*, *Weekender*, *Tattler*, *Flash*, and *Scoop*, and any other newspaper, publication, pamphlet, magazine, periodical, or other printed matter, from publishing any more articles deemed "obscene, immoral or otherwise injurious to public morals."[17]

Earlier in the week, Conant's representatives had met with provincial and city police representatives at Queen's Park in Toronto to discuss the topic of filthy literature. "We will go as far as the law will allow," Conant pledged in invoking his war against the tabloids, a declaration that was eventually swept into the dustbin of history due to the continuing public demand for such "literature." In 1939, circulation figures for *Scoop* alone reached forty-two thousand.

Only the negative publicity surrounding Eaton's employee Alfredo Bassonesi eclipsed that of Zwahl. Unlike Zwahl, however, Bassonesi was a long-time employee, had an impeccable work record, and was a favourite of Lady Eaton.

Italian by birth, Bassonesi gained employment in Eaton's furniture department in 1924. He became not only one of their top furniture salesmen, but a section head. On June 10, 1940, the very day war was declared against Italy by Canada, Bassonesi, along with hundreds of Italian employees from other stores, was detained first at Toronto's Exhibition Centre, then moved to the Petawawa, Ontario, internment camp. The reason for Bassonesi's detainment was anti-British sentiments he was alleged to have made to other Eaton's employees, as well as to officials, upon his detainment at Exhibition Place.

Because Bassonesi was never placed under formal arrest, he immediately began writing increasingly exasperated letters to members of Eaton's management, including the personnel director, Ivor Lewis, as well as the general manager, O. D. Vaughan. In every letter Bassonesi implored them to prevail upon authorities to release him from Petawawa.

In July, Bassonesi's wife visited Ivor Lewis to plead her husband's cause further. Lewis informed her that Eaton's was helpless to intercede, but suggested that, to find a resolution to her financial crisis, she should contact the Custodian of Alien Property, who handled such matters. In a letter to Mr. Bassonesi, Vaughan assured him that, should his wife fail to find satisfactory financial resolution to her problems through the government, Eaton's would endeavour to help her "in any way which seems possible."[18]

The Bassonesi saga only became truly noteworthy, however, when Lady Eaton personally enlisted Ivor Lewis to take up the case, worrying that, if Eaton's did not reinstate Bassonesi, it would make Bassonesi bitter toward Canada and Canadians. In December 1940, Bassonesi was freed, though it would be several more months and take several more despairing letters to Vaughan before he was reinstated in the furniture department in spring 1941.

Almost immediately, Canada's tabloid press assailed Flora McCrea for her guardian-angel-like intercession in Bassonesi's case, arising from what they implied were her pro-Fascist sympathies. "Lady Eaton Italian Intern Back on Job," the March 15, 1941, *Hush* headline blared, adding:

> It is said that Eaton's directors are up in arms over the whole thing. But what are they to do about it? Lady Flora is the big boss now, and she can tell them all where to go if they are dissatisfied. Gradually the story is spreading. It is common talk in the City Hall. Civic employees, Masons, Orangemen – thousands of loyal Canadian citizens – express disgust and openly declare that they will boycott Eaton's.

The article further reminded readers of statements made by Flora McCrea in an infamous August 16, 1930, interview with the *Toronto Star*. Opining on a wide variety of topics, including music, people, and travel, Lady Eaton had waxed rhapsodic about the wonders of Italy, where she owned a summer villa, as well as about the personal magnetism and charm of Benito Mussolini, whom she admired for having "the most beautiful smile" and a "fearless" personality. Impressed by his bearing during a military parade, Flora McCrea concluded that Mussolini was "a man who knew what he was going to do and was not to be swerved to right or left."

In language sure to make Monday-morning quarterbackers cringe, Flora McCrea recommended that those who accused Mussolini of tyrannizing his people "should be shot." In her opinion, Mussolini had "saved not only Italy but the whole of Europe from Bolshevism and had made the cities and towns cleaner and the people more prosperous and contented. There were no beggars to be seen now compared with those of some years ago,"[19] she noted.

Despite the drubbing Flora McCrea received in the popular press, she valiantly forged ahead with her War Auxiliary work. In 1940, the Auxiliary published a report of the progress made during its first year of operation. It noted that a large number of Eaton's girls were learning formerly exclusive male trades such as motor-vehicle mechanics, sponsored by corporations like Ford and General Motors. Others completed St. John's Ambulance Association training, and Red Cross first-aid courses, or took air-raid precautions courses, which included map-reading and rifle practice.

The 1940 report featured a letter from an Auxiliary worker based in Cheyne Hospital in Chelsea, England. Describing the horrendous deprivations suffered by refugee families who had fled their war-ravaged homelands, the letter's author beseeched Eatonians to donate small items such as blanket ends to use for coat lining and children's underwear, as well as felt hats to make children's slippers. Even the smallest items, down to buttons and balls of wool, became invaluable. The worker wrote:

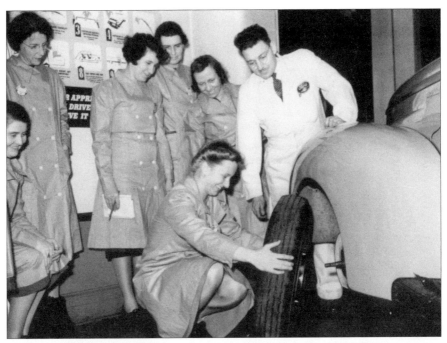

Mechanics course for women, 1940. During the Second World War women were desperately needed to fill men's jobs.

You are asking is there anything you can send for the Refugee work. May I have the good bits out of everyone's old towels? They are useful for so many things – for the babies, for the children's face cloths, – even for use in the kitchens in the houses we have taken over for our refugee families. We are perpetually short of "bits" like that, and we have so many babies. I didn't really know before what "Destitute" meant. Now I've learnt that it's not having a bit of rag to wash your baby with, or the napkins to put on him or a towel to dry your hands on. "Destitution" means not having little things – and strangely enough, they are the hardest to get! I had been running Cheyne hospital for weeks before I remembered about toothbrushes before night. We suffer daily and nightly bombardment, which makes me think that silence must be the most precious gift in the world. We have hurried meals and shortened hours of sleep. We have no theatres and precious little relaxation of any sort, but still we are carrying on. Sometimes I forget for a long time that we are at War, or why, or with whom, there is nothing left but the effort to relieve suffering.[20]

By the early 1940s, the number of employable single women in Canada was so low that National Selective Services continued to canvass

Gloria Swanson participates in Eaton's Victory Loan Drive (1939–45).

for married women with children. Those who chose to work were urged by Flora McCrea to donate as much of their salaries as possible toward the purchase of Victory Bonds, a recommendation that was also castigated by the tabloids, who stated: "One thousand dollars means less in the financial economy of Lady Eaton than 25 cents does to an average housewife or an average clerk in the Eaton store. By what right, then, moral or otherwise, does she advise Canadians to invest in War Savings Certificates?"[21]

Ignoring the criticism, on the first and second Sunday of every September, Flora McCrea Eaton held fundraising lunches at sprawling Eaton Hall. The house served as a second home for refugee children sent to Canada during the worst of Britain's bombing. It was also opened up to servicemen on leave. By 1944, Flora McCrea invited the Royal Canadian Navy to use the home as a convalescent hospital for over seventy wounded sailors. On another occasion a serviceman who attended a party at the hall recalls that, no matter how minor a veteran's status in the organization, he was individually announced at the head of a red carpet. "They made you feel like a king, there was no question about it," he says.

The work of Eatonians in war canteens was stellar. Lady Eaton was a great admirer of Mrs. Schuyler Snively, who inaugurated the first Active Service Canteen in Toronto in November 1939. The canteen eventually catered to more than three million men of the navies, armies, air forces, and merchant marines of British and Allied countries. It served as a model for all other canteens operating not just across Canada, but also further afield. The use of books, sports equipment, and board games were free in canteens. Cigarettes and soft drinks cost only nominal sums.

The first canteen employed five workers; within three years the staff had grown to five thousand workers, serving over seventy thousand servicemen per month. Snively also oversaw the implementation and operation of recreation centres for troops in training, complete with a stage, where a guest artist could sing or play the piano. Girls were asked to dance and play card games and quizzes with the servicemen. Wives and girlfriends were also welcome at the canteens.

One unidentified soldier spontaneously composed a poem in pencil on a napkin and left it on a table where a canteen worker found it and forwarded it to Lady Eaton. Lady Eaton subsequently forwarded it to Major General Leo R. LaFlèche DSO, Minister of National War Services in Ottawa, to illustrate how well the canteen was regarded by service-men. The soldier had written:

> I dropped into the A.S.C.
> For a bite and to rest a while –
> The first thing that greeted me
> Was a friendly word and a smile.
>
> There's a warm and comfortable feeling
> For us who are far from home
> No friendlier place will we find
> Wherever our steps may roam.
>
> I'm sure that you who serve,
> Without thought of renown –
> Some day will be rewarded
> With a beautiful golden crown.[22]

Helen Buik, the manager of restaurants for Eaton's College Street store, had enlisted in April 1942 and became a flight officer in the RCAF,

Inside an Eaton War Auxiliary's Active Service canteen

along with Kathleen Jeffs, the head of Eaton's Montreal restaurant service, who also became an RCAF flight officer. Both women raised servicemen's morale by planning variable menus that served well-seasoned and nourishing food. The women also ensured that mess halls within canteens were well-aired and clean.

Predictably, the seamier side of canteen life was explored by the tabloid newspapers of the day. The April 15, 1941, edition of *Hush* trumpeted the dangers active servicemen faced from the "loose women" who lay in wait just outside the canteen's gates. The paper noted that any active serviceman who had been "out" with a woman during his period of leave was required to report to his medical officer for precautionary treatment immediately on his return to barracks, and that failure to do so was a military offence.

The second plague afflicting servicemen in training, as identified by *Hush*, was the commercial racketeers who were "hanging around Salvation Army and YMCA canteens, charging enlisted men inflated prices for goods." Camp Borden in Ontario was singled out as a hotbed of graft.

Hush suspected that a few unsavoury firms run by "Christian" racketeers were paying off camp employees to look the other way as they orchestrated the sale of worthless junk at twice the normal cost. As evidence, the paper cited the fact that ladies' compacts, for sale in Toronto for $1.59, cost $2.50 in Camp Borden, while cushion covers with crests on them, costing 50¢ in Toronto, were $1.50 at Camp Borden. "On pay day, their first impulse is to buy something to send to mother, wife, or kiddies. Any salesman who is privileged to approach them may reasonably count on making some sales,"[23] the paper said.

Men stationed in the camps were occasionally called upon to pose for Victory Bond posters, or to appear at other public-relations events. To accomplish the dual objective of raising the profile of Eaton's and supporting the war effort on November 11, 1940, to mark the armistice of the First World War, a member of Toronto's Irish Regiment and employee of Eaton's, who was stationed at Camp Borden, sounded the last post on his bugle over the grave of Timothy Eaton.

On the evening of September 10, 1939, Canada's first evening at war, members of Eaton's volunteer acting troupe, the "Masquers," met in the College Street store to plan upcoming performances for troops in training. The troupe was originally formed in 1918 under the name "The Eaton's Players," and was composed entirely of current and former employees of the Toronto and Winnipeg Eaton's stores. Performances had been held yearly at the Dominion Drama Festival, where, in 1937, the group won the Bessborough Trophy in a field of five hundred different troupes from across Canada. In 1939, the troupe included twenty-one elevator girls, a deliveryman, two top executives, and a company electrician.

To kick off their fundraising tour in September 1939, the Masquers performed the plays *The Guardsman* and *The Silver Cord* at various auditoriums throughout Toronto. Over the course of the war, the Masquers would cumulatively travel over 40,000 miles and give over 300 performances for Eaton's troops in training camps across Canada and Europe. After each performance, the members passed around a hat to collect donations for the Eaton's Employees' War Auxiliary.

Masquer Ivor Lewis, designer of the Victory Bond statue that stood in front of Toronto City Hall during the First World War and the Timothy Eaton statue donated to the store by employees in 1919, won a Dominion best actor award in 1936 as "Lark" in *Napoleon Crossing the Rockies*, which was performed at Toronto's Arts and Letters Club. Eaton's resident magician, Johnny Giordmaine, was a member of the troupe; later on it also included radio and TV personality Bill Walker.

Eaton's always applauded its success stories. A jewellery saleswoman, Janet Nagy, would leave the Masquers in 1946 to train at the Royal Academy of Dramatic Art in England, and eventually played opposite Orson Welles in the *Harry Lime* radio series. Later, Nagy starred in films such as *Meet the Navy*, and *I Was a Male War Bride*, co-starring Cary Grant.

In a 1945 issue of the Montreal in-store magazine *Entre Nous*, a store employee, who had travelled all across Europe entertaining troops with the Masquers, provided verbal images of some of the countries she had visited. In Ghent, Belgium, she had walked through fish stalls. In Sluis, Holland, she had photographed the ruins of demolished churches. In one church she attempted to play the damaged organ, and noted that the only object remaining untouched was the crucifix hanging by the altar. In Ypres, meanwhile, she admired the Memorial Arch, erected in tribute to the men who served in the First World War.

———■———

In the anxious days leading up to the signing of the Armistice between the Allies and Germans, which ended the war in Europe, Eaton's attempted to mobilize its Security Department to be on guard against overzealous revellers. Employees were instructed to remove all valuable merchandise from the counters and windows, store all furs in safety vaults, and leave the stores with a minimum of commotion.

When the news finally flashed in Toronto at 8:45 a.m., May 7, 1945, that Germany had categorically surrendered, all calm preplanning went out the window as Eaton's employees dashed, whooping and hollering, through the store. Abandoning all their best-laid plans for decorum, they surged toward the exits and onto the street.

Caught up in the excitement, employees of Toronto's Merchandise Display department hastily assembled a series of cardboard-cutout figures of Mussolini, Hirohito, and Hitler, which were cartwheeled over the heads of the jubilant crowd before finally being torn to pieces. Victory Loan flags, which had hung from the windows of the Queen Street, College Street, Montreal, and Winnipeg stores, were hastily dismantled and replaced with victory flags that had been created by the Merchandise Display department in the weeks leading up to the event. Hundreds of huge flags hung from windows, symbolizing Eaton's patriotism. One employee cut so much fabric for use in these flags that she temporarily lost the use of the muscles in her right arm.

Inside the Queen Street store, elevators were switched to down-traffic only to handle the crush of ecstatic employees who surged towards street level. Outgoing telephone calls were prohibited. Delivery-truck drivers on their routes were signalled to return to their warehouses.

A mass of humanity congealed around the steps of Toronto's City Hall, next to the Toronto store, where they burned an effigy of Hitler made by employees of the Department of Labour. Mayor R. H. Saunders stepped up to a platform to urge the crowd to remember that the war in the Pacific still raged. His words were swiftly drowned out by the music that blared from Victory Loan loudspeakers mounted on trucks parked on the streets.

Damage from Halifax VE *Day riot, May 8, 1945*

Under a clear blue sky, the crowd surged down Bay Street, dancing, waving flags, and singing. Blizzards of paper were tossed from planes circling the sky, while strips of torn paper drifted down from office windows at Yonge and King streets.

Inebriated young women sang and danced. Uniformed servicemen impulsively embraced and kissed them full on the mouth. Commuters wriggled out of streetcar windows and balanced, cheering, on the windowsills.

A piper and a drummer led one boisterous group through the lobby of the King Edward Hotel, right past a wounded soldier, one of his arms shot off above the elbow, the other arm wedged in front of him with splints, from which dangled two canes.

The price of war was even more visible at an almost-empty Union Station, where a reporter noted the presence of two sombre-looking soldiers reading the headlines, their crutches leaning against the bench they were sitting on. Both had only one good leg each.

The Timothy Eaton Memorial Church, which Margaret Eaton had commissioned to be built in honour of her late husband in 1914, was festooned with flags from forty-nine nations hanging from the side and rear galleries. Church bells chimed the anthems of several Allied countries.

That night, the Reverend Dr. D. A. MacLellan officiated at a special evening service.

Similar celebrations occurred in Winnipeg and Montreal, where, as in Toronto, government offices were closed for the day. In all, Eaton's spent $7,500 on decorations for the Winnipeg, Montreal, and Toronto stores and branches to celebrate VE day. With the exception of a few broken windows, the celebrations were incident-free.

The scene in Halifax, however, was less good-natured. Thousands of rioters smashed and ransacked almost every store in the city core. Two buildings were totally burned and gutted. Liquor stores were broken into and vandalized. Every window in the Eaton's store was broken, most of the fixtures and showcases on the main floor were smashed, and thousands of dollars of merchandise were snatched. One eighteen-year-old navy man drank himself to death in the dockyard, while a soldier was beaten to death by throngs of rioters.

The devastation only ended once police imposed an 8 p.m. curfew, which they enforced by driving down the streets in trucks, reading the Riot Act through loudspeakers mounted on the hoods of their vehicles.

When asked for a reason for the violence, one sailor called it "vengeance" for "the way the city had treated them."[24] His complaint was based on what he considered the unreasonably high prices charged for goods and the scarcity of affordable accommodation. When the city-wide melee was over, damage to property was estimated at over $100,000, an amount rivalled only by the destruction caused by the *Mont Blanc*'s explosion.

To ward off similar misadventures, during the anticipated celebrations to mark the August 14, 1945, announcement that Japan had surrendered to the Allies, Eaton's spent $7,190 on barricades and shutters for all its stores. Police were also placed outside all major stores as a deterrent.

However, apart from a guardrail being ripped off the window of the Market Square store in Hamilton, where twelve thousand citizens participated in a street dance, and a stone being thrown through the Sudbury store window, there was no recurrence of the mob violence that had marred some of Halifax's VE-day celebrations.

As soon as the country was assured that peace was truly at hand, John Craig's Eaton's son, John David Eaton, now company president, instructed his staff to begin planning a series of luncheons to honour the contributions made by his company's employees.

The first "large family party," as the hostess, Lady Eaton, referred to it, occurred on September 12, 1946, between 2:30 and 6:00 p.m., at Eaton Hall, where John David Eaton, assisted by R. Y., handed out ten-karat-gold signet rings, which had been designed by Ivor Lewis, to representatives of the twelve military divisions, including the air force, merchant marine, navy, and army. All together, over 2,500 veterans were bused in from Toronto at Eaton's expense for the event. John David's wife, Signy, also attended.

Once the ring ceremony ended, William Palk, who had been a former prisoner-of-war in Germany, spoke. A tribute to the Eaton Employees' War Auxiliary followed. Margot Bodwell, who had served with the Women's Royal Canadian Naval Service during the war, was the next speaker. Lady Eaton then gave an address, after which a sumptuous supper was served. The Royal Canadian Air Force Central Band from Ottawa provided stirring music. The official ceremony lasted slightly over an hour, after which a gunshot signalled the release of hundreds of balloons over the property's man-made lake, named *Jonda* after

Reception for Second World War veterans at Eaton Hall, September 12, 1946

*A mother who lost
her son in the Second
World War meets
Flora McCrae Eaton
after a dinner in
Montreal honouring
Eatonians who
served in the armed
services, 1946.*

*Ceremony for Eaton's Winnipeg war veterans,
Fort Garry Hotel ballroom, September 30, 1946*

T. R. C. Adams
R.C.A.F.

A. C. Aitken
R.C.A.F.

D. Allen
R.C.A.F.

G. K. Armstrong
R.C.A.F.

F. J. Ashford
Q.O.R.

H. G. Baggs
R.C.A.F.

F. Bailie
R.C.E.

Harold Best
R.C.A.F.

W. H. Bowler
R.C.A.F.

G. R. Boxall
R.C.A.F.

B. Brock
R.C.A.F.

J. W. Burns
R.C.A.F.

R. Chisamore
R.W.R.

H. Clarke
R.C.A.F.

R. Cockburn
Royal Reg.

A. Code
C.A.C.

K. Coles
R.C.N.V.R.

J. Cornwall
R.C.E.

Paul Coté
Irish Reg.

M. L. Davis
48th Highlanders

A. Duncan
R.C.N.V.R.

A. R. Dunlea
R.C.A.F.

R. G. Eaton
R.C.A.F.

W. J. Elder
R.C.A.F.

S. Finlayson
R.C.A.F.

E. W. Folliott
R.C.A.F.

G. Freeman
R.C.A.F.

N. L. Glynn
R.C.A.F.

A. Grant
R.C.A.F.

H. A. Grant
R.C.A.F.

J. H. Gunyon
R.C.A.F.

F. Halliday
R.C.A.F.

E. D. Hawkins
R.C.A.F.

R. W. Hisson
R.C.A.F.

S. Japp
Merchant Navy

J. Kavanagh
Q.O.R.

W. D. Larmouth
R.C.A.F.

J. Lawson
Ont. Reg.

J. B. Leitch
R.C.A.F.

A. F. Low
R.C.A.S.C.

D. MacNeill
R.C.A.F.

J. H. McCappin
R.C.N.V.R.

B. W. McClennan
R.C.A.F.

H. P. McKee
R.C.A.F.

R. W. McLaren
R.C.A.F.

H. S. McRae
Q.O.R.

J. Martin
R.C.N.V.R.

J. M. Mitchell
Q.O.R.

A. Morgan
R.C.A.F.

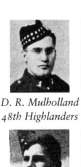

D. R. Mulholland	N. F. Notley	R. E. Nutter	J. Parker	T. A. Partridge	J. Paton	W. Pearce
48th Highlanders	R.C.A.F.	R.C.A.F.	R.C.A.F.	48th Highlanders	R.C.A.F.	48th Highlanders

Harry Pope	D. Roddy	H. H. Sealy	W. J. Sewell	J. K. Shallhorn	F. J. Simpson	R. G. Smith
48th Highlanders	R.C.A.F.	R.C.A.F.	Irish Reg.	R.C.A.	R.C.A.F.	R.C.A.F.

G. R. Somers	A. Standley	A. Stephen	J. J. Stephen	J. W. Stephens	R. B. Stuart	A. Swain
R.C.A.F.	P.L.D.G.	R.C.A.F.	R.C.A.F.	R.C.A.M.C.	R.C.A.F.	R.C.A.F.

W. Tait	W. G. Taylor	G. W. Tompkins	R. C. S. Upton	E. C. Vickers	J. White	J. Winter
R.C.A.F.	R.C.A.F.	R.C.A.F.	R.C.C.S.	R.C.A.F.	R.C.A.F.	R.S.A.S.C.

In the May 21, 1945, issue of Flash *magazine, Eaton's honoured its war dead.*

C. A. Wright
R.C.A.F.

John David Eaton. A calamity was barely avoided when two veterans accidentally capsized their canoe.

After the war, the Eaton family converted the ten-acre Eaton Hall property into picnic grounds for Eatonians' families. The grounds featured a baseball diamond, teeter-totters, and a volleyball court, among other attractions. A special picnic was thrown each year for veterans. In the event of rain, there was a covered pavilion, which came equipped with an electric refrigerator and outdoor barbecue.

From the Eaton Hall event, John David, his wife, Signy, and Lady Eaton embarked by private plane on a rock-star-like series of personal appearances at similar luncheons across the country. The schedule included Moncton on September 16, Montreal on September 18, Winnipeg on September 30, Regina on October 1, and Calgary on October 3.

The gold signet rings were distributed to representatives of the armed services at each stop. Each ring was specially sized to fit both male and female employees. Following the luncheons, rings were sent to every veteran who had worked for the store. Tactful requests for finger sizes were sent to the families of deceased servicemen, whose rings were distributed to their survivors. Following the luncheons, replicas of the rings were sold, with small-sized rings priced at $3.97. Purchasers were later given the choice of buying either a crest or lapel pins, though in an exasperating bit of officialdom, government agencies reminded Eaton's that it was a crime for non-veterans to wear either the badges or the rings.

The Montreal luncheon to honour veterans was held in the ninth-floor restaurant on September 19, 1945. The event attracted over five hundred male and female veterans. The general bonhomie was washed down with such nourishing menu choices as chilled Montreal melon, consommé, fried chicken with bacon, corn fritters, spiced peaches, sweet potatoes, broccoli, hollandaise sauce, relish, ice-cream meringue with sauce, salted nuts, rolls, and coffee.

The Winnipeg ceremony took place in the ballroom of the Fort Garry Hotel. The menu included seafood cocktail Ostendaise, roast beef tenderloin with fresh mushroom sauce, château potatoes, and apple pie à la mode for dessert.

Eaton's donated a total of $25,000 toward placing war memorials in the Winnipeg, Toronto, and Montreal stores. The bronze tablet in Toronto to honour its 263 dead cost $11,469, and the Montreal one, honouring its 268 dead, cost $12,094.20. The remainder of the money went toward the purchase of the Winnipeg plaque, which was placed at the front of the main floor in the centre bay.

Commemorative plaques were also placed in Eaton's smaller stores. In Moncton, 9 casualties were cited; in Halifax, 5; in Brandon, Manitoba, 9; Saskatoon, 5; Calgary, 4; and Edmonton, 6. The plaques contained the following quotation:

They were Faithful unto Death
In proud remembrance of the ——— members of the EATON staff

who made the supreme sacrifice in World War II, having gone forth valiantly to fight for the survival of freedom. Their names are here inscribed that all may read who pass this way. 1945.

Eaton's war veterans did not forget John David Eaton's generosity. By the end of 1948, three Second World War veterans' committees were established in the Toronto, Winnipeg, and Montreal stores. Their sole objective was to bestow a suitable token of appreciation on John David.

A one-of-a-kind gift was commissioned, consisting of an enormous silver punch bowl, handcrafted in Copenhagen by the Georg Jensen Company. The bowl came with twenty-four silver goblets and a tray engraved with crests of the three armed forces, as well as that of the merchant marine.

Canvassers approached veterans in each store for donations toward the making of the bowl, with excellent results. Over 95 per cent of employees donated money, bringing the final total to $6,680.98.

Eaton's Second World War veterans donated money
to buy this silver serving bowl for John David Eaton.

There were, however, some holdouts. Store manager Jim Matthews, who had served in the RCAF, warned the canvassers that union members, who were just beginning to try to gain a foothold in the Eaton's stores, might exploit the employees' purchase of such an extravagant gift. "I said, if you want to collect money, go right ahead, but leave me out of it," says Matthews. "First of all, I knew John David Eaton was not the kind of guy who'd accept a gift like that, and second, I told them the union would just use the bowl against the company, and that's just what happened. Next thing you know, pictures of the damn bowl were plastered all over union pamphlets."

Shortly after the bowl arrived at the Montreal store in November 1948, the veterans' committees tried to arrange a convenient time and place for it to be presented to John David. Sensing that he would not appreciate a media circus, some veterans suggested that a quiet ceremony could be held in the boardroom of the Queen Street store in Toronto.

In the end, no presentation ceremony ever took place. Instead, the bowl was wrapped in Cellophane and placed on a storage shelf in the silver department of the Queen Street store.

Fred Eaton recalls, "When my father died, the manager came over and said, 'Fred, we've got his bowl,' and he told me the story. 'What should we do?' he asked. I said, 'Give it to my mother.'"

Fred's mother, Signy, kept the bowl until her death. When Fred became High Commissioner to London, he used the bowl at formal functions. "It's a very special bowl," he says, explaining that his father's refusal to accept the bowl was based on modesty rather than arrogance. "What happened was the veterans said, 'We want to present this to you.' 'I don't want it,' my father said. 'You don't owe me anything and I'm certainly not accepting a gift for something that should have been done anyway.' Well, it was slightly upsetting to the people, but they could understand in a way. My father was a private guy, and he certainly never wanted any thanks for what he did. He would not go to any ceremony where he knew they'd give it to him, and they knew he was a man of fixed opinion and if *they* surprised him, he might surprise them with something *he* would do. . . . Of course, we are very thankful for that gesture, but father didn't think he was deserving of any gift from them. Those guys fought in a war."

CHAPTER 9

Union Battle

First attempt to unionize Eaton's, 1948–51
• Second attempt, 1983–87

J UST AS THE WAR OVERSEAS was coming to an end, an internal war was erupting throughout the Eaton's empire. In a situation of supreme irony, at the same time that Eaton's war veterans were raising money to purchase the silver bowl as a tribute to John David Eaton, militants within the store were initiating what turned out to be a five-year battle to unionize the company's employees.

Beginning in 1948, the Retail, Wholesale, and Department Store Union (RWDSU), funded by the mighty Steelworkers of America, engaged John David Eaton in a prolonged game of mental poker. The prize was no less than securing the hearts, souls, and minds of Eaton's forty thousand front-line workers from coast to coast. From the outset, John David Eaton held an ace in the form of the seemingly bottomless reservoir of goodwill built up by his father, John Craig Eaton, whose beneficence during the First World War generated amongst Eatonians an almost religious devotion. Not even John Craig's lockout of factory workers during the 1912 garment strike could dim the halo he took to his grave.

A story repeated so often that it bordered on the apocryphal had John Craig Eaton walking through the Queen Street store and spotting an elderly woman scrubbing the floor. Appalled by the sight of senior citizen labouring for her money, John Craig promptly secured retirement for her, with a pension.

Another example of the Eaton family's benevolence involved the sterner R. Y. When College Street employee Bill Hamilton had a kidney removed in 1931, he spent four weeks recuperating in Toronto General Hospital. R. Y. Eaton sent him a basket of fruit. Eaton's Welfare Office, meanwhile, paid for all of Hamilton's medical expenses. Hamilton's recovery at home took six weeks, and during that time he was visited by an Eaton's nurse, who personally delivered to him his salary of eight dollars a week.

As a College Street employee recalled years later, "Old R. Y. knew every employee in this store. He knew the guy who cleaned the floor and the guy who cleaned the floor knew him."[1]

The family further enhanced its appeal by inviting employees to their home for seasonal banquets or other special events. Staff members came away feeling like a member of society's privileged class.

"The word went out that hurting the family personally just wasn't done," says Barbara Redlich. "There were grumblings of discontent, but women would look appalled at the idea of actually betraying any member of the Eaton's family."

Members of the RWDSU countered happy stories such as this with horror stories designed to illustrate the callousness of Eaton's management. Timothy Eaton's prejudice against unions was duly observed, yet Timothy got off relatively unscathed, mostly because even unionists appreciated that he would never ask a man or woman to do what he wouldn't have been willing to do himself. John David Eaton was another story. One of the union's favourite examples of the company's unfairness under John David involved a sixty-year-old employee named Everett Manning.

Desperate for male employees during the Second World War, the Eaton's store under John David Eaton hired Manning as a trucker in the Mail Order Assembly department. In addition to working as a trucker, Manning tossed heavy parcels onto conveyor belts and filled out COD order forms. After a serious eight-week bout with pleurisy, Manning discovered that he could no longer lift heavy parcels onto the conveyor belts. When he approached his manager about obtaining lighter work, the manager refused, suggesting instead that Manning retire. When

Manning argued that he could still fill in COD orders, the manager informed him that Eaton's would not be willing to pay Manning twenty-nine dollars a week for what, in his words, was "a girl's job."[2]

On June 12, 1942, Manning was given two weeks' vacation pay and a week's salary, and was relieved of his job. Ready to sweep down on the disgruntled Manning as he left the store were members of the Retail, Wholesale, and Department Store Union, who found him work at General Bakeries, where he received five dollars a week more than he earned at Eaton's. Despite becoming a poster boy for the RWDSU, however, Manning never joined.

Leading the RWDSU's charge to fell the retail giant was a petite blonde dynamo named Eileen Tallman (later Sufrin). She had her work cut out for her. To apply to the Labour Board for certification status, the union had to sign up 45 per cent of employees in each bargaining unit. If 55 per cent were secured, the board could certify the union without a vote. Should a vote be necessary, however, the union had to obtain a majority among those eligible to vote, rather than merely a majority of votes among those casting ballots. As a result, the union had to try to drum up interest, even in notoriously anti-union areas, such as commission selling.

In exchange for ten-to-eighteen-hour workdays, the Steelworkers paid Tallman a measly $3,000 a year, a salary that elicited not a whisper of protest among labour activists. Had the Steelworkers been a commercial establishment, or Tallman a man, her salary would almost certainly have raised the ire of labour representatives. The cost of the RWDSU's entire five-year campaign against Eaton's would eventually amount to over $100,000, most of it underwritten by the Steelworkers.

Tallman tried to recruit female employees to the union's cause by promising to rectify the wage disparities between male and female employees – as well as to eliminate some of the clean-up duties women were expected to perform in addition to selling – such as dusting and getting coffee for their male superiors.

In 1949, female sales clerks were earning twenty-four dollars a week, as opposed to their male counterparts, who earned thirty-eight dollars. Wages fluctuated according to which employees were involved and what merchandise they sold. A woman who sold furs in Toronto's Queen Street store, for example, earned less than her male counterpart in the College Street store, while employees of the budget Annex store received even less than the other two employees.

Commission selling, which Tallman decried because it fostered competition instead of co-operation, was almost exclusively the province of
men, while women accepted lower-paying straight salaried positions.
Not surprisingly, as the union drive dragged on, commission salesmen,
particularly those selling high-priced furniture in the College Street
store, were among the union's most vocal opponents.

Despite her best efforts to lobby for equal pay for equal work,
Tallman was stymied by the sexist prejudice of her own union, who
steered female employees off the issue by offering the consolation prize
of attaining a minimum flat weekly salary of thirty-five dollars. Before
long, vigorous infighting erupted between the union's male leaders and
high-profile female labour activists, such as the MPP for East York,
Agnes Macphail.

A March 1951 broadcast on radio station CKEY, sponsored by the
Retail Workers Union, contained the following embarrassing exchange
between Ernest Arnold, a staff representative of the union, and Macphail:

Arnold: Miss Macphail, it must give you a good deal of personal satisfaction to see equal pay for equal work getting into
the legislation stage after you have campaigned for it for so
many years.

Macphail: Yes! I would be very happy if we had passed a bill providing for equal pay for equal work, but unhappily, such is not
the case. Equal pay is only given in the case that women are doing
the *same* work, not comparable work of an equal quality or
quantity of work.

Immediately following this exchange, Arnold inadvertently impugned
the motives of his own union, while giving Macphail the chance to
deliver a death blow to his dignity:

Arnold: It looks to me as if employees will need a union to help
them put any teeth into this bill – both to help the employee
present her case and to make sure her job is protected afterward.

Macphail: I shouldn't think it would have any effect. It is approv-
ing of what they are doing.[3]

For the duration of the Eaton's drive, the RWDSU's headquarters were set up directly across the street from the company's Queen Street store. The union figured that, once Toronto's employees cracked, the rest of the empire's employees would soon follow suit.

Along with a team of five other union workers, including future Steelworker President Lynn Williams, Eileen Tallman toured the Toronto stores, assessing how many departments might be receptive to union representation. The answer was daunting by any stretch of the imagination. Tallman counted at least 250 separate departments and realized almost immediately that the only way to engage the employees was by calling them at home in the evenings. Over 250 shop stewards were enlisted to the cause through this method, several of them later fanning out across the company's stores, trying to convert the unconverted.

The goal of organizing department-store workers was complicated even further by the rapid turnover rate among employees, especially younger, short-term employees. As fast as Tallman could tabulate a list of union supporters, they retired, married, or moved to other companies, forcing her to begin her tally again.

The union used several stunts to attract new members. In one stunt, the wives of all union cardholders shopped at Eaton's on the same day, carrying bags upon which were written the words, "Join Local 1000." Employees' wives also wore badges which read: "My husband is a Union Man. Join Local 1000."[4] Peanuts were carried into the stores in bags to symbolize the low wages employees received.

On another occasion, the wives and children of union supporters carried dozens of helium-filled yellow balloons with the words "Join Local 1000 Now" written on them into the Queen Street store. One child lost his grip on his balloon, and watched it sail up to the ceiling. To the delight of union supporters, a flustered Eaton's manager was forced to climb a stepladder to retrieve it.[5]

During the union drive, Tallman stood at the James Street entrance to the Queen Street store every morning and distributed leaflets to employees, as well as to John David Eaton. In a gesture even some union members found amusing, every time John David received a leaflet, he would grin, pass it to a nearby caretaker, and say, "Here, you need this more than I do."[6]

Throughout the late 1940s, the union steadily made gains. By the fall of 1950, Tallman claimed she had signed up 6,500 of the store's 13,000 employees. Tallman later said that she felt she had to reach the magic number of 7,000 members before she would have a mandate to approach the Labour Congress about certification.

The union's perseverance was particularly impressive in light of the countermoves John David Eaton made in an effort to derail the union drive. In 1948, for example, John David announced a two-dollar pay raise to employees across the board. Small but regular pay raises continued over the next several months. That same year, John David also created the first corporate pension plan, which was open to any member over thirty years of age who had worked for the store for at least five consecutive years. Part-timers, left out of the first draft pension plan, were included within a year. John David claimed he had personally donated fifty million dollars to kick-start the pension fund, which Tallman dismissed as no more than a tax dodge.

The company also announced an increase in welfare-pay rates for employees absent from work through illness, married or single employees who had worked for Eaton's for more than ten years receiving 75 per cent of their wages, with a minimum weekly payment of fifty dollars for twelve weeks. Those who had worked for more than twenty-five years received the same amount for six months.

"John David Eaton was smart," says College Street store drapery salesman Reg Collins. "He matched the union deals with increased vacation time, wages, the works."

Under its March 13, 1950, headline "Eaton's Labour Fight," the tabloid *Hush* proclaimed that John David had cleverly defused the union's power by applying its recommendations, but modifying them to suit Eaton's long-term economic objectives. Many new employees, who formed the bulk of the union supporters, had not worked long enough to qualify for Eaton's benefits, and so quit the store, diminishing the union's numbers each time they did so.

The union's biggest goal was to secure a five-day, forty-hour work week, with Saturday off, hours it claimed were offered by the unionized Macy's store in New York. John David Eaton argued that Macy's policy allowed its employees one day off during the week, but that on Saturday, by far the store's biggest selling day, most employees were required to be on the job.

Those Eaton's employees who turned down the union confessed to feeling reasonably satisfied with their lot at Eaton's. One man told the *Hush* newspaper:

> You know everyone is by nature a griper. This isn't a bad spot to work in. I do my job and seldom have I been refused any favor that I have asked for. Suppose I want to get away early some night for some worthwhile reason. I go to the store manager and tell him, and maybe I can knock off an hour or an hour and a half early if business is slow. That wouldn't be with the Union.[7]

While decrying the low salaries females earned, Doris Anderson nevertheless felt that most supervisors, even of the most unsavoury variety, could be manipulated, and so there was a bit of flexibility. "There was a funny little guy with brown teeth who ate soda crackers all day. He really threw his weight around. When you first joined Eaton's, he really loaded you with work. If you couldn't do it, he would say you wouldn't work out. Once you pulled your load, though, you could start to kid him a little bit, and then you were okay," she recalls.

Eaton's wielded two particularly effective weapons in its fight against the union drive. The first involved highlighting the American origins of the RWDSU, as well as exploiting the communist leanings within the union. Eaton's reminded Eatonians that the RWDSU was almost decimated in 1948, when several of its union officials in the United States refused to sign affidavits denying they were members of the Communist Party, as required under the Taft–Hartley Act. That was all the information some Eatonians needed to turn the union down.

"I couldn't go with outright communism," says merchandise display artist Sheila Wherry. "I suspected it would turn into a dictatorship and be against individuality. I couldn't afford that mentality, considering what it was I did."

Wherry, who received, in her words, "the lowest goddamned wages the company was willing to pay me," had worked her way up to the top of her profession by concentrating solely on her work. "I didn't bat my eyelashes or work any female charms on the men I worked with. They would have taken advantage of it," she says, adding," I gradually won them over one by one, by getting the work done honestly and fairly." Wherry attained some measure of revenge against her male superiors by painting some of the papier mâché window-display figures in their likenesses.

Doris Anderson, who had her own brushes with sexism at Eaton's, still had serious reservations about the union. "I met with Eileen Tallman and I thought no one needed a union more than Eaton's, but I got kind of soured on it," she says. "The men held forth in the union, while the women did the donkey work like taking notes and making coffee."

It didn't help matters that the very male union members who criticized the sexism they claimed was rampant within Eaton's themselves conducted regular Miss Local 1000 beauty contests. Among the awards distributed were coffee pots – in which, presumably, contest winners could make cups of coffee for their men.

In spite of setbacks such as these, by October 18, 1950, the union had collected a sufficient number of names to formally request certification status from the Ontario Labour Relations Board, a move that threw Eaton's representatives into overdrive. Using its own printing press, Eaton's began printing up broadsides entitled "An Important Personal Message to You from Eaton's," detailing how employees could withdraw from the union. The union countered with an "Open Letter to John David Eaton," in which they warned him not to engage in any pressure tactics against employees sympathetic to the union.

On May 28, 1951, the board established Local 1000 as the official bargaining unit, with one stipulation. The board asked the union to perform a cross-check of the union's membership cards against the Eaton's payroll cards.

After months of delays, and arguments attempting to prove that cross-checking the payroll cards would be too time-consuming, on October 9, 1951, Eaton's finally presented the OLRB with a list of employees the board ruled were eligible for the bargaining unit.

Armed with Eaton's precious payroll list, the Labour Board set the voting date for December 3 and 4, 1951. With the spirit of his late grandfather Timothy Eaton looking over his shoulder, John David suddenly confronted a vision of a future in which he would no longer exert complete control over his employees, the most cherished power the Eaton family had enjoyed for over seventy-five years. Just when fate looked the bleakest, however, the momentum began to quickly veer away from the union. And the union had only itself to blame.

Over the course of six weeks, the union committed a series of public-relations blunders that couldn't have been more damaging if Eaton's had planned them itself. Perhaps the biggest blunder was in attacking Eaton's employees personally. The first to be targeted was House Furnishings employee Alfredo Bassonesi, whom, ten years before, Lady Eaton had helped release from Petawawa internment camp.

Faced with the December 3 and 4 voting dates, Bassonesi had formed a group of Eaton's employees called the "Loyal Eatonians." Subsidized by the employees themselves, the group printed up their own pamphlets using Eaton's in-store presses and distributed them to employees as they entered and exited the store. The pamphlets speculated that the $1.50

Italian employee Alfredo Bassonesi became a favourite target of Local 1000's wrath during Eaton's contentious union battle of 1948-52. He is pictured here as an organ grinder with a monkey who has the name Mussolini written across his chest.

union dues that employees would have to pay would net a bonanza for the union of over $200,000.

As soon as the union got a whiff of Bassonesi's activities, it designed posters entitled "Come, Come, Alfredo," that depicted Bassonesi as a hairy-legged organ grinder, holding a nickel-and-dime tin cup in one hand, and a monkey in the other. On the monkey's head was a hat bearing the name Mussolini. Bassonesi was not the only one insulted by the poster. So were "Loyal Eatonians," who were referred to derisively in the poster as members of Bassonesi's "flock," and therefore implicated as being pro-Fascist. The poster began:

> A New Leader has arisen at Eaton's. His flock refer to themselves anonymously as "Non-Union Employees," or "Loyal Eatonians," or "Eaton's Children". His followers apparently prefer to leave their salaries and working conditions to the whim of a "Great White Father" than to participate in anything so modern as collective bargaining through those "agitating" union organizations to which almost a million Canadians belong.[8]

Eaton's swiftly capitalized on the anti-union sentiment the poster had stirred up among some employees. A November 13, 1951, pamphlet, entitled "What Are They Selling?" contained a copy of the union's Bassonesi poster, along with a public letter of apology from Eaton's that read:

> The Company deeply regrets any embarrassment which may have been suffered by a long service, and independent-minded employee as a result of the cowardly attack to which the professional outside organizers of Local 1000 stooped in their special leaflet of last Thursday. Possibly, however, its publication is not an unmixed evil. It serves to illustrate as clearly as anything can, the sham nature of the so-called "brotherhood" which these professional Unioneers profess.[9]

"The union blew it big-time with the Bassonesi attack," says Rita Marofsky, who was employed at the cosmetics counter in the Queen Street store. "Everyone I worked with rolled their eyes, knowing that's where the union completely fumbled the ball."

"It was cowardly," agrees Marg Morison, who herself became a member of the Loyal Eatonians. "Nobody seriously thought the union had a chance," she says. At the height of the 1951 Christmas rush, Morison distributed anti-union leaflets to employees as they walked into the store in the morning. The combination of the leaflets and Morison's respected reputation did much to discourage established employees from committing themselves to the union. Nevertheless, her influence generated mixed opinions among the store's more iconoclastic employees.

"Marg was a toady of management, that's how many saw her," says Sheila Wherry. " 'Look out – Gestapo' was her nickname."

The union soon resorted to tricks to try to prevent the Loyal Eatonians from making any significant impact. When some Loyal Eatonian's grew exhausted from handing out leaflets, pro-union supporters posing as Loyal Eatonians stepped in and offered to distribute the leaflets. Instead, they threw them in the trash.

One Eaton family member in particular exhibited great support for the Loyal Eatonians. One morning in late November, a limousine glided up to the College Street doors and disgorged Lady Eaton herself, who proceeded to give the Loyal Eatonians a pep talk. As she recounted in her memoirs: "If those people who worked all day for us could stand at the Store doors from 7:00 a.m. until 8:30 to prove their loyalty to the Company, then I felt I could very well get up and go down among them to give them a nod of encouragement."[10]

As shop stewards struggled to drum up votes, the union committed a second public-relations faux pas with the publication of a "spoof" leaflet, which belittled the intelligence of Loyal Eatonians. Entitled "We Stand for Eaton's," it contained a final paragraph that mocked Loyal Eatonians' readiness to go down with the store. The final paragraph of the leaflet read: "Leave your fate COMPLETELY in the hands of the Company and stop thinking, as we have done. Then we can all stand and stand and stand until we all go down together. Wouldn't that be wonderful?"[11]

Responding to a flurry of protests from Eaton's anti-unionists, or "lily-whiters," as Lynn Williams called them, the union desisted from expressing such sardonic humour again. They soon discovered, however, that the damage had already been done.

While the union was busy ridiculing long-time employees, Eaton's concentrated on the positive and distributed to staff members a list of all the employees who had begun working at the bottom and had worked their way to the top of the corporate ladder. O. D. Vaughan, who came to Eaton's to work as a drapery salesman, had eventually become a vice-president; Fred Walls started as a messenger boy in 1909, and worked his way up to become a company director; C. M. Leishman, who started off selling men's clothing, became head of the department, and was finally made a director in 1943. For Eaton's, it was "every man a king" propaganda at its finest.

A November 14, 1951, pamphlet entitled "It's Always Opportunity Day for Eaton Employees," drove the point home one last time. It read:

> Yesterday, and all the yesterdays even back for 80 years, people just like you came to work here in stock rooms, in the mail order, in offices, as salespeople. They were your counterparts and they progressed up and in the Company, not because they belonged to a union, but because of EXPERIENCE, TRAINING, and ABILITY to do whatever job they now hold: section heads, foremen, adjusters, assistants, department heads, supervisors and directors. They are as you yourselves can be. On December 3rd you are going to have to make a choice between the people you know and can trust and strangers whose chief concern is collecting union dues and building union power. Your decision rests to a large measure on your future and the future of this Company.[12]

As its number of supporters dwindled in the days preceding the final vote, the union scrambled to rehabilitate its image as a voice for the voiceless. Shop stewards frenetically canvassed the store's departments and reported, erroneously, that there was no backlash against the union's publications.

What union organizers might not have factored into the equation was that, anxious to receive their Christmas bonuses, Eaton's employees had cooled on the idea of a union. In addition, Eaton's had begun effectively deflating the union's promises, which they termed "grub-riddled Local 1000 fruit," or "shiny apples filled with worms."[13]

In language sure to frighten long-serving employees, Eaton's explained that, should the union succeed, employees with seniority, even Quarter-Century Club members, might be outranked by short-service stewards. Regarding welfare and pensions, Eaton's warned that all the extras employees now enjoyed, including having sick pay delivered to their homes by a company nurse, might be placed in jeopardy and subjected to collective bargaining. And then there was the spectre of possible strikes – an image particularly demoralizing to senior employees, who considered themselves as white-collar as Eaton family members themselves.

Finally, on the evening of December 3, the vote ending five years of anxiety finally took place. The sliver-thin victory that Eaton's obtained could not have been more devastating for the union. The Yes votes numbered 4,020, while the No votes totalled 4,880.

At the time of the vote, dietician Dorothy Ferguson shared the upper floor of a duplex with two other anti-union employees. On the floor below lived three pro-union mail-order employees. When the telephone call came announcing the results of the vote, pandemonium erupted. "Upstairs we began hooting and hollering with happiness," recalls Ferguson. "Downstairs we could hear loud groans and cries. It was kind of embarrassing. Eventually everything was smoothed over. After all, we had to continue to work together at the same company, so we just had to learn to put it behind us."

Other employees reacted more bitterly. Shoe salesman Len Horrocks, who had served on the union's executive board, blamed married women, part-time employees, and older female employees for destroying the union's hopes. He said, "The married women and part-timers killed us. Then there were old maids, Loyal Eatonians, who had been at Eaton's since they were fourteen. There was no way people like them were going to change."[14]

Other employees, who had served as union stewards, admitted that some of the employees they had recruited ended up not voting for the union because of the bonuses, raises, and pension promises they received from management in the final days of the union drive. Meanwhile, employees viewed the regular payment of union dues as an unnecessary additional expense.

The *Globe and Mail* ultimately attributed the union's failure to "the revulsion most Eaton employees felt at the tactics used by the union." Accusing the union of stooping to "vituperation of the meanest sort," the paper added, "On the radio, in leaflets and pamphlets, the union conducted a campaign so scurrilous and vehement that loyal, long-term employees of the Eaton staff formed their own organizations to defeat it."[15]

Reg Collins was among those who agreed that the union had made itself an enemy of those it was trying to help. "The union just got very nasty. They turned a lot of people off and caused them to turn back toward Eaton's. After all, people could get no-interest loans at Eaton's, and nurses would come out to pay them when they were sick."

Others saw a silver lining. "Eaton's broke the union, but softened things up after the union action, so the union was beneficial," Doris Anderson concludes.

Though the drive to unionize had forced Eaton's to improve pension and welfare payments, some of these improvements were short-lived. Reg Collins recalls, "John David had matched the union deals, twenty-five years of service, seven weeks vacation, and so on, then for nine years after that, there was no wage increase, so the company ended up looking bad."

Even worse, within two years of the vote, John David Eaton announced that Saturday half-days were being cancelled in favour of full days, and that the store would remain open Mondays to Fridays until 5:30 p.m., rather than 5:00 p.m.

When the first union drive failed, the RWDSU retired to lick their wounds. Thirty years later those wounds would still be festering.

◼

During the deep recession of the early 1980s, the hugely successful Eaton Centre in Toronto helped keep the Eaton's empire solvent. The financial stability of the company was further sustained by deep cuts in spending implemented by Executive Vice-President and Chief Operating Officer Greg Purchase, who had been imported from Winnipeg to try to solve Eaton's cash-flow crisis. Staff members did not greet his actions with unanimous praise, though.

Purchase began by imposing wage freezes on Eaton's staff. He also cut back on expenses by centralizing the entire company's merchandising and distribution functions. Forced to accept the fact that Toronto was now calling all the shots, many regional executives quit in protest.

When Purchase finally lifted the wage freeze after two years, employees were dismayed to discover that the amount of their paycheques increased in some cases by only three or four cents an hour. Eaton's had also increasingly seen the cost-saving value in employing part-time workers, many of them students or working mothers. The lower the salaries these employees received – sometimes no more than $5.50 an hour – the more expensive long-term employees seemed.

One by one, the handful of winning cards once held by John David Eaton began losing its critical aces. Despite owning 110 stores coast to coast and possessing a workforce of over 36,000 employees, much of what had defined Eaton's as the premier shopping store in Canada – and bound it to local communities – was being eliminated. The Santa Claus Parade was history, while, after 1976, the Eaton's catalogues were wracking up value only as collectors' items on the shelves of antique stores. Most inconceivably, American-owned Simpson's-Sears began overtaking Eaton's as the most profitable store in the country.

"First Greggy [Greg Purchase] cancelled the Santa Claus parade, then he killed Eaton's buying operation, then he eliminated the Trans-Canada Sales," says Peter Glen. "Everything that made the store distinctive and linked it to the community around it was removed."

"All Purchase understood was the concept of stack 'em and rack 'em," complains one Eaton's Centre employee.

Fred Eaton disagrees. "Yes, Greg Purchase did streamline and cut costs in a lot of ways, but there was more to it than that, there was this idea of promoting and selling. Greg knew that every department had to have something special. Every spring and fall we'd have reviews, where we'd ask, 'What is the plan? What are you going to do? What is the item you're going to get?' The biggest one was the sheepskin you put on top of your mattress. We used to pile those things high in the store, and have a TV running. It must have driven people crazy. 'From the land of twenty-three-million sheep comes the . . .' the ad would begin, and the mattresses sold. Other times it might have been knives. We would make it exciting. People would come in and see we have lots of this and they'd say, 'Oh, they have confidence in that.' We sold thousands of gloves, scrapers, so Greg was very good at that."

For over forty years, the RWDSU had waited patiently for just the right opportunity to attempt to unionize Eaton's again. They got their chance in the fall of 1983 in the form of Bramalea TV sales employee Paul Wannamaker, who complained to a customer about his low salary and commission. The "customer" in question was none other than Mike Danyluk, a representative of the RWDSU, who rushed back to the union with the news that all was not well in the Eaton's stores.

Bramalea workers celebrate their victory.

In less than twenty-four hours, union representatives fanned out throughout the store, searching for other discontented employees – and they weren't hard to find. By February 1984, the union had signed up 80 per cent of the Bramalea store's 185 sales-office clerical employees.

The press pounced on the story. Emboldened by the number of Bramalea store employees showing support for the union, employees of Eaton's other stores soon followed suit. In quick succession, the Scarborough Town Centre store, the Yonge-Eglinton store, the Shoppers' World store on Danforth Avenue, the Centre store in St. Catharines, and the small Warehouse Store in London, Ontario, all gained union certification.

Eleven other stores in Ontario became the target of unions, including the Yorkdale store and the Toronto Eaton Centre, but neither ultimately unionized. To protect against financial losses in the event that the union might gain a foothold at the Eaton Centre, managers and executives were trained to man the cash registers. Company architect Hank Hankinson remembers he and another high-ranking Eaton's employee competing to see who rang up purchases the fastest. "This fellow was quite arrogant and swaggered around boasting that he was a whiz with mechanical things. Finally we started training on the cash registers. Whenever we made a mistake, a buzzer would sound. Well, his buzzer ended up going off more often than mine. That made me feel a little bit better," he laughs.

Another member of Eaton's management recalls that pranksters placed odd-sized shoes in the wrong shoe boxes. Meanwhile, anti-union supporters handed out pamphlets entitled "Stop the Union Now."

Unfortunately for pro-union sales staff members, their bargaining position was less strong than it had been in the days when selling was more of an art than a skill. Despite their best attempts to get excited about their products, and to convey this excitement to their customers, in the end, sales clerks were obliged to do little other than scan barcodes into the company's computer. Long-term employees were the only ones who maintained relationships with their customers. Generally speaking, the days when customers and staff members knew each other on a first-name basis had become a distant memory. Meanwhile, the domination of designer labels and brand names also made selections less unique than in the days when buyers from individual stores bought merchandise from out-of-the-way suppliers in small towns and villages throughout the world.

Some Eaton's stores fought hard for a union, and lost. The cost to employee relations was incalculable. The London, Ontario, store was the site of some particularly contentious battling between pro- and anti-union staff. At one time, the store's convivial sales staff threw birthday parties for each other, sometimes in the manager's office itself. The end of the voting process strained many of these friendships to the point of breaking.

Rose Askin fought hard to unionize Eaton's employees of the London, Ontario, store.

Participating in the London store's charge to obtain union representation was housewares sales clerk Rose Askin. Askin had worked at Eaton's for twenty-seven years and had chronicled her career with the company in two large scrapbooks containing photographs, letters, and news articles. Her home was decorated with Eaton's furniture and accessories. To mark her quarter-century with the firm, Askin proudly picked the biggest commemorative diamond ring available. By the early 1980s, however, Askin had grown disillusioned with the number of untrained staff members the firm hired, most of whom she felt diminished the store's reputation. "Customer service went kaput," she says today.

Askin signed up co-workers to the union with the same impressive energy she devoted to her sales job. Before long, the store manager accused her of trying to sign up employees on the store's premises itself.

"I told him, 'I'm smarter than that. What I do outside my business has nothing to do with my job.'" Askin says management's presence outside the lunchroom where the vote ultimately took place intimidated many employees from voting in favour of the union.

"I don't agree with Rose," says Ivan Fry, who served as one of the union co-ordinators. "It was a secret ballot, but we had a pretty rough idea beforehand who would vote for or against the union."

Anti-union activists were less sure than Fry of which direction the vote might take. "I'll never forget the day of the vote," says Marion McLaughlin, a commission sales clerk of twenty-three years. "It took place on a Saturday. My hands were sweating, my heart was pounding, it was incredible. At 5:00 p.m., they did a count." When tallied, the votes revealed that 55 per cent of the store's employees voted against the union, while 45 per cent voted for it.

Using money contributed to her by the company, McLaughlin had printed up anti-union flyers and buttons and distributed them to employees of the store. "The union tried viciously to get into the store," she says. "But what they had to offer wasn't that spectacular."

"After the vote, we just said, 'Oh, well, it's water under the bridge, we lost, maybe next time,'" says furniture salesman Glen Baker, a pro-union supporter. "The store was a pleasant place to work. They gave you lots of days off."

Even Ivan Fry has kind words to say about the store. "I wasn't as down on Eaton's as a place to work. It wasn't as bad as we said it was. I stayed until '98," he says. "No one truly understood the pension plan, that was a source of a lot of the problem. It was very Mickey Mouse. No one represented you like they would have with most pension plans."

Fry feels that straight commission sales staff generally fared better financially than non-commission staff, and points out that those who fought the hardest for the union might not have been up to the challenge of selling without a safety net. "Sometimes, not the best employees want protection," he says. "Weak ones often want the most protection."

In retrospect Fry believes that the union deserves to share some of the blame for failing to entice employees to the cause. "The people who organized didn't do as good a job at the first. You had construction workers talking to women earning a second income. Some of these guys had tattoos on their bodies and they came to women's doors like that. That part of it was wrong," he says.

Askin believes that, following the vote, her fellow employees, as well as members of management, took revenge on her for her pro-union sympathies. Shortly after the vote, she was transferred to the chinaware

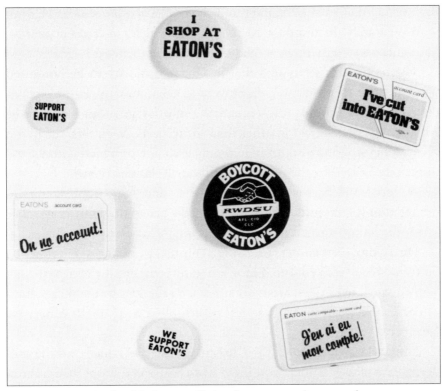

Battle of the buttons. Various buttons worn by pro- and anti-union activists in the 1980s union drive.

section, a move she viewed as a demotion. By 1987, she tendered her resignation, three years short of her mandatory retirement age of sixty.

At her retirement party, Askin discovered that many co-workers had refused to sign her farewell card. She suffered an even more traumatic blow upon discovering that she was not entitled to any employee allowance, because she had never contributed to the pension plan. "I was devastated," says Askin, who insists that her superiors steered her away from the plan because they thought it was so deficient.

By contrast, some of Askin's fellow pro-union employees praised Eaton's for refusing to take revenge on union activists. "To give Eaton's credit, they didn't chase pro-union people out after the vote," says Ivan Fry.

———■———

Once the six stores were certified, union leaders pressed hard to amalgamate all the Ontario stores into a single contract. Eaton's countered by insisting that each bargaining unit within each store should be dealt with separately. In response to the union's call for increased salaries, Eaton's countered that they would offer a flat 7.8-per-cent increase.

The union also stipulated that it wanted seniority to be honoured when it came to promoting employees in the company. Eaton's countered that they would only recognize seniority in promotions if the employee were qualified in other relevant respects. With this, the union accused Eaton's of bad-faith bargaining, a charge of which Eaton's was ultimately cleared by the province's Labour Relations Board.

Negotiations between union members and store representatives dragged on for months. When they finally broke down in November 1984, the union, against its own better judgment, voted to strike.

On Friday, November 30, 1984, employees of the six unionized Ontario stores walked out. Eaton's had already hired extra part-time staff to work over the Christmas season, so the loss to the picket lines of the striking employees was not as crippling as it might otherwise have been.

Fireworks erupted after the Christmas rush had ended and the doldrums of a new year had begun. On March 2, 1985, more than a thousand female protestors, gleaned from the Federation of Women Teachers as well as other special-interest groups, bore down on the Eaton's

Centre, and screamed "scab" at the employees working there. "Boycott Eaton's" stickers were affixed to the surface of display cases. At one point, someone released mice on the premises.

Several Toronto employees were livid at being called scabs, since the store had already voted against forming a bargaining unit. In an article entitled "Eaton's Strike a Scam," Garth Turner, Business Editor of the *Toronto Sun*, reacted with rage to the women's incursion into the private property of the Eaton family. Accusing the RWDSU of being unable even to organize "a sock drawer," he wrote:

> Last Saturday, in a spectacle I couldn't believe, more than 3,000 people stormed the Eaton Centre, and paraded through the store disrupting business, offending shoppers and slinging verbal abuse on the workers. But the store isn't unionized. The workers who took the slurs aren't involved in the strike. And neither were the people marching through the aisles. No, they were participants in an International Women's Day Parade, made up of women's groups, various left-wing splinter political groups and unions. There may have been 50 legitimate Eaton's strikers, but the other 2,500 were women downtown for a good time . . . What right did they have to bust up Fred Eaton's store? They had none.[16]

Like his father, grandfather, and great-grandfather before him, Fred Eaton had no intention of capitulating to union demands. "I remember as a very young person when the first round went around and my father was the Head, and then I was the Head the second time it came around, and I said, 'Not on my watch you don't get in.' Well, they didn't in the end."

Rather than duck and hide, Fred made a point of visiting those stores being picketed, sometimes serving behind their counters for more than an hour. He recalls, "I remember we used to visit the stores right through the strike, especially the ones on strike, and wave to the strikers as we rolled in. I thought, 'Oh God, we're not going to hole up in the offices while you guys are doing this . . . we'll just walk right across the lines and the hell with it.'"

"We could have used him on our side," one union member laughs today. As the months dragged on with no resolution in sight, more and more striking workers returned to their jobs. Under Ontario labour

legislation, those strikers who hadn't returned within six months –
namely by May – would lose their jobs. By March, less than half the
original number of strikers remained on the picket lines.

In spite of its victory, Eaton's did suffer some notable dressing-downs
during the union drive. The United Church of Canada castigated the
chain for failing to bargain with union organizers in good faith for
securing improved wages and working conditions, particularly for
women, who comprised 80 per cent of Eaton's employees.

Complicating the RWDSU's fight to sign up Eaton's employees was
the presence across Canada of other unions trying simultaneously to do
the same thing. In Quebec, the Union des employés de commerce began
a drive to organize 6,000 Quebec workers, particularly 1,300 located in
the downtown Montreal store, as well as 200 in Sherbrooke. Only
Sherbrooke succeeded in gaining certification.

At the Brampton store, meanwhile, security officers joined the United
Plant Guard Workers of America. The security guards weren't allowed to
join the RWDSU because of an Ontario law prohibiting them from being
members of the same union as fellow employers, because of their sur-
veillance activities.

In Guelph, Ontario, two competing unions, the United Food and
Commercial Workers Union and the RWDSU, approached Eaton's
employees. The same situation occurred in Hamilton, prompting
George Ross, a Hamilton-based organizer for the RWDSU, to complain
that the competition only served to confuse workers.

Various union drives also took place in Winnipeg and British
Columbia. John English, a Winnipeg delivery driver, recalls, "The union
was just for younger people, not for older ones. My biggest mistake was,
I went to one of the meetings. I paid for it afterwards, because management found out and thought I was thinking of joining a union. But the
union wasn't offering any better than company rates. People didn't
realize that delivery drivers were some of the better-paid employees,
better even than some assistant managers."

Alfred Judt of Winnipeg saw any hopes of a union shrivel up due
to conflict of interest between two competing unions. "Two unions
tried to simultaneously outfox each other and that's why they failed,"
he says.

When the Brandon, Manitoba, store succeeded in being certified,

Eaton's management retaliated by threatening to close the store altogether. Along with some other Winnipeg employees, Alfred Judt was sent to move all the store's merchandise down from the upper to the lower floors prior to removing it from the store altogether. What merchandise remained was priced down. Judt was also instructed to close down the cafeteria and lay off the staff. When the union was ultimately voted out on a Friday, Judt and his fellow employees had to quickly reverse what they had done and reopen the store by the following Monday. Their work didn't come cheap. "Our bill was $60,000," says Judt, who adds facetiously, "It was a ridiculous waste of money, with what they paid us, they could have paid the staff for ten years."

The Brandon store certification turned out to be an anomaly. By the time pro-union momentum swung to the West Coast, Eaton's had already taken the preventative action of offering regular salary increases to employees. "We got three raises in a row," says Donna York of the Abbotsford store. "We wondered why, until we heard about the unions."

For at least one manager of a large British Columbia Eaton's store, the pro-union supporters left a lasting negative impression. He says, "They [the unions] picked on stores when they felt there were problems. They did interviews in my store. It was a difficult time for management. We couldn't say or do anything at the end when they aggressively went after the store and made everyone's life hell. It was very unpleasant. On the other hand, the Eaton family believed everyone was looked after and protected. I believe the boys felt deeply for people in the company. But the people in senior management didn't care."

"I don't think we needed a union," says Fred Eaton. "It's probably the last thing we needed. I don't think unions serve much of a useful purpose in this day and age. I mean we're not talking about keeping children out of slave labour or something like that."

As Toronto's picketers dwindled down to less than fifty, Tom Collins, negotiator for the RWDSU, finally capitulated and accepted an offer from Eaton's that was not substantially different than the original offer. With the exception of seven employees of the London, Ontario, warehouse store, by the end of 1987, all certified stores had been decertified.

Eaton's victory must have seemed pyrrhic. Over the next ten years, most Eaton's stores would consistently lose money, due in part to the arrival of U.S. discount competitors, such as Wal-Mart, as well as to its frustrating inability to change its image from a store for older Canadians. By the 1990s, several stores would be forced to close. In 1997, when it finally filed for Company Credit Agreement Act (CCAA) protection, it was clear the Eaton merchandising empire had struck back for the last time.

CHAPTER 10

The End

Bankruptcy protection • Attempt at restructuring
• Eaton's closing • Staff reactions

T HE TORONTO EATON CENTRE'S final auction proved to be an anti-climactic stage of grief that had its beginnings on February 27, 1997, when Eaton's filed for CCAA protection. The move gave Eaton's protection from its creditors, while allowing it to find a way to reduce its debt and increase future sales. The filing rocked Canada's employees and customers alike.

Just a few days prior to the filing, a "Salute to the Staff" party celebrating the Centre's twentieth anniversary was thrown on the main floor of the Eaton Centre store. Wearing brightly coloured paper hats, unsuspecting staff members gathered to hear store executives reassure them that the company was alive and well and looking towards the future.

Chief Operating Officer Peter Saunders took to the stage to praise the staff for achieving excellent sales-volume figures and concluded that successful stores depended not merely on "bricks and mortar, but on good people."

Fred Eaton was next to speak. "I wonder how many of you were here twenty years ago as I was and my brothers were?" he said. A significant percentage of those assembled waved their hands. "That's marvellous," he responded in his smooth baritone. "Congratulations to all those twenty-year-olds. We're all twenty years old now, and congratulations to everyone else who works in this store and makes it the landmark it is – Happy Anniversary," he said, blowing heartily on his tasselled noisemaker.

Shortly after Fred finished speaking a pre-taped VHS film retrospective of the Eaton Centre store flickered on a television monitor located to one side of the stage. At the film's conclusion, an ear-splitting bang signalled the release from the ceiling of hundreds of orange, pink, and purple balloons. Several balloons bounced off staff members' heads before being playfully kicked into corners.

Employees picked up goody bags, and departed down the store's main aisle, passing through a gauntlet of Eaton family members, consisting of Fred, John Craig, and George, who shook hands and smiled through what must have been their tears. Coincidentally, in big white letters in the upper-left-hand corner of the television monitor by the side of the stage flashed the word "Ejecting."

"I walked away from the event and everything started to spin," recalls Sigi Brough, the MC of the event. The day before, a member of Eaton's legal team had warned Brough that "something was amiss" in the company and that she would know more over the next few days.

Like most others within the executive inner circle, Brough had heard of rumours that the store was suffering financially, but confirmation of trouble so close to this celebration was nevertheless devastating. "I looked out at all those nice people holding their clackers and thought, 'How deceiving for these good people,'" she says.

Hank Hankinson, the architect responsible for designing the Eaton's Centre, attended the event, but failed to engage the interest of Fred Eaton in a book he was compiling on the history of the Eaton's stores across Canada. "He told me it wasn't a good time," says Hankinson. Later, upon hearing about the CCAA filing, Hankinson admitted that he "kind of gave up on the project." Afterwards, Hankinson entitled his moribund project, "Eaton's: Death of a Dream."

As soon as Eaton's filed for creditor protection, Ernst & Young stepped in to administrate the proceedings, which gave them unprecedented access to previously confidential reports concerning assets, liabilities, and the basic financial condition of the company. At this stage, Eaton's hoped they could still reverse the downward spiral by restructuring their store operations. To do so, they accepted a deal with the people who had always shown them the most loyalty: their employees.

Shortly after the CCAA filing, representatives of the law firm of Koskie, Minskie began approaching members of the Eaton's Retirement Annuity Fund about sharing in a 50–50-per-cent pension-surplus-sharing agreement that would allow Eaton's pensioners to receive their benefits, while sharing the rest with the company to help it bail itself out of its debt. Within just a few months, Koskie, Minskie had signed up a majority of the members of the Eaton's Retirement Annuity Plan. Membership in the ERAP had been compulsory for all regular full-time Eaton's employees over the age of twenty-five, or those with five years continuous service.

When the deal was finalized, a sum of 237 million dollars was distributed to ERAP members. Eaton's retained a balance of 208 million dollars, which they topped off by raising additional funds through real-estate sales and the selling of their credit-card division. The Eaton family donated 50 million dollars from its own pockets, a gesture that earned respect from at least some employees.

"It says a lot that the family contributed their own money to bailing out the company," says Winnipeg employee, Jim Thomson.

A Toronto employee wasn't so impressed. "What they did with the pension money was a disgrace," he says. "What did they spend it on but marble floors and chandeliers? How did that help the quality of products?"

Indeed, after paying off their creditors, Eaton's did proceed to allocate a portion of the money received from the pension-surplus-sharing agreement to renovating some of their stores. Another large expenditure went toward hiring George Kosich, aged sixty-two, as the company's new CEO, to replace George Eaton. Prior to arriving at Eaton's, Kosich had just retired from his position as President and CEO of the Hudson's Bay Company.

Kosich had worked miracles at the Bay and its chain member Zeller's throughout the 1980s, raising their sales by more than 50 per cent by the time he retired. Vowing not to close any Eaton's stores until he had assessed their viability, Kosich immediately embarked on a cross-country store-by-store review.

By the time his tenure ended a mere eighteen months later, Kosich had closed twenty-one Eaton's stores and laid off more than two thousand employees. At the same time, he attempted to attract younger shoppers by eroticizing Eaton's staid image through suggestive television and magazine ads. Entitled "Times Are Changing," the ads featured semi-clothed females posing in submissive positions.

Increasingly, brand names such as Liz Claiborne and Tommy Hilfiger filled floor spaces formerly reserved for more meat-and-potatoes items such as stoves and microwave ovens. "Diversity" became the catchphrase of the reborn fashion departments.

Melinda Mattos, whose first retail job was working in Yorkdale's "Diversity" fashion shop, recalls in-store instructors encouraging sales clerks to develop a passion for their products. Handed a heart-shaped piece of construction paper, Mattos was asked to write a valentine to her product, in her words, "a puke-green towel." Despite the cornball nature of these sorts of projects, Mattos quickly developed a familial kinship with her co-workers, some of them older women, who were amused yet accepting of Mattos's fuchsia-coloured hair and polyester, plaid bell-bottom pants. Even after Mattos's job came to an end, she continued to refer to herself as a "recovering Eatonian."[1]

If shoppers had been handed heart-shaped pieces of construction paper and asked to write valentines to the products being offered to them, they might have written instead: "Can buy it cheaper at Sears." For staple goods, in particular, customers now chose to shop at Business Depot or Wal-Mart. Some of Eaton's smaller stores were particularly hard-hit during Kosich's tenure, when style was emphasized over substance.

"Kosich was an asshole. He promised us that our store was not going to be closed," says Charlottetown Store Manager Gary Briand, whose store held the regional monopoly on the sale of hard goods such as washing machines and other household appliances.

Desperate to save his store, Briand enlisted the aid of Mayor Pat Bois to call George Kosich to convince him that the store was worth keeping. In response, Kosich promised to fly to Charlottetown to personally assess the situation.

Kosich's trip did not result in the stay of execution Briand had hoped for. Starting on a bad foot, Kosich arrived on a Saturday, Briand's day off. "If a staff member hadn't taken the initiative of calling me at home, I might never have known Kosich was there," he says today.

As soon as Briand was informed of Kosich's presence, he hurriedly donned a suit and rushed to the store. Practically bursting through the front door, he approached Kosich and extended his hand in introduction, only to have Kosich say to him, "What are you doing here? I really don't need you."

Despite the best efforts of Briand and his staff, by the third week of April 1998, the Charlottetown store became one of the first casualties of Eaton's restructuring. Today, since there have been no offers to buy it, the once picturesque store still stands boarded up, its exterior spraypainted with graffiti. Though gone, however, the store is far from forgotten.

In 1999, Helen Hughes, a former sales clerk of thirty-five years, decided to place an ad in Charlottetown's local newspaper, advertising a get-together for ex-employees of the Charlottetown Eaton's. A sudden burst of rain failed to discourage over thirty former employees from bringing their own lawn chairs and home-made snacks into Hughes's garage, where they sat for the afternoon reminiscing about the store's good times, taking their reminiscences onto the driveway once the rain abated.

"Some were disappointed when the reunion was over," says Hughes, who asked each participant to sign a guestbook. Hughes has repeated the reunions each year since, and remains amazed that the number of attendees, rather than shrinking, miraculously seems to grow.

Kosich's reign ended when it was found that, despite his drastic spending cuts and the sprucing up of marquee stores, sales figures and profits continued to slip. Some analysts claimed that Kosich had failed to close enough stores. Others theorized that Eaton's had abandoned its core customer base: women over thirty, who shopped at the store for a variety of items, including both hard and soft goods.

Ads that had appeared during Kosich's reign stressing that Eaton's was no longer "your grandmother's store" not only alienated older customers but also failed to attract young shoppers. It seemed that no matter what tactic the family tried on the advice of outside consultants, it could not find a way to simultaneously draw on its past while looking towards its future.

◼

If the shock of the 1997 CCAA filing rocked Eaton's employees, then the announcement on August 20, 1999, that negotiations for the purchase of at least some of the chain's outlets by Federated Departments Stores, owners of Macy's, had fallen through, finished any hopes of saving Eaton's from ruin.

Upon hearing the news, Fred Eaton put his phone down and poured himself a drink. Sigi Brough, meanwhile, opened her desk drawer and removed a tin cookie jar she had picked up on a recent promotion tour to Macy's. "I looked at the tin jar and thought, if only." She continues, "I don't think anyone can grasp the kind of loyalty long-term associates had towards the company. It was almost like a virus that got into you. It was the people connection that made the company what it was – period, no ifs, ands, or buts. I was part of the executive team and I knew where we were in terms of the insolvency, but I never thought it would come to that. I kept keeping my fingers crossed that we could sell it."

As soon as the Federated deal fell through, Eaton's served its 13,000 employees with termination notices, effective November 30, 1999. Only those needed during the liquidation process were invited to remain.

When customers approached Eaton's stores, photocopied notices taped on the glass doors read, "This Individual Is Insolvent." "My stomach dropped to my knees when I saw it," says Eaton's customer Carol Bouquet of Montreal. "I remember cupping my hands and looking through the glass, but all I could see were empty hangers. They looked like scarecrows in the dark, with clothes hanging half-on and -off them."

Thunder Bay natives Jim Pole and Nicole Pelletier arrived at the downtown Montreal store on August 20 to pick up Jim's pants for their wedding which was scheduled for the following day, only to be told by a security guard that the pants could not be located. Refusing to leave, the couple received their pants only when after more than a hour the guard opened the front door a crack and passed the pants to them.

Gordon Brothers Retail Partners of Boston, who were appointed as Eaton's liquidators by the Ontario Superior Court, prided themselves on being, in the words of its president, Bobby Sager, the "liquidators with a heart." Not long after the August 25, 1999, announcement that Eaton's was closing for good, 120 members of Gordon Brothers' staff fanned out across the company's remaining sixty-four stores, with the objective of selling off every item not nailed down in order to raise the over 320 million dollars Eaton's owed its creditors.

At least some of the liquidators arrived at stores minus their much-ballyhooed hearts. "In the beginning, the liquidators came in like storm troopers," says Carmel Neighbour, who worked in the chinaware section of the Seven Oaks store in British Columbia. "Someone would come in and say, 'We're taking your toaster.' We'd say, 'Can he do that?' and the answer was always 'Yes.'"

Kathy Henkinson, a sixteen-year employee of the Abbotsford, B.C., store, recalls her store's liquidator as "an arrogant jerk. He went into the manager's office and put his feet up on the desk like he was saying 'I'm the boss. This is what I say.' While we were trying to get things down and sorted, he was reading a paper, or playing solitaire on the computer. The new manager didn't have the balls to move him along." As fast as Henkinson could mark down merchandise, the liquidator would hoard it for himself. "He had quite a stash," she recalls.

During the first few weeks of the liquidation sales, markdowns began at 20 to 40 per cent. But if Eaton's sales staff expected loyal customers to arrive clutching their sodden hankies, they were sadly mistaken. In their place appeared ruthless retail predators, who had come to pick the carrion off the store's bones. Some of the hungriest predators were teenage girls, ironically the very demographic group Eaton's had once been eager to attract.

"People saw the sign saying 'Liquidation Sale,' and they thought they would find one huge garage sale, but the sales were less good than regular sales," says Janice Downey, an employee of the Guildford, B.C., store. An ugly moment occurred when a young woman decided she wanted to return the item she had just purchased on sale. "I told her, 'I'll be happy to send the liquidator out to you,'" says Downey, "but she had a fit. She started banging on my name tag, saying, 'This says Eaton's.'" Finally, security was called and the woman was forcibly ejected from the store. That night at home, Downey discovered a huge bruise on her chest where the name tag had been pounded into her.

For Downey, the pain experienced by the customer's assault paled in comparison to the pain experienced upon recalling the store's glory days, when staff members and customers shared an emotional symbiosis. "Eaton's was the only place I've ever worked where it was a pleasure to work every day," she explains. "I never woke up and said, 'Oh, God, I have got to go to work today.'"

In the store's glory days, customers bonded with employees and trusted them to recommend purchases. "One lady ran a bed-and-breakfast, she would only deal with me," says Downey. "When she needed new cookware, I found it, I said 'I guarantee you'll love it.'

Eventually, I outfitted her whole bed and breakfast. You didn't need files on your customers, you'd phone them and suggest items. That customer and I still meet once a month for dinner," she says.

Even in the store's darkest days, there were some glimmers of kindness. Peter Nash, owner of a local hair-styling salon, felt so sorry for employees of the Seven Oaks store that he asked a representative of the Human Resource Department to distribute seventy-five gift certificates offering discounts on haircuts. One dispirited female employee arrived at his salon and announced, "I'm fifty-nine years old, and people won't recognize my hidden talent." "What is your hidden talent?" Nash asked. "Doing my husband's books," she said. Taking her by the shoulders, Nash sat her down at a desk and said, "Now you have a job." For the other employees who turned up at his salon, Nash tried to ensure that they maintained a certain look and image essential to obtaining work with the public. A close-knit group to this day, Seven Oaks employees meet for dinner every couple of months

From coast to coast, from big to little stores, Eaton's staff members forged lifelong friendships. Many were single women, whose diamond ring, awarded for twenty-five years of loyal service, took on the symbolism of a wedding band. For women such as these, the Eatonian ideal of prompt, respectful, and efficient service was a mantra they transferred into every aspect of their lives. Long-term employees, true Eatonians, were not merely employees of the store, but also members of an exclusive community, and when that community became threatened by outside influences, they bonded together even more strongly to fight the common enemy.

In the last days of the Winnipeg store's existence, cosmetic sales clerk Amy Langsdine took a break from marking down merchandise to plan a surprise birthday party for a favourite co-worker. Using a back staircase, she sneaked a picnic basket filled with a home-baked casserole and a bottle of wine up to the already abandoned fifth-floor Grill Room restaurant. To lend an air of celebration, Langsdine also placed two candles on the table and lit them. "I walked my girlfriend up the dark staircase to the restaurant, and when she saw what I had done, she literally fell on her knees and cried," says Langsdine. In the midst of the women's lunch, the liquidator appeared, but this one did have a heart. Instead of remonstrating them for potentially creating a fire hazard, he took Langsdine's camera and photographed the two women for posterity.

*Amy Langsdine gives her co-worker a last supper
in Winnipeg's Grill Room restaurant, 1999.*

Six weeks before the store's final closing, Langsdine decided to place a journal at the foot of the Timothy Eaton statue in her store, the ultimate symbol of paternalism. For years, in a curious gesture of respect, a uniformed man had approached the statue every morning, saluted it, and then disappeared into the store.

To Langsdine's astonishment, mementoes soon began appearing around the base of the statue, along with a homemade floral wreath bearing the words "Rest in Peace." Many of the mourners were immigrants, whose first introduction to Canadian culture had been through the Eaton's catalogue.

When a single journal proved insufficient to contain all the memories that were scribbled in it, Langsdine replaced it with two, then three more. What started as a modest gesture soon evolved into a phenomenon. One after the other, customers searched for Langsdine to thank her for providing them with the journals. "Older people would call out, 'Amy, which one are you?' and when they found me would fall in my arms crying," says Langsdine. Those who wept included widowed husbands and wives who had met their spouses at "Timmy's Toe" and now returned alone to reminisce. A wartime bride told Langsdine about how her husband had brought her to Eaton's to select her first bottle of perfume.

A woman who travelled to Winnipeg from Victoria, B.C., described in the journal her one and only meal in the Grill Room in 1946, when she was five years old. Two guardians had taken her to the restaurant for a last meal before depositing her on a train that ultimately delivered her to her new foster home in Dauphin. Fifty-three years later, and only days before the store was to close for good, the women returned with her four adult children to show them, in her words, "where I came from."

Former Junior Executive Gary Filmon phoned up his wife, Janice, and made plans to take a final stroll through the Winnipeg store before it closed for good. The former Manitoba premier remembers that in the early 1960s his boss at Eaton's would give him a discount on new clothes.

By the final week of the liquidation sale, grieving staff members shifted all remaining store merchandise to the first floor. At one point, Langsdine and her co-workers were pulling display material from windows, including baskets, furniture, and sleighs, all of which, in her words, "sold like crazy." The contents of Santa's village, including his miniature elves, rabbits, and cartoon characters, were donated to the Winnipeg Children's Museum, where they remain today.

On one of her last days at work, Langsdine toured the store's underground tunnels, walking in and out of an old safe, where cash had once been kept. She then walked up and down the ramps where, decades before, Eaton's horses had moved from floor to floor. On a chalkboard located within what had once been a children's basement playroom, she wrote a short description of her history with the store, which she dated and signed. Once the liquidation sales ended, overcome by emotion, Langsdine went to bed, where she remained on and off for two weeks.

A few hundred loyal customers, including a man singing "Auld Lang Syne" a cappella, gathered at the foot of the statue as the store's closing bell rang for the last time at 6:00 p.m., October 20, 1999. The matching statue of Timothy in Toronto's Eaton Centre was also decorated with dozens of flowers, cards, and letters, although in its case, the store it guarded would reopen for business immediately.

Eventually, Osmington, Inc., the new owners of Winnipeg's downtown store, had to decide what to do with the venerated Timothy statue. Former store employees wrote letters to the Eaton's family in Toronto begging them to allow the statue to stay in Winnipeg.

"There was no way we were going to allow it to end up in Toronto," says Jim Thomson. Like other Winnipeggers, Thomson had formed a grudge against Eaton's management in Toronto after it appropriated all of Winnipeg's regional buyers, then dumped merchandise it couldn't sell on the Winnipeg store.

Thomson currently acts as treasurer of the Eaton's Retirement Club in Winnipeg, which he co-founded in 1989. Its 550 members represent the largest organized club of former Eaton's employees in Canada. Close to two hundred members of the club still meet once a month at various lodges and retirement homes throughout the city, where homemade sandwiches are served up at the events, along with a rich garnish of Eaton's reminiscences.

Thanks in part to the efforts of the Eaton's Retirement Club, Winnipeg's Timothy statue was moved to the Polo Park store in the fall of 2000, Polo Park being run by Sears, but operating under the name eatons. To mark the move, Osmington Inc. organized a "Farewell to Timothy" luncheon to which they invited members of the Eaton's Retirement Club.

Lieutenant Governor Peter Liba, himself a former store employee, delivered a speech and distributed special Millennium Medals to attendees of the event. "The new owners really went all out," says Jim Thomson. "There were sandwiches served. It helped to heal a lot of old wounds."

The wounds were not allowed to heal for long. At the behest of Fred Eaton, Sears began preparations to ship the Timothy statue to St. Mary's, Ontario, in July 2002, St. Mary's being the site where Timothy had operated his second store in 1860. The intended move came in response to Sears's decision to drop the eatons name from the Polo Park store, as well as in response to the news that the Polo Park might be taken over by the Hudson's Bay Company. At the eleventh hour, however, Thomson and his fellow Retirement Club members interceded and saved the statue from the clutches of Ontario decision-makers. Fred Eaton confirmed that, due in part to the vigourous campaigning by Loyal Eatonians, including members of the Retirement Club, the statue would stay where it was.

For Winnipeg's Eatonians, the store remained their touchstone to the past, as well as being the closest thing to a second home many of them have ever known. Nevertheless, petitions to the provincial government requesting the Eaton's building to be designated as a heritage site were denied.

Eaton's Retirement Club members lobbied hard to find a proper home for the war memorial plaques that had hung on the wall beside the Timothy statue. Now under the guardianship of the Retirement Club, the plaques are either to be weatherproofed and moved to St. James

Park, which is situated near a veterans' hospital, or placed in a special area within a proposed sports arena that is scheduled to be built on the Eaton's building site when the store is torn down in July 2002.

In Toronto, the question of who owned Timothy's statue sparked a protracted tussling match between the Eaton's family and Sears Canada, Inc., who purchased the Eaton Centre store along with nineteen other Eaton's stores for approximately 80 million dollars in October 1999. Some Eatonians worried that Sears only wanted to keep the statue as a talisman, symbolizing its vanquishing of a retail giant. The dispute ended only when the Eaton family served Sears's lawyers with legal documents, proving the family's irrefutable ownership of the statue.

Some acquisitive former customers even stepped up to the plate to bid on the statue. Businessman Dan Moorehouse, who attended one of the Danbury auctions of Eaton's assets, briefly toyed with buying the statue simply as a souvenir. "What something's worth is what someone's willing to pay for it," he reasoned.

Eventually, the Eaton family itself settled the question of where Timothy's statue would reside, by choosing Toronto's Royal Ontario Museum as its permanent home. In the dark, early-morning hours of November 4, 1999, seven ROM employees struggled to move the 1,125 kilogram statue, along with its metal base, to Eaton Hall, located on the first floor of the museum. Loading the statue itself onto the truck was easy, but the marble base, consisting of forty different sections, had to be rocked off its moorings with crowbars, and fork-lifted piece by piece onto the truck before it could be transported to the museum. Due to a light drizzle, Timothy's head had to be wrapped in plastic. Museum officials hoped that, once the statue was in place, visitors would continue to rub its toe for good luck.

In Winnipeg, CBC radio host Ron Robinson, a former Eaton's bookstore employee, chose to honour Timothy's statue in a different way. As soon as he heard of the retail giant's demise, Robinson composed a forty-five-minute one-man play simply entitled "Timothy Eaton." In it he played the statue, which comes to life with the words, "I may be bronze, but I'm not deaf."

The play was performed at Winnipeg's Fringe Festival during the summer of 2000, as well as at some smaller venues in and around Winnipeg. As Timothy, Robinson called upon audience members to share their memories of Eaton's glory days, in between snacking on Tim-Bits, doughnuts provided by the local Tim Horton's shop. The play concluded with Timothy transforming once again into bronze and returning to a world of silence, where once "dreams were in the making."

"Life is a series of goodbyes, but you don't expect to see the skeleton of things turned over to the public," says former model and *Toronto Sun* columnist Joan Sutton. "First there was the catalogue, then the stores, they were institutions, but their personalities will lodge them forever in our memory."

Today, Eaton's empire has been officially declared dead, yet its legacy has never been more fashionable. Online auctions sites such as eBay currently sell Eaton's memorabilia, including Quarter-Century Club watches, Punkinhead bears, and Eaton's catalogues. The Eatonia Train, which John Craig Eaton used to transport blankets and medicine to victims of the Halifax Explosion, was purchased in 1990 from Calgary's Heritage Park Society by private collector Gordon Bell, and relocated to a tourist town named Three Valley Gap in Revelstoke, British Columbia – ironically, the place where, just as the CNR's last spike was driven in, Eaton's cross-country catalogue operation both ended and began.

The wide variety of buildings located in Three Valley Gap include a church, two bars, a theatre, and a one-room schoolhouse constructed entirely out of lumber recycled from nearby early-twentieth-century structures. Bell's town also features a two-hundred-room hotel, located close to John Craig Eaton's train.

From coffee shops to country clubs, groups of former Eatonians continue to meet weekly, monthly, and yearly. At the Don Mills store in Toronto, each week employees meet to share memories along with their morning coffee. Also in Toronto, an all-male group of former managers, buyers, and executives, who call themselves the "Irregulars," get together yearly to eat dinner and trade war stories as well as ribald jokes. One year, an Irregular received a specially designed plaque depicting him as the back end of a horse. "Many of the members have become Masters of Industry, but no matter where they went, they came together like a group," says Dr. Walter Prendergast, Eaton's former company physician, adding, "Even when they were out years ago, they still talk about the company as 'we' and that feeling is still there. I compare this to an organization like the armed forces."

Eatonians did get at least one last laugh. In February of 2002, Sears Canada, Inc., announced that, after only sixteen months, it was relin-

TO ALL ⟨E⟩ OLD BOYS

Wednesday, November 22, 1995

THE ANNUAL 'GET TOGETHER'

of

Invitation to meeting of the Irregulars, drawn by Eaton buyer Alan Boothe.

quishing the name "eatons" on five of the seven Eaton's stores it had acquired in the fall of 1999, with the exception of the Toronto and Victoria Eaton centres. Sears had boasted that they would do what Eaton's had been unable to do, namely make its conservative image trendy again. It proved to be a costly mistake. In the end, upgrading Eaton's conservative legacy was like trying to put hot pants on the Timothy statue to make him look more cool.

"It was ridiculous that people grieved the passing of the Eaton name the second time," says Jim Matthews. "The name died in 1999, pure and simple. Anything operating under that name after that was just an imitation."

Fulfilling dreams was the vision to which Timothy Eaton aspired: the dream of millions of immigrants to buy their first home through Eaton's catalogue, plant gardens using Eaton's seeds, and to have a safe and hospitable place to bring and raise their families, filled with good food and friendly conversation. Until almost the end of its existence, Eaton's remained the biggest corner store in the country. From waitresses to delivery drivers to sales clerks and janitors, hard-working Eatonians subscribed to the ideal "one for all and all for one." It was an ideal which, while archaic, certainly, and perhaps even sentimental, had its roots buried deep in English Canada's Protestant soil. There is no question that Eaton's *was* the Eatonians, and in the memories of those who worked for it and shopped in it, "Eaton's *was* Canada."

Notes

Several authors' books about Eaton's provided me with valuable background information. Among them are those by Joy Santink, William Stephenson, Barry Broadfoot, Flora McCrea Eaton, Eileen Sufrin, and Rod McQueen. Where specific quotations have been used, they are identified in the notes; otherwise, all reference material appears in the Sources section. The bulk of the information came from letters, diary entries, Eaton's in-store magazines, and other documents found in the Eaton Collection at the Archives of Ontario, identified as EA throughout the notes. Quotations that appear without footnotes were obtained from author interviews.

CHAPTER 2: *Learning from the Bottom Up*

[1] EA F229-162-0-476, Box 12. "Timothy Eaton Address, New Year's Banquet Address," 1898.

[2] EA F-229-162-900, Box 28. "Mr. Fryer Begins Fiftieth Year with Firm," April 3, 1939.

[3] Provincial Archives of Manitoba, Manitoba Labour Education Oral History 1986, anonymous interview.

[4] Provincial Archives of Manitoba, Manitoba Labour Education Oral History 1986, Noreen Rooke interview.

[5] EA F229-162-0-901-1, Box 28, Employee Reminiscences, Frederick William Story, 1891–1897.

[6] EA F-229-Series 6, Box 1.

[7] EA F-229-6-Box 1, Private Office Correspondence – Employment.

[8] EA F-229-141-0-211, Box 8, *Entre Nous*, "How Does a Young Person Get Ahead at Eaton's?" April 1960, p. 4.

[9] EA F-229-Series 6, Box 1

[10] *Evening Telegram* ad of March 30, 1912, "Let Your Easter Clothes Be Eaton-Made."

[11] EA F-229-162-0-901-1, Box 28, Employee Reminiscences, Agnes Pollock.

[12] Provincial Archives of Manitoba, Manitoba Labour Education Oral History 1986, anonymous interview.

[13] June 13, 1934, *Winnipeg Tribune*, "Eaton System of Bonuses and Pay Explained."

[14] June 14, 1934, *Winnipeg Tribune*, "Eaton Company Wage System Again Reviewed."

[15] *National Tattler* (Toronto, Ont.), February 1, 1939, vol. 2, no. 2, p. 3.

[16] Wright, Cynthia Jane, "The Most Prominent Rendezvous of the Feminine Toronto: Eaton's College Street and the Organization of Shopping in Toronto, 1920–1950," doctoral thesis, University of Toronto, 1993.

[17] EA F-229-162-0-476, Box 12, "Timothy Eaton Address, New Year's Banquet Address, 1898."

[18] Provincial Archives of Manitoba, Manitoba Labour Education Oral History 1986, Noreen Rooke interview.

[19] EA F-229-69, Box 48, "Low Productivity Summaries."

[20] Ibid.

[21] Ibid.

[22] Provincial Archives of Manitoba, Manitoba Labour Education Oral History 1986, Charlotte Lepp interview.

[23] Ibid.

[24] *Eaton's News Quarterly*, "Mrs. Martin's New Bill," p. 6.

CHAPTER 3: *Santa and Other Extravaganzas*

[1] How, H. R. "The Santa Claus Parade's a Year-Round Job," *Canadian Business* magazine, November 1955, p. 88.

[2] Ibid.

[3] "She's Toyland's Unsung Heroine," Marilyn Linton, *Toronto Sunday Sun*, December 22, 1985, p. A23.

[4] EA F-229-162-0-907, Box 28, Jack Brockie Exercise Book, 1965.

[5] EA F-229-162-0-538, Series 151, letter written in 1957.

[6] EA F-229-162-0-539, Box 15.

[7] Ibid.

[8] Ibid.

[9] Letter from George Anthony to Fred Eaton, February 11, 1971.

10 "The Grinch Stole Our Christmas Parade," *Toronto Star*, August 10, 1982, p. A8.

11 "Santa's Elves Stop Working," by Kelly McParland, *Toronto Star*, August 10, 1982, p. A13.

CHAPTER 4: *Feasts for More Than the Eyes*

1 McCrea Eaton, Flora, *Memory's Wall: The Autobiography of Flora McCrea*, with a Foreword by Arthur Meighen, Toronto: Clark, Irwin, c. 1956. p. 145.

2 EA F-229-0-158, 1968-74, Box 5, Interview with Mr. J. A. Brockie, October 1968, Anecdote re. Mr. R. Y. Eaton.

3 EA F-229-162-0-1027, Box 32, "Sew to Show."

4 Stephenson, William, *The Store That Timothy Built*, McClelland & Stewart, Toronto/Montreal, 1969. p. 164.

5 EA F-229-162-0-158, Auditorium – Confidential, 1968-74, Box 5.

6 Ibid.

7 Ibid.

8 Ibid.

9 EA F-229-162-0-1058, *Toronto Telegram*, September 11, 1968.

10 Sutton, Joan, "Together Now – Toronto's Glamour Greats," by Joan Sutton, *Toronto Sunday Sun*, March 3, 1974, p. 12.

11 *Toronto Telegram*, July, 1975.

CHAPTER 5: *The Wish Book*

1 EA F-229-162-0-503, *Contacts*, 1944.

2 Kasper, Isabel and Ed, *By-gone Era*, Eaton's Retirement Club Newsletter, vol. 10, no. 5, December 1999–January 2000.

3 EA Series 117, Box 1, Testimonials.

4 Ibid.

5 Ibid.

6 EA F-229-162-0-669, Box 18. Recollections of Mrs. Emily Cowley, July 25, 1962.

7 EA F-229-0-669, Box 18, Letter from Frank Beecroft to Lady Eaton, Jan. 1957.

8 Ibid.

9 Ibid.

10 EA F-229-162-0-669, Box 18, Eaton Co. – History – Employee Reminiscences.

[11] EA F-229-162-0-669, Box 18.

[12] EA F229-162-0-901-1, Box 28, Employee Reminiscences, Frederick William Story, 1891–1897.

[13] EA F-229-162-0-1268, Box 39, Brigden, Frederick, Essay by the President of Brigden's, March 31, 1955.

[14] EA F-229-6, Box 1, Private Office Correspondence.

[15] Stephenson, *The Store That Timothy Built*, p. 192.

[16] Letter from Eugène Brochm to M. O. Advertising Department, undated, provided by Judith McErvel.

[17] Maynard, Fredele, "Satisfaction Guaranteed," *Eaton Quarterly*, Winter 1969, p. 14.

[18] EA F-229-162-0-508, Box 18, Testimonials and Complaints, Series 117.

[19] Ibid.

[20] Maynard, Fredele, "Satisfaction Guaranteed," *Eaton Quarterly*, Winter 1969, p. 14.

[21] Ibid.

[22] Broadfoot, Barry, *The Pioneer Years, 1895–1914*, Toronto, Doubleday Canada Ltd., 1976, p. 280.

[23] EA F-229-162-0-614, Customer Letter.

[24] Maynard, Fredele, "Satisfaction Guaranteed," *Eaton Quarterly*, Winter 1969, p. 14.

CHAPTER 6: *Closing the Book*

[1] "No Room in the Lifeboat," *Winnipeg Tribune*, January 15, 1976.

[2] Ibid.

[3] Mardon, Harry, "Why Catalogue Operation Ending," *Winnipeg Tribune*, March 26, 1976.

[4] Meakin, Darlene, "Rural Buyers Will Miss Catalogue Most," *Winnipeg Tribune*, January 16, 1976.

[5] *Winnipeg Tribune*, January 15, 1976.

[6] Burton, Allan, *Store of Memories*, Toronto, McClelland & Stewart, 1986, p. 253.

[7] DeFoe, Bill, *The Way We Were* (courtesy of Manfred Buehner).

[8] EA F-229-162-0-508, Letter, January 19, 1976.

[9] Ibid.

[10] Ibid.

[11] Ibid. Letter from Mrs. Maurice Johnson.

CHAPTER 7: *The Maharajas of Eaton's*

[1] EA F-229-162-0-476, "Timothy Eaton Address, New Year's Eve Banquet," Statement by Mr. Ecclestone, 1878.

[2] EA F-229-06-162, Box 1, Letter from Timothy Eaton to Frank MacMahon, File – Private Office, London Buying Office.

[3] Ibid.

[4] EA F-229-162-0-476. "Timothy Eaton Address, New Year's Eve Banquet Address."

[5] EA F-229-162-0-491, "Buyers Instructions," 1901.

[6] EA F-229-78, Box 1, Eaton's General Merchandise Office, Foreign Buyers' Records, Notebooks (3), J. A. C. Poole.

[7] Anonymous, "Footprints in the Desert Sand."

[8] EA F-229-221-0-16, Box 19, James Forster bio.

[9] EA F-229-8-0-325, Box 13, "Accidents & Disasters," Letter From Tom Somerset to A. McPherson, Esq., Belfast, December 5, 1915.

[10] Ibid.

[11] EA F-229-8-0-325, Box 13, Letter from Mrs. Powell to J. J. Vaughan, June 14, 1915.

[12] EA F-229-8-0-325, Box 13, Letter from Mrs. MacLean.

[13] EA F-229-8-0-325, Box 13, Letter from Charles MacLean to John Craig Eaton.

[14] EA F-229-8-0-325, Box 13, February 18, 1916 letter from Mr. McGillvray to J. J. Vaughan.

[15] EA Letter from B. C. Walker to R. Y. Eaton, October 5, 1923.

[16] Ibid.

[17] EA F-229-162-0-476, Box 12, Febuary 7, 1968 letter from Yagi to G. Carlson, Company Merchandise Office.

[18] EA F-229-8-0-334, "Letter of R. Y. Eaton to Percy Portlock," June 20, 1939.

[19] EA F-229-141-0-171, *Flash*, 1935-1943, June 13, 1938.

[20] Ibid.

[21] Ibid.

[22] EA F-229-141-0-79, Box 3, "Buyers Abroad," *Contacts*.

[23] EA F-229-141-0-188, Box 8, "If I Were A Buyer," *Entre Nous*, 1937.

[24] EA F-229-162-0-1258, Box 39, *Buyers' Memo*, "Eaton's Is Well Represented."

CHAPTER 8: *The War Years*

[1] The Scribe, *Eaton's Golden Jubilee, 1869–1919: A Book To Commemorate the Fiftieth Anniversary of the T. Eaton. Co. Ltd.*, T. Eaton Co. Ltd., Toronto and Winnipeg, 1919, p. 113.

[2] EA Series 141, Box 6, December 14, 1944, *Flash*, p. 45.

[3] EA F-229-162-0-972, Box 30, "Employees' War Service & Letters to Miss Rymal, 1915–17."

[4] Ibid.

[5] Ibid.

[6] EA F-229-162-0-972, Box 30, "Letter from G. A. Hunter to Secretary of Eatonia."

[7] Stephenson, *The Store That Timothy Built*, p. 74.

[8] EA F-229-8-0-324, Box 8, "Complimentary Banquet Tendered by the President and Directors of the T. Eaton Company Ltd., to Their Returned Men."

[9] Ibid.

[10] August 8, 1996, letter from Doreen O'Dell to John Craig Eaton (courtesy of Phil and Doreen O'Dell).

[11] EA F-229-Series 36, T1/81/1, Box 10, Enemy Trading Act.

[12] *Daily Star*, "Ringer Girls," June 24, 1942.

[13] Provincial Archives of Manitoba, Manitoba Labour Education Oral History 1986, Charlotte Lepp, Winnipeg store.

[14] Provincial Archives of Manitoba, Manitoba Labour Education Oral History 1986, Charlotte Lepp, Winnipeg Store, Anonymous.

[15] EA F-229-Series 37, Box 21, Correspondence re. Otto Zwahl.

[16] Ibid.

[17] *Toronto Telegram*, November 6, 1939, "Conant Asks Supreme Court to Ban Five Toronto Tabloids."

[18] EA F-229-8-0-336, Box 13, July 18, 1940 letter from O. D. Vaughan to Mrs. Bassonesi.

[19] Pyper, C. B. "Woman Has Qualities for Business Success, Lady Eaton Declares," *Toronto Star*, August 16, 1930. p. 6.

[20] EA F-229-162-0-972, Box 30, "Report on Eaton's War Auxiliary."

[21] *Hush*, vol. 3, no. 47, March 15, 1941, "Lady Eaton Back on Job, Italian Interns: Interned Italian Employee Freed From Concentration Camp and Re-installed in Big Store," p. 4.

[22] EA F-229-162-0-972, Box 30 "Employee War Service."

23 *Hush*, Vol. 4, No. 8, June 14, 1941, "Canteen Graft Gyps Soldiers, Military Authorities Should Take Over Direction of Civilian Conducted Canteens in Army Camps," p. 4.

24 *Globe and Mail*, May 9, 1945, "Riots Sweep Over Halifax," p. 1.

CHAPTER 9: *Union Battle*

1 Woodcock, Connie, "Eaton's College: Toronto's Extinct Taj Mahal," *Toronto Sunday Sun*, January 25, 1976, M3.

2 Sufrin, Eileen, *The Eaton Drive: The Campaign to Organize Canada's Largest Department Store, 1948–1952*, p. 66–67.

3 National Archives of Canada, MG-30 (B-125) vol. 13–126, Radio Scripts n.d. 1950–51, file no. 2.

4 Callwood, June, "She's Organizing Eaton's," *Maclean's*, October 1950, p. 48.

5 Ibid.

6 Ibid.

7 *Hush*, "Eaton's Labor Fight," March 13, 1950, August 12, 1950, vol. 1, no. 8., p. 4.

8 EA F-229-8-0-336, Box 8-13, "What Are They Selling?" November 13, 1951.

9 Ibid.

10 Eaton, Flora McCrea, *Memory's Wall*, p. 241.

11 Sufrin, Eileen, *The Eaton Drive: The Campaign to Organize Canada's Largest Department Store, 1948–1952*, p. 180.

12 National Archives of Canada, MG 30 CB-125 B-126, Company Leaflets, n.d., 1950–51.

13 Ibid.

14 Sufrin, Eileen, *The Eaton Drive*, p. 189.

15 Ibid., quoting December 5, 1952, *Globe & Mail* editorial.

16 Turner, Garth, "Eaton's Strike a Scam," *Toronto Sun*, March 15, 1985.

CHAPTER 10: *The End*

1 Mattos, Melinda, Reality Sandwiches, "memoirs of a gold standard plus eatonian." Internet essay, <http://www.realitysandwiches.com/melinda/eatons.html>.

Sources

Archives:

Eaton's Archives, Archives of Ontario
National Archives of Canada
Provincial Archives of Manitoba
University of Manitoba Archives

Newspapers:

Daily Star
Globe and Mail
Toronto Star
Toronto Sun
Toronto Telegram
Winnipeg Free Press
Winnipeg Tribune

Eaton's In-House Magazines:

Contacts
Eaton News Quarterly
Entre Nous
Flash

General Magazines:

Canadian Business
Financial Post
Hush

Maclean's
National Tattler

Dissertations, Letters, and Essays:

Anonymous essay "Footprints in the Sand."

Aylward, Sandra Elizabeth, "Experiencing Patriarchy: Women, Work, and Trade Unionism at Eaton's," doctoral thesis, McMaster University, Hamilton, Ontario.

DeFoe, Bill. "The Way We Were".

Eaton's Retirement Club Newsletter, letter entitled "By-Gone Era," from Isabel and Ed Kasper.

Internet essay entitled "memoirs of a gold standard plus eatonian," Melinda Mattos (booklet) <http://www.realitysandwiches.com/melinda/eatons.html>.

Letter from Doreen O'Dell to John Craig Eaton, August 8, 1996.

Letter from George Anthony to Fred Eaton, February 11, 1971.

Wright, Cynthia Jane, "The Most Prominent Rendezvous of the Feminine Toronto: Eaton's College Street and the Organization of Shopping in Toronto, 1920–1950," Ph.D. thesis, University of Toronto, 1993.

Books:

Broadfoot, Barry, *The Pioneer Years 1895–1914, Memories of Settlers Who Opened the West*, Toronto/Garden City, N.Y., Doubleday Canada Ltd., 1976.

———, *Ten Lost Years 1929–1939, Memories of Canadians Who Survived the Depression*, Toronto, A Douglas Gibson Book, McClelland & Stewart, 1973.

Burton, G. Allan, *A Store of Memories*, Toronto, McClelland & Stewart, 1986.

MacPherson, Mary-Etta, *Shopkeepers to a Nation: The Eatons*, Toronto, McClelland & Stewart, 1963.

McCrea Eaton, Flora, *Memory's Wall: The Autobiography of Flora McCrea Eaton*, Toronto, Clarke, Irwin & Co., 1956.

McQueen, Rod, *The Eatons, The Rise and Fall of Canada's Royal Family*, Toronto, Stoddart Publishing Co., 1998.

Nasmith, George G., *Timothy Eaton*, Toronto, McClelland & Stewart, 1923.

Purchase, Gregory R., *Hard Rock Retailing*, published privately, Toronto, 1996.

Santink, Joy L., *Timothy Eaton and the Rise of His Department Store*, Toronto, University of Toronto Press, 1990.

Starowicz, Mark, "Eaton's: An Irreverent History," In *Corporate Canada: 14 Probes into the Workings of a Branch-Plant Economy*, edited by Mark Starowicz and Rae Murphy, Toronto, James Lewis and Samuel, 1972.

Stephenson, William, *The Store That Timothy Built*, Toronto, McClelland & Stewart, 1969.

Stevens, G. R., *The Incompleat Canadian: An Approach to Social History*, published privately, Toronto, 1965.

Sufrin, Eileen, *The Eaton Drive: The Campaign to Organize Canada's Largest Department Store 1948 to 1952*, Toronto, Fitzhenry & Whiteside, 1982.

The Scribe, *Golden Jubilee 1869–1919, A Book to Commemorate the Fiftieth Anniversary of the T. Eaton Co. Ltd.*, Toronto and Winnipeg, T. Eaton Co., 1919.

List of Obtained Permissions:

The author wishes to thank the following companies and individuals:

George Anthony for permission to use quotation/quotations from his letter to Fred Eaton dated February 11, 1972.

Barry Broadfoot for permission to quote from his book *The Pioneer Years 1895–1914*, published by Toronto, Doubleday Canada Ltd., 1976.

Sharon Landry of Sears Canada, Inc., for granting permission to use material from the Eaton's Archive at the Archives of Ontario.

Melinda Mattos for permission to quote from her Internet essay, "Memoirs of a Gold Standard Plus Eatonian."

Phil O'Dell for permission to quote from the August 8, 1996, letter from Doreen O'Dell to John Craig Eaton.

Scott Reid, Archivist, Moving Images and Sound, Provincial Archives of Manitoba, for allowing quotations to be used from the Provincial Archives of Manitoba, Manitoba Labour Education Oral History Project, 1986.

John Sullivan of the *Winnipeg Free Press* for permission to quote from the *Winnipeg Tribune*.

The Toronto Sun Publishing Company for the right to use four quotations from articles in the *Toronto Sun* written by Connie Woodcock, Joan Sutton, Garth Turner, and Marilyn Linton.

Illustration Credits

p. 57 Top, EA, Archives of Ontario, F 229-308-0-792-1; bottom, EA, Archives of Ontario, F 229-308-0-794-1

p. 58 EA, Archives of Ontario, F 229-300-1-77-1, AO5497

p. 60 Top, EA, Archives of Ontario F 229-308-0-787-1; bottom, EA, Archives of Ontario, F 229-308-0-779-1

p. 64 EA, Archives of Ontario, F 229-308-0-778-1

p.67 EA, Archives of Ontario, F 229-305-1-19, #67359

p.68 EA, Archives of Ontario, F 229-308-0-738, AO5502

p.71 EA, Archives of Ontario, F 229-308-0-738, AO5503

p.73 Top, EA, Archives of Ontario, F 229-308-0-1049-1; middle, EA, Archives of Ontario, F 229-308-0-1050-1; bottom, EA, Archives of Ontario F 229-308-0-725-1

p.75 EA, Archives of Ontario, F 229-308-0-1720-2

p.76 Top, EA, Archives of Ontario, F 229-308-0-735-1; button, courtesy Jim Matthews; bottom, courtesy Joseph Giordmaine

p.81 EA, Archives of Ontario, F 229 308-0-2304-1

p.82 EA, Archives of Ontario, F 229-312-0-127

p.84 Top, EA, Archives of Ontario F 229-308-0-2309-1; bottom, EA, Archives of Ontario, F 229-312-0-58-1

p.86 EA, Archives of Ontario, F 229-308-0-2310-1

p.87 Courtesy: Dorothy Ferguson

p.88 EA, Archives of Ontario, F 229-300-1-114-1, AO5496

p.91 Courtesy: Sigi Brough, Judith McKervel

p.92 EA, Archives of Ontario, F 229-308-0-2310-2

p.93 EA, Archives of Ontario, F 229-312-0-77-1

p.94 EA, Archives of Ontario, F 229-308-0-1663-1

p.96 EA, Archives of Ontario, F 229-308-0-2335-1

p.98 EA, Archives of Ontario, F 229-308-0-2325-1

p.99 EA, Archives of Ontario, F 229-300-1-85-6, AO5498

p.100 EA, Archives of Ontario, F 229-308-0-61-2

p.102 Top, EA, Archives of Ontario, F 229-308-0-64, C6784-6; bottom, EA, Archives of Ontario, F 229-308-0-61-4, AO146

p.106 Courtesy: Norman Scudelleri

p.107 Courtesy: Barbara Duckworth (66154-14)

p.108 Courtesy: Jim Matthews

p.110 Top, courtesy: Marg Morison; bottom, courtesy: Lilian Vadeboncoeur; Jean Macdonald, courtesy: Jean Macdonald p.111   Courtesy: Lilian Vadeboncoeur

p.113   Courtesy: Sigi and Michael Brough

p.115   Photo: Barbara Redlich

p.118   Top, William Wardill; bottom, courtesy: William Wardill.

p.119   Courtesy: Jim Matthews

p.122   EA, Archives of Ontario, F 229-308-0-990-1

p.124   EA, Archives of Ontario, F 229-308-0-998-1 AO1103

p.125   EA, Archives of Ontario, F 229-308-0-2191-1

p.126   Top left, courtesy: Sigi Brough, Judith McKervel; top right, courtesy Jim Matthews; bottom, courtesy Sigi Brough, Judith McKervel

p.129   Top, EA, Archives of Ontario, F 229-308-0-685; bottom, EA, Archives of Ontario F 229-308-0-925

p.132   EA, Archives of Ontario, F 229-308-0-1037-1

p.134   EA, Archives of Ontario, F 229-308-0-973-1

p.142   Courtesy: Lilian Vadeboncoeur

p.143   EA, Archives of Ontario, F 229-308-0-1656-6

p.144   EA, Archives of Ontario, F 229-305-1-16, #68162

p.145   Courtesy: Sigi Brough, Judith McKervel

p.149   Courtesy: Manfred Buehner

p.163   EA, Archives of Ontario, F 229-300-1-335-1, AO5500

p.165   EA, Archives of Ontario, F 229-308-0-463-2

p.166   Courtesy: Dennis Benoit

p.168   Photo: Lynn Spurway

p.170   EA, Archives of Ontario, F 229-308-0-663-3

p.174   Top, EA, Archives of Ontario, F 229-308-0-663-2; bottom, EA, Archives of Ontario, F 229-308-0-662-2

p.178   EA, Archives of Ontario, F 229-312-0-22

p.182   Top, EA, Archives of Ontario, F 229-308-0-675-2; bottom, EA, Archives of Ontario, F 229-308-0-675-1, AO5456

p.189   Courtesy: Heinz Boehlke

p.190   EA, Archives of Ontario, F 229-308-0-664

p.195   Courtesy: Musée McCord/McCord Museum, Montreal

p.202   Courtesy: Dorothy Strype

p.203   Top, EA, Archives of Ontario, F 229-308-0-1447-1; middle, EA, Archives of Ontario, F 229-308-0-1090-2; bottom, Archives of Ontario, F 229-308-0-1090-1

p.204   EA, Archives of Ontario, F 229-308-0-1437-1

p.208 Top, EA, Archives of Ontario, F 229-308-0-2457-1; bottom, EA, Archives of Ontario, F 229-308-0-2458-1

p.211 Top, EA, Archives of Ontario F 229-308-0-1266-1; bottom, courtesy: Fred Eaton

p.213 Courtesy: Norah Forster

p.216 EA, Archives of Ontario, F 229-308-0-1441-1

p.218 EA, Archives of Ontario, F 229-308-0-1003-1

p.223 EA, Archives of Ontario, F 229-308-0-1447-2

p.224 EA, Archives of Ontario, F 229-308-0-1102-1

p.226 EA, Archives of Ontario, F 229-308-0-1438-1

p.230 EA, Archives of Ontario, F 229- 308-0-1731-1

p.232 EA, Archives of Ontario, F 229-308-0-1292-2

p.233 Top, EA, Archives of Ontario, F 229-308-0-1295-2; bottom, Archives of Ontario, F 229-308-0-1293-1

p.234-235 Courtesy: Jim Matthews (From *Flash* magazine, May 21, 1945)

p.237 EA, Archives of Ontario, F 229-8-0-366

p.247 EA, Archives of Ontario, F 229-8-0-336

p.254 Courtesy: *Toronto Star*

p.255 Courtesy: Rose Askin

p.257 Courtesy: Jim Matthews

p.271 Photo: Amy Langsdine

p.276 Courtesy: Alan Boothe

Index

Page numbers in italics indicate an illustration.